# THE
# LEADING
# EDGE

## CEOs Who Turned
## Their Companies Around:
## What They Did and How They Did It

MARK POTTS
PETER BEHR

McGraw-Hill Book Company

New York   St. Louis   San Francisco
Toronto   Hamburg   Mexico

2 3 4 5 6 7 8 9 D O C D O C 8 7

ISBN 0-07-050599-3


LIBRARY OF CONGRESS CATALOGING-IN-PUBLICATION DATA

Potts, Mark.
  The leading edge.
  1. Organizational change—Case studies.    2. Success
in business—Case studies.      I. Behr, Peter.   II. Title.
HD58.8.P68 1987       658.4'06        86-10567
ISBN 0-07-050599-3

BOOK DESIGN BY PATRICE FODERO

# CONTENTS

# 1

# THE LEADING EDGE

## A New Breed of CEO

They call him Neutron Jack. It's a nickname John F. Welch Jr. detests, one hung on him a few years back by some unknown wag in the company Welch heads, General Electric Co. A $29-billion-a-year colossus even before its recent acquisition of RCA Corp., GE employs 300,000 persons worldwide making everything from lightbulbs to jet engines, AM radios to CAT scanners, tiny electronic chips to 150-ton railroad locomotives.

They call him Neutron Jack because in the past five years he has cut a swath through the huge company, overseeing the closing of more than a score of plants and the idling of tens of thousands of workers.

When Neutron Jack hits a GE plant town, they say, the people disappear, but the building still stands.

Through layoffs and attrition, GE's work force has been slashed by 25 percent from the 400,000 level Welch inherited, a searing change for a company whose loyalty to employees and communities had seemed an inviolable part of its culture.

Under Welch, GE is undergoing the most profound change in its century-long history, a change that Welch says is made necessary by the grim requirements for survival in faster-changing, less predictable, and far tougher global markets.

His orders to the company's managers are to make their businesses first or second in their markets or see the businesses closed or sold. It is no idle threat. More than 150 businesses have been jettisoned under the "fix, sell or close" commandment imposed by Welch, a tough, resourceful chemical engineer from a working-class Massachusetts family who rocketed up through GE's managerial ranks to become chairman at 45.

Over the past half-decade, Welch has pushed GE into the highest technologies, aided by billions in ready cash, the product of being a successful industrial giant. He has dismantled what may be the most celebrated and copied corporate planning mechanism in American business and replaced it with a more dynamic system that puts an emphasis on forcing managers to stay one step—at least— ahead of competitors, to react to that competitive world marketplace, indeed, to be in first or second place in their respective industries or be shown the door. He is attempting to foster a spirit of entrepreneurialism inside a vast, corporate bureaucracy, to give those with a potentially money-making idea a chance to take a shot at it—without fear of being penalized for failure. In short, Welch has attempted to put the behemoth known as General Electric onto the fast track occupied mostly by much smaller high-technology companies.

In the process, he has made the company into even more of a behemoth. By engineering the takeover of RCA Corp., Welch has almost doubled GE's size and added a new layer of business and technologies to GE's already long list.

But Welch is no wild-eyed renegade on an ego trip bent on shaking up one of America's most important industrial powers, its ninth-largest company, just for the sake of it. His overhaul of GE, heartily endorsed by both the board of directors that appointed him and the highly respected predecessor who handpicked him as chairman, is bringing General Electric up to date in an economic, business, and technological environment that has changed more profoundly in the past few years than in any comparable period in the history of American industry.

The business world now is a very different place from what it was not long ago, just as GE is a very different place—and that's no coincidence. All Welch is doing, he argues—backed up by statistics, confirmation by outside analysts, and validation on Wall Street, where GE is a stock market favorite—is making the changes needed to make GE competitive and successful in that rapidly changing world.

"I think the world is increasingly smaller, more competitive by the hour," Welch says. "I think more than anything, we're trying to see ourselves in everything we do as being world-competitive in cost, quality and services."

The course Welch has charted is taking GE increasingly away from the consumer and smokestack product lines that made GE literally a household name. GE's future lies in other businesses where its technological strength provides the greatest leverage, namely high-tech defense contracting, credit and financial services, medical systems, space-age materials, and other state-of-the-art areas. These businesses have been made lean and hard under Welch, given more agile management, and infused with $22 billion in new technology and modern equipment over the past five years as GE has searched for critical competitive advantages in each of its markets. The advantages may be unique technology, or a more efficient plant, or a commanding financial edge, but whatever the source, they must give GE businesses a greater flow of profits for each dollar of investment that GE's rivals can muster. Or else they will be closed or sold.

Welch likes to think of GE as a microcosm of the American economy—before the RCA addition roughly one-third of its profits came from older manufacturing businesses, one-third from high-technology businesses, and one-third from a range of services, including financial, engineering, and information. (Now, only one-fifth is manufacturing.)

But GE is a microcosm of another sort. The challenges confronting the company provide a vivid picture of the mounting competitive forces and financial pressures now bearing down on corporations and their employees in the 1980s. Welch's combative response to these challenges has set a theme that now runs throughout the business world.

At other major corporations, executives with similar visions also are dragging their companies kicking and screaming into the tough world of business in the 1980s. This is a particularly challenging time in American business history, an era in which the United States has lost its once-dominant position in many key old-line industries, such as steel and automobiles, and is in danger of being outflanked in many newer areas, such as silicon-chip-based electronics and biotechnology. Years of inefficient management and manufacturing are taking their toll, as other countries prove they can make products better and cheaper—and sell them in the U.S. market more effectively.

Overwhelmed by this challenge, many American companies are either going out of business or selling out to stronger competitors. Others are foundering, seemingly unable to cope with the deep changes in their environment. Still others are appealing for government help or market intervention.

But the top executives of corporations on the leading edge of American industry are adjusting their companies to recognize—and take advantage of—the revolutionary changes that have buffeted virtually every major American company in recent years: the internationalization of the world economy; the advent of cheap, easily usable computers leading an onrush of high technology; the accelerating shift from a predominantly industrial economy to one increasingly reliant on services; the lingering effects of back-to-back worldwide recessions; and the deregulation of many of the nation's major industries. Welch's predecessor as GE's chairman, Reginald H. Jones, puts it this way:

"If any CEO looks at today's environment thoughtfully and dispassionately, he is going to have to say to himself, very honestly, that life is tougher today than it was when he took over. He's got to realize that through the '50s and '60s, America presented its corporate sector tremendous opportunities—opportunities for growth and profitability. The rest of the industrialized world was pretty much in a shambles following World War II, and it took a long time for them to rebuild. The world was our oyster.

"By the time we got to the 1970s, we had seen the so-called economic miracle in West Germany, and we had seen this remarkable growth of the Japanese economy. We were therefore encountering the beginnings of the really tough competition that exists today. And it got steadily more difficult through the '70s. We began to see the less-developed countries want their own industrial base, we began to run into all kinds of problems with local content laws on the part of the [lesser-developed countries], which required us to invest abroad because we could not export from the United States willy-nilly as we saw fit, we saw other nations willing to make those domestic investments . . . we began to run into the problems of our own very high-priced labor vis-à-vis that of other countries, our own sloppy management styles that had just sort of developed because we had not been forced to compete as we are today, and we had all through the '70s, in particular, not made the capital investments, the R&D investments, that we should have made.

"The net result was that our productivity was slipping, whereas it was growing by leaps and bounds in Japan. So as we came to the '80s, it was time to pick ourselves up by our own bootstraps and really go to work."

The decade of the 1980s began with the worst recession since the Great Depression of the 1930s, and even the long recovery that followed did not halt the grim procession of plant closings throughout the nation's industrial sector, a procession that spread from core industries like steel to the computer and silicon-chip industry as the combined effects of tougher foreign competition and declining American productivity took their toll. The problem was compounded by a foreign-exchange imbalance between the dollar and the Japanese yen that had the double-whammy effect of making Japanese imports cheaper in this country and American goods more expensive abroad. Although the yen-dollar imbalance finally began to right itself in 1985, the damage was already done. By mid-decade, just about everybody in business knew that the combination of these problems was having devastating effects.

"Both at home and abroad, the United States is beginning to lose market position in such sophisticated industries as machine tools and electronics. We now live in an age of competition, not merely among companies, but among entire national economies," says Edward G. Jefferson, the recently retired chairman of one of the nation's leading technology firms, E. I. du Pont de Nemours & Co. Inc.

The result is apparent to anyone looking into a parking lot or a consumer electronics store or a clothing outlet—a dramatic change in the presence of imports. In the 1960s, total trade in goods and services amounted to about 11 percent of the U.S. gross national product. Two decades later, that percentage has doubled, and three-quarters of all American manufactured goods are facing foreign competition.

For consumers and manufacturers alike, this has brought an expanding array of products and components at competitive prices that have helped take the sting from the inflation of the 1970s. But the costs include the toll on the 11.5 million Americans who lost jobs between 1979 and 1984 because of imports, plant closings, and the impact of automation.

"We have to be able to produce at world-scale competitive prices, in spite of the yen-dollar differential and in spite of the wage differential," says Thornton F. Bradshaw, chairman of RCA. "We've got to overcome those with superior manufacturing and superior innovation, superior product delivery, superior service, and by the very large advantage we have by being right here with the world's largest market. It's not impossible to do. . . . I am an optimist, in spite of the fact that I can give you as long a list as anybody as to why American industry is in a hell of a spot today."

Many large American companies are reacting to this maelstrom of change in the same way as General Electric. They are revamping virtually every aspect of their businesses to enable them to compete more effectively. By doing so, these corporations are making a place for themselves at the leading edge of corporate America.

These companies understand the critical advantage that technology offers, whether in the form of new products, or faster, more efficient processes, or a surer handle on vital information inside and outside the organization. Most are making the same hard choices that GE has made, to close down antiquated manufacturing lines or to discontinue products or businesses that cannot meet the market's challenge. Others are looking at the healthier, expanding services sector for opportunities to balance their threatened manufacturing core. Many are redrawing their organizational charts to put a premium on decentralized decision-making and quick reaction to mercurial market conditions, while at the same time they are focusing harder than ever on the intrinsic strengths that arise from the culture and values of the organization. And many are opening their doors to partnerships with competitors at home and abroad, recognizing that such alliances are essential to fill gaps in their technology, marketing skills, and product lines. If Welch's insight is right, these strategies are the keys to success for major corporations in this new age of global competition and fast, unpredictable technological change.

The focus of this book is not on macroeconomic policies—although these have profoundly affected the business environment in recent years. It does not explore answers to the most serious trade challenge that the world has faced since before World War II. And it does not offer a blueprint for easing the pain that individuals and communities are suffering because of the rapid pace of change. Rather, it is an examination of what a group of corporate leaders is doing to strengthen their companies and, in that way, to strengthen the economy as a whole.

The challenge these executives are tackling is the creation of companies that will not only outperform the competition, but that will outstrip the growth of the surrounding economy. As Jones and many others have noted, the world's economic engine has slowed noticeably from the inflation-fueled pace of the 1970s. To reach the leading edge and remain there, companies must concentrate their resources in products and services that offer the best prospects for immediate growth and profitability, while they carefully develop new businesses for the future. At the same time, mature businesses must be lubricated with productivity improvements, reducing costs so that they too will grow more rapidly than the economy around them.

Changing the core of a company is more easily said than done, for a large corporation is much like an ocean liner, slow and difficult to turn. For that reason, many of the executives following this course refer to their corporate makeovers as "sea changes." "I was so sure when I started on this that in 5 to 10 years it would be all over and it would be perfect," says James F. Beré, the chairman of Borg-Warner, who has been adding service businesses to his company's traditional industrial manufacturing base. "And I met a Japanese friend of mine, who was then in his 80s, and he said, 'I think I've learned something in my management. I used to think I could change things in 10 years. You really need 20.'"

This book describes how America's corporate leaders are effecting these needed changes to adapt to the environment around them—and gives those leaders' philosophies and rationales in their own words. Readers of this book will see Jack Welch and his lieutenants at GE as they try to wrestle with the wheel of the giant company, trying to turn and head the company toward an uncompromising emphasis on winning, a new approach to strategic planning, and an unrelenting search for the telling technological or financial advantage.

We will meet Roger Smith, chairman of General Motors Corp., the nation's largest company, who, through GM's Saturn project, is trying to reinvent the way automobiles are made and sold. This book also recounts the effort of Gould Inc. to shift out of the slow-moving battery and electrical equipment businesses and into high-tech electronics in an attempt to grow at a pace faster than that of the general economy. We will see how Borg-Warner Corp., formerly an old-line supplier of automobile transmissions and equipment for Detroit's car factories, has smoothed out the ups and downs of business cycles by moving into service-oriented industries like consumer and corporate financing and protective services—while retaining and rebuilding its more traditional businesses.

Similarly, this book tells how National Intergroup has torn up its roots in the faltering American steel industry and is putting down new roots in healthier service businesses. And we'll see how Coca-Cola, recognizing the increasingly important role of leisure activities in the world economy, has expanded its share of the world's leisure time beyond "the pause that refreshes" into such fields as movie and television production and clothing—while at the same time discovering that if you tinker with the taste of what is arguably the world's best-known consumer product, you can be guilty of changing too much.

Not all companies are changing solely because of the new environment around them. Some are reacting to other stimuli as well. This book describes how American Telephone & Telegraph, its tight grip on the United States telecommunications industry now broken by government fiat, is reaching out into new businesses demanding new technologies and skills that were stunted by years of regulation and monopoly. We'll see how Martin Marietta Corp. and Walt Disney Co., awakened by fierce takeover raids, have gone through revolutions of their own—Martin Marietta with bold steps into high-technology and service businesses that are logical extensions of its older businesses, Disney with a renewed commitment to dominate the American entertainment industry after years of lethargy. And we'll see how RCA made itself attractive to Welch and General Electric by shaking off the effects of years of inept management and ill-advised diversification and making an effort to regain its technological leadership in the rapidly changing electronics and communications fields in which it competes.

The stories of these leaders and their companies document the forces of change that have uprooted so much of the quieter, more controlled life that corporate America enjoyed in the postwar era of industrial dominance. A major company that cannot outperform the economy risks coming under siege from corporate raiders and dissatisfied investors. Yet within this slower-flowing river of growth are fast-moving currents of opportunity that must be detected and seized before domestic and foreign rivals find them. It's a fair question why any employee, supervisor, or investor would welcome this pressure-cooked environment. But for the major American corporations that play in this global arena, there is no avoiding it. "The spread between winners and losers is widening," says Michael Carpenter, GE's chief strategist and one of Welch's top aides. "There is no middling ground. Long-term, unless American industry is competitive worldwide, there are no jobs. The strategy for GE and the country that creates the greatest number of jobs is one that maximizes our world competitiveness in each of our businesses."

All the corporations in this book are on the leading edge in the way they are transforming themselves, making changes that all American companies will have to make in coming years to survive in the new business environment of the rest of this decade, the 1990s, and the new century. This kind of adaptation must become a continual process, because as different as the business and technological climate is now from what it was a few years ago, it will be even more different in a few more years. Success will go to the company that can catch the crest of the wave of change and make the continual adjustments needed to stay on it.

Says Gould's chairman, William Ylvisaker, "All you've got to do is look at the earnings reports of corporations today." Companies that 5 or 10 years ago were the stars of the Fortune 500 are now scrambling to regain momentum or stay independent. "Caterpillar's a good example," Ylvisaker says. "Great company—what's happened to it? The same is true of the major steel companies. . . . You go right down the line and you say, what's happened?" Ylvisaker provides one answer: "Maybe it's management that hasn't got the guts to make adjustments to the world competition that's been created."

Managements that have the guts are making over their corporations into dynamic entities that are hardly recognizable when compared to their earlier incarnations—with tremendous consequences for managers, employers, suppliers, customers, and the national economy. Those able to comprehend, accept, and lead these changes will be the most successful managers in years to come.

Examining the major companies that have undergone or are undergoing transformations reveals several major common philosophies. These are not technical business-school recipes for success; instead, they are strategies that have evolved within the top management of these companies as reactions to the fundamental changes underway in the world's business environment. In many cases they represent not only a change in the company's lines of business or management and manufacturing processes but also of that elusive quality known by the buzzword "corporate culture"—the very spirit with which a company's human relationships and values are infused.

The lessons that emerge are:

• Anticipate changes in your competitive surroundings and be prepared to react quickly to them. This requires both a broad view of larger market forces and a flexible, decentralized environment that allows quick decision-making at all levels of the company—and especially at those levels closest to customers and clients.

- Know your company's strengths and take advantage of them. Do what you do best. Stick to your basic businesses, or logical extensions of them, and, when possible, seek out and exploit high-quality market niches in which your company has some sort of unique advantage.
- Recognize that technology is a powerful weapon for corporate change, both as a source of new products and services and as a way of dramatically increasing productivity. Embrace it with enthusiasm and realism by applying it to existing businesses, using it to create new businesses, and bringing its fruits to market as quickly as possible.
- When possible, enter into mutually beneficial alliances with other companies at home and abroad, thus increasing your competitive ability, adding technology or other know-how, joining complementary strengths, or providing access to new markets.
- Create a partnership between management and employees through respect, trust, and candor, recognizing that a secure group of employees will accept and take advantage of change.
- Take calculated risks in an attempt to improve your company's competitive position, and foster an environment that encourages risk-taking by others—through compensation plans, in-company entrepreneurial programs, and reluctance to punish failure after valiant attempts to improve the company meet with failure.
- Managing in today's more competitive world and being able to adapt to the constantly changing environment demands a new kind of leader: someone who is not just a manager, but who also has the vision to understand what is changing in the business world and can adapt quickly to take advantage of that change.
- Never lose sight of the future. At the same time, don't forget the present. Ideally, balance long-term advantages and goals against short-term performance pressures to create a business that is strong today—and will be stronger tomorrow.

Over the course of this book, we will look at the common themes infusing these leading-edge companies, examining in-depth how 10 companies are changing themselves to react both to those general shifts in the environment and to their own individual pressures. In addition, we will examine in-depth the eight lessons outlined above, using the 10 companies and others as examples. The strongest voices in this book are those of the top managers who are leading their companies through the difficult straits of the 1980s and pushing their organizations onto the leading edge of American business.

# 2

# GENERAL ELECTRIC

## Charting a Fast New Course for
## a Once-Stodgy Corporate Giant

In Louisville, Ky., one of the most advanced assembly lines in the world
is turning out dishwashers of unprecedented quality with previously un-
heard-of efficiency. In Erie, Pa., a decades-old factory is turning out
state-of-the-art railroad locomotives using similarly modern production
techniques. And in Winchester, Va., a sprawling plant is cranking out
lightbulbs at a pace twice what anyone in the industry thought possible
a few years ago.

These are not sexy, high-tech products—indeed, few fruits of American industry are as simple as a 60-watt lightbulb—but they are all examples of the transformation of one of the nation's largest companies, a
company that is supplying all sorts of modern manufacturing, management and planning techniques to its thousands of businesses in an attempt
to stay on the leading edge of the changing markets in which it competes.

General Electric's annual revenues of more than $29 billion make it
one of the nation's most imposing corporate behemoths. It is a widely
diversified conglomerate, its products integral parts of everyday life. From
lightbulbs to electric motors to televisions to jet engines, some GE product
touches Americans on a regular, and most likely daily, basis. The com-

pany's 300,000 employees are spread throughout every corner of the country and most parts of the world, making it one of the key employers at home and abroad, a company acutely intertwined with the economy around it. In short, GE is one of the good-old-fashioned American industrial giants.

But there is nothing old-fashioned about General Electric these days. Under the leadership of Jack Welch, it is rethinking every facet of the way it does business.

"We're not changing GE for the sake of changing GE," Welch says. "We'll try to adapt GE to a world that we see is on fire."

The Welch-led transformation of General Electric has included the modernization of those factories producing such seemingly mundane products as dishwashers, locomotives and lightbulbs. It also includes a commitment to apply technology in the most opportunistic ways to products and production, to try to steal a march on competitors using that technology as well as to strive for low-cost operation and other competitive edges. Finally, the transformation has produced a new planning process that replaces GE's time-proven and oft-emulated planning system with a more dynamic system that tries to stay closer to fast-moving businesses and urges managers to think like their competitors—and then think of ways to foil that thinking.

Welch's makeover of GE has even included a little empire-building, with the $6.4 billion acquisition of RCA Corp., which will give the company a new infusion of technology, service businesses, defense contracts, and access to industrial and consumer markets.

The acquisition of RCA, announced in late 1985, is the single most visible sign of the revolution Welch is leading at GE. It also has been the most heavily criticized, seen by many, even in the business world, as another example of the big getting bigger. "I don't see anything constructive at all in GE and RCA getting together," Pepsico Inc. Chairman Donald Kendall told the *Wall Street Journal* shortly after the deal was announced. "I'm sure [Welch] has figured out something, but it escapes me. It's just creating a $40 billion giant. [RCA Chairman Thornton] Bradshaw has done a great job of turning RCA around, and it ought to stay alone."

But Welch sees the RCA acquisition as being an integral part of his campaign to strengthen GE. To him, the merger is justified on at least two major counts. First, it greatly expands the roster of potential winners at GE by adding RCA's established businesses and budding technologies to GE's. It permits a pooling of technology by two companies whose parallel expertise creates opportunities for the elusive quality of synergy. "We don't know any one business well," Welch says. "We know management and how to allocate resources and how to pick winners and people and markets, which makes us different."

Secondly, the combination with RCA gives GE a stronger, more protected base that can generate profits to help the operations that are exposed to stiff competition from abroad, or that are awaiting technological breakthroughs or market rebounds. Like the large Japanese companies that are able to challenge GE on many fronts, RCA has its American enclaves that face no serious foreign challenges: defense contracting, the NBC television and radio network, and a diversified service business.

While the two companies seem similar—as a matter of fact, they can trace the same corporate ancestry—they are not really mirror-image electronics and communications giants. Rather, many of their businesses complement, rather than compete with, each other—a fact that surprised many who raised initial antitrust qualms about the deal. Where GE has pursued industrial electrical and electronics markets, RCA has gone for communications and consumer electronics. GE was building large electrical turbines; RCA was building satellites. GE made toasters; RCA made video-disc players. And as defense contractors, while GE made jet engines, RCA assembled sophisticated military communications systems. And so on.

In acquiring RCA, Welch sees an opportunity to extend the General Electric philosophy to new businesses—and to bring RCA's know-how to bear on GE's existing lines. And the merger helps fulfill Welch's dream of getting GE into the No. 1 or No. 2 position in as many businesses as possible—and then using that dominant position to earn money to increase its share across the board. With the RCA acquisition, Welch says, "We're the best now in broadcasting; we are the best in engines; we'll be the best in aerospace; we're the best in lighting; we're the best in appliances; we're No. 1 in motors; No. 1 in engineering materials; we're No. 1 in medical diagnostic imaging. There isn't another company, when you look across it, that looks like this."

In many senses, the new GE seems a repudiation of the stolid company run by Welch's predecessor, the legendary Reginald H. Jones, who during the 1970s was the stately exemplar of all that was right about the modern American chief executive. The peripatetic Welch, and the thoughts he espouses, are quite different—which an enthusiastically supportive

Jones says was just what he had in mind when he recommended Welch as his successor. "I became very concerned that the technologies in which GE was most involved were changing and changing fast," says Jones, now a consultant to GE. "We were looking at slower growth, intensified competition—particularly international—and a much higher technological content. So it seemed to me that we should be looking for people that would fit that environment and would be able to produce against that environment."

Jones saw the feisty Welch—with his demonstrated interests in technology, marketing, and battering the competition—as the embodiment of where GE had to be taken in the next decade and beyond. And Welch has used those qualities to put his own personal stamp on GE's corporate culture. Just as Jones implemented a system of corporate financial controls and planning that first rescued the company from an early 1970s financial morass and then became a model for corporate management systems, Welch, the engineer/entrepreneur, is making his own mark on GE.

In many ways, Welch seems to be trying to set the stage for others at GE to repeat his career. Constantly preaching about the entrepreneurial spirit, urging managers to take chances, recounting like a proud mentor anecdotes of managers who are pushing pet projects just as he nurtured engineering plastics into a billion-dollar business, Welch is trying to get his infectious enthusiasm to permeate the entire organization.

Most strikingly, he says he will not punish failure if it is in the name of taking a chance. As long as a manager will give a sound idea a try, Welch says, he or she will not be penalized for vagaries of the marketplace that cause failure. "We've got to take the punitive aspects out of the management process in order to get enough bubbling-up of ideas," Welch enthuses, "because the bubbling up is in fact the only way for us to make it, to win."

Other GE executives say Welch is obsessive about this idea of boosting risk-taking. "Jack grew up in an environment that encouraged people to take chances, and I think he didn't punish you when you missed," says Frank P. Doyle, GE's senior vice president for corporate relations, who has responsibility for personnel development. "That's almost religious with him now. He almost goes overboard. You find a guy who took a big swing and didn't make it, he gets management awards."

One of the celebrated stories Welch and others around the company tell to illustrate this concerns the failure of the company's Halarc project to develop a practical version of an efficient light bulb that would last

5,000 hours, five times the normal life of a standard bulb, using one-third the energy. Conceived during the energy crisis of the late 1970s and developed at a cost of several million dollars, the project failed when the energy crunch abated and consumers weren't willing to pay $10 or more for a long-lasting light bulb.

At other companies, those involved in an ill-fated project might have gone looking for new jobs. At GE under Welch, they were celebrated. "We had a big dance, a big party, promoted the fellow who was running it, gave VCRs to all the employees that were involved in it, and promoted [some of them]—and closed the project," Welch says. In what may be a first in corporate America, the failure of the Halarc effort was even written up in glowing terms in GE's house magazine, *Monogram*.

"We felt everybody gave it a reasonable shot, and people worked damn hard at it," says Paul W. Van Orden, GE's vice chairman, who headed its consumer-products sector at the time. "We made a very big effort to understand that you could take a run at something with the management's blessing, give it your best shot, and if the market wasn't there, or we couldn't crack the technology, the individuals didn't end up losing."

"That's a role model," Welch says. "Trying to get people to try it. And we publicized it, gave management awards for a good try, made it a big deal, because we've got to get more and more people constantly reaching out. . . . What we're trying to do is create more role models so people within [GE] will do it—more ventures within the business."

Welch says that in addition to tempering the risk of failure, one key to allowing entrepreneurial managers to flourish is to give them a sense of "ownership" of their business—again, an echo of Welch's own reputation for running parts of the huge GE bureaucracy as if they were small, autonomous businesses answerable to him. "I think my background, clearly, has something to do with how I feel about managing businesses," Welch says. "I'm a believer in somebody who fights for an idea. If somebody comes to me in this company who wants to try something, and I can sort of feel pretty good about it after he gets through with me, I will think, oh, that's great."

One GE employee who convinced Welch to take a flyer on a project was Gary Carlson, a middle-level manager in the company's huge lighting division. Carlson believed that GE could create a hot new business by buying a small Minnesota Mining and Manufacturing Co. ceramics subsidiary that appeared to be going nowhere. Carlson believed that a new company combining the 3M unit's technology with GE's know-how could produce a strong product line of ceramic settings for semiconductors—a fast-growing market. Welch, won over by Carlson's determination, approved the acquisition. Soon, Carlson was running a business worth about $50 million annually. But the experiment fell far short of expectations. Carlson was transferred to another assignment and later left the company. His experience shows the flip-side of the new atmosphere at GE: a manager who shoots for the moon and misses may pay a price, even in an environment that exalts risk-taking.

Although Welch has been advocating high technology at GE, he has not neglected the company's other, lower-technology manufacturing businesses. In fact, some of the company's largest recent investments have gone for product and manufacturing improvements for such conventional items as dishwashers and railroad locomotives.

And Welch applies the same management standards to these businesses. Carl J. Schlemmer, manager of the company's huge Erie, Pa., diesel locomotive plant, has been given increasing bonuses as a reward for implementing a half-billion-dollar modernization of the locomotive assembly process—even though the locomotive business, until recently, was horrendous.

"Carl Schlemmer, who has a booming 1980 and is a hero, then modernizes his factory and orders go down to nothing in the '81-'82 recession, is as good a guy in '82 with lousy numbers as he was in '80 with great numbers," Welch said. "I gave him a bonus in '82 that was an incremental improvement over what he had in '81, although his numbers were down 40 percent, because he was implementing the best against his external world. I try to measure people not on some internal numbers, but on how they are doing against their environment. . . ." GE officials believe the modernization of the locomotive plant will reap huge benefits when the railroad market finally rebounds.

Welch believes that by urging his managers to take such chances and to react more strongly to perceived market forces rather than to internal expectations or corporate political considerations, he is improving GE's already impressive pool of managerial talent—a group rated as "outstanding" by 93 percent of securities analysts surveyed by GE a few years ago.

"I think that people get put into environments and come out of them a lot better," Welch says. "We sometimes measure our managers in the old system of management by the numbers—'He made $41 million this year and had 6,000 employees, so therefore he's at level so and so at this pay.' Well, some of those businesses, my kid could have been in a rocking chair making $41 million. Some of the businesses that we're losing money in were managed by better managers who were fighting a tougher competitive environment, who weren't lucky enough to be placed in that job at that time."

In return for his support, Welch demands that his subordinates do their homework, and woe to the executive who enters the chairman's office unprepared. Welch is known as a tough, unrelenting questioner who uses his considerable intelligence to get quickly to the center of a question.

"He gives one of the most rigorous business reviews I've ever seen," Doyle says. "One of the things you learn when you deal with him is that he's going to be rigorous and he's going to be forceful and emotional. . . . If I'm in there with a central issue that I'm not all over, then that's a tough afternoon. . . . Those are not tea parties." Still, Doyle says, Welch doesn't seem to hold a grudge over such incidents. "If I've had a really tough headknocker with Welch on an important issue, I may be seething about it years later. That's behind him two hours later," he says. "He is far more likely to put it behind him than most of us are."

Welch's style and philosophies haven't gone down well in some parts of GE. His search for go-go managers, some critics say, has rewarded younger executives while pushing out older employees who are finding it harder to adapt. Despite success stories like Schlemmer's—who after 33 years with the company admits that he is an old dog learning new tricks—GE faces at least four dozen age-discrimination suits filed by older managers and employees who were told the company no longer needed them. There is also evidence of strain among those who remain. A recent employee-attitude survey gave management mediocre marks for internal communications, reflecting an uneasiness among some parts of GE over the drastic change in environment within the company, some insiders say.

All in all, Neutron Jack Welch has earned his name. But Welch argues, with justification, that those steps were needed to improve productivity and profitability. And in many communities where the axe has fallen, GE has won praise from some union and civic officials for the measures it takes to cushion the blow, including generous severance benefits, transfer opportunities, and counseling to help former employees find new work. A management bent on GE's brand of hard-nosed restructuring is obliged to try to set the casualties back on their feet, out of fairness to them, and to buttress the morale of the remaining work force.

There have been many changes for those who remain. Among the most important is the way in which Welch has revolutionized GE's strategic-planning process. For the better part of the decade of the 1970s, General Electric was the unchallenged leader in the field of corporate planning. GE literally wrote the book on the subject—the bound set of worksheets used by GE managers to predict and assess their businesses' performances were the basis of the planning processes at countless other companies.

In the past few years, however, GE has been radically restructuring its vaunted corporate planning system. The planning staff at corporate headquarters in Fairfield, Conn., has been reduced from 85 members a year before the arrival of Michael Carpenter, GE's vice president for corporate business development and planning, to 30 today. The number of local planners at GE's farflung operations has been pared proportionately, or more. The company's major appliance group, for example, has reduced its 50-member planning staff to exactly zero in the past few years.

This is not to say that GE has abandoned the kind of future-thinking that is essential to the success of any business venture. Far from it. The company has changed radically the way it looks at its crystal ball, and how it reacts to what it sees. "We think we brought planning to life, not scuttled it," Welch says emphatically.

The change reflects a shift in philosophy under Welch—yet another manifestation of the company's perception of a changing business environment. With world markets relentlessly becoming more competitive and GE increasingly involved in high-technology businesses whose elements seemingly change hourly, the rigorous planning system of the past just couldn't keep up, GE officials say. Shifts in markets for high-tech products can render plans obsolete in a matter of months, a period the old system—which operated on an annual cycle—couldn't cope with.

Instead, GE has now adopted a more flexible system that adjusts the planning cycle to the needs of a particular business—requiring managers of a fast-moving high-tech operation to update their plans every few months, while asking for updated plans from slower-moving businesses much more infrequently. At the same time it is trying to reduce second-guessing by top management and give line managers more flexibility in adapting their businesses to rapidly changing market conditions.

The new GE system puts more of an emphasis on pure strategy, defined by Carpenter as "thinking through the fundamental keys to success of a business: What is competition doing, how do the economics work, how do you create competitive advantage, and how do you nail the other guy. That's what strategy is." Such a strategy, which often can be distilled and expressed in a few paragraphs, forms the basis for actual operational planning, which has also been simplified at GE.

In strategic planning, as in many other areas, GE under Welch is attempting to move away from the sloth caused by its bureaucratic weight and essay a more free-wheeling, fast-reacting, entrepreneurial style that might normally be seen in a much smaller company. Not lost in the change are GE's famed controls on spending and other financial and managerial restrictions that help the company run efficiently. But the way the company looks at and reacts to the world around it has undergone fundamental change.

Carpenter, a tough but affable Englishman, says, "The challenge we faced, and that Jack began to deal with before I arrived, was the challenge of how you preserve what's good about strategic thinking while eliminating what's bad."

To Welch's management team, GE, like many companies, had become preoccupied with imaginary planning targets that had little or no relationship to actual market conditions. "The thing that always bothers me is that setting up a numerical target doesn't make it happen," Welch says. "It is nothing more than a discussion of numbers between the two of us."

On the other hand, targets based on the marketplace, formulated after a detailed analysis of what the competition is doing, offer more realistic measures of success, Welch believes. As a result, he's trying to instill in his managers an obsession with what their competition is doing, and urging them to stay a step or two ahead.

"It's better for us to look back over the last three years and clearly analyze how we performed against our competitive world," he says. "The degree to which we outperform industry will be the measure of our success. I'd rather be a historian than a prognosticator of success. . . . If we underperform industry, we will not have been successful in implementing our strategy." The biggest target Welch has set for his managers is to try to make their operations No. 1 or No. 2 in their industries—or else.

In addition, GE hopes its new planning system will instill an important spark in the company's strategy-making. "You've got to allow for creativity," Carpenter says. "One of the problems with the bureaucratic process was that creativity, which is the essence of strategy, of continuing to rethink your business and how to play the game, diminishes under the weight of big, thick leather binders."

The results of the new planning philosophy are being felt in many corners of GE's far-flung empire—from Cleveland, where worries about imports and other competition have been the impetus for a major overhaul of the company's lightbulb division, to Louisville, where concentration on staying ahead of the competition has led to the spending of tens of millions of dollars to modernize the company's major appliance produc-. tion lines, to Lynn, Mass., where the products of a strategy to wrest a key military jet engine contract from an archrival are now rolling off the assembly line.

One of the key tools GE's managers have is technology, in all of its forms—as a way to create new businesses, to update traditional products, or to improve manufacturing productivity and efficiency. In an effort to keep the huge company globally competitive for the next decade and beyond, GE officials have embarked on a furious program of research, development, and acquisition designed to transform General Electric into a high-technology superpower. GE's management wants the company to be as well-known for microchips and sophisticated medical equipment as it is for lightbulbs and dishwashers. And GE, bolstered by a strong corporate balance sheet, is not afraid to make some short-term sacrifices in the name of long-term gains. "We're not here for six months," Welch says. "We have an institution that has to be a winner over a long period of time."

As part of his reordering of GE's corporate culture, Welch is urging his managers to scrap their search for small business improvements in favor of a quest for the big hit. "We've got to have a lot of people who are willing to go for the quantum change, who are not willing to do a little better than last year every time—who are willing to change the nature of the business they are in," Welch says.

Central to the new philosophy of GE's management is a realization of fundamental changes going on in the business and economic environment in which GE operates. "You can't be a world-class competitor with a domestic headset," Welch says. "You've got to think of selling not in 50 states, but in 50 nations. You have to think of sourcing not in one state or one country, but in 50 countries. You've got to have a world view of this whole thing."

GE has the financial resources to fund its vision of the future. At one point, it had $5 billion in cash—the largest corporate war chest ever assembled without debt—and even with heavy spending on capital improvements and acquisitions in recent years, the company's nest egg was about $3 billion when it made the $6.4 billion acquisition of RCA in late 1985. Borrowing the rest of the money to buy RCA was no problem.

GE had accumulated the money over several years from profits and from the sale of scores of businesses that GE executives didn't think fit the company's future—including its Utah International mining division, sold in 1984 for $2.4 billion just a few years after GE had acquired it. "I had a predecessor who saved all his nickles and dimes for me," Welch says. "That was marvelous, because I like to spend money." GE has attempted to spend its money to develop and market new technologies, to expand and modernize its existing businesses, and to make acquisitions—small ones that will give GE access to business niches and big ones, like RCA, that will position it in scores of businesses at once.

By adding RCA, Welch believes that GE has further strengthened its financial underpinnings by adding additional businesses that are not as vulnerable to economic cycles as GE's more traditional industrial businesses. Together with GE's own financial-services powerhouse, they provide the cushion for the kinds of chances Welch wants to take, allowing the company to make riskier investments or to carry a money-losing business until it can reach its full potential.

Much of the money has been targeted for investment in technology to improve the lot of both GE's older businesses and its newer high-tech ventures. "Technology is in old businesses, it's in new businesses, it's everywhere to get competitive. It's in every corner of the place," Welch says. "If you look at a company like General Electric, we can only win in games that require technology [and] investment."

"The priorities, as I see it, are first of all reinvesting in the existing businesses to make sure they're as attractive 10 years from now as they are today," Carpenter says. "That's the first priority: make sure the foundation is secure. . . . The second priority is to fund all of the good internal ventures."

"The technology investments are the only way the core can survive," Welch says. "We can't have anything in our core—in GE—that doesn't require, or doesn't have the opportunity for, technological leapfrogs, process technology, wins, and investment."

The list of research projects underway at GE's first-rate corporate research and development center in Schenectady, N.Y., reads like a *Scientific American*-to-Silicon Valley tour of the high-technology frontier, including engineered materials, interactive graphics, very large scale integrated (VLSI) circuits, artificial intelligence, and "seeing" robots.

Some of the various technologies carry higher priorities than others, as reflects the various characteristics of the many GE businesses to which they may be applied. "Various industries have their clocks ticking at different rates," says Roland W. Schmitt, GE's chief scientist. "What's short-term with a large turbine business is infinity for electronics."

"I call them the runners and the joggers," he says. Some are "flat-out" sprinters, like magnetic-resonance medical imaging—a fast-growing business GE pioneered—or complex integrated-circuit technology. "But then there are a number of other things that are progressing at a nice clip, but clearly could be speeded up," he says.

"There's a growing recognition of the value of speed in moving technology into products," Schmitt says. "Three or four years ago, we took a look, with operations, at several different programs, and we started asking ourselves the question: Suppose we turn up the resources in these programs to bring them to market a couple of years earlier? That would obviously cost a lot of extra money; the question is, would that pay off?

"Even with our hard-nosed operations guys at it, we came to the conclusion that in a lot of cases it paid off," he says. "It paid off because you got to market faster, you've got a bigger market share, and so on, so the extra cost is more than paid. Now we're trying to push that."

In an effort to hasten new technology to market, Welch is urging managers of GE's various businesses to draw more fully on the resources of the corporate labs to bring closer together technologies and markets for maximum speed in reacting to business changes.

In some cases, GE has found itself playing catch-up in the technology race, particularly in the semiconductor and computer-related fields—the legacy of Jones' decision a decade ago to pull the company out of most sectors of the computer business. Although there's no question that the decision, on the whole, was a sound one, even Jones concedes that GE may have retrenched too far. "I think where we made a mistake was in not continuing, to the degree we should have, the emphasis on the semiconductor, on the electronic approach to controls, because controls are at the heart of so many businesses in General Electric," says the former chairman. "We've had to fight our way into that."

To be sure, GE has had other setbacks—small ones like Carlson's ceramics effort and larger ones like a full-scale effort to become a leading provider of factory automation, which has fallen short of GE's ambitious expectations. "Did we screw up and go down some blind alleys? Absolutely," Welch says. But by listening harder to its customers and reacting decisively, GE now has a refocused, smaller effort that has begun to grow rapidly.

To Welch, one of the crucial keys to success is identifying the businesses in which you can do best and vowing to dominate them. Prior to the takeover of RCA, Welch had identified 15 major GE businesses as the foundations of the company's future. Those were broken into three groups, each of which contributed roughly equally to GE's revenues: the company's traditional "core" businesses, such as lighting, electric motors, and appliances; high-technology lines, such as jet engines, electronics, and factory automation; and services, including credit, insurance, and leasing. "I've got 15 businesses that I've got a chance to be a powerhouse in," Welch said then. "They're not all No. 1, they're not all clearly defined winners, but they're businesses [to which] we can bring these assets . . . technology, money, people, resources, to win. And they're big games, not small games." Acquiring RCA gives GE several more businesses to add to that core.

The success or failure of Welch's efforts are measured by the numbers that reflect GE's performance. So far, the company's stock price, sales, and earnings growth far exceed the norms of American Big Business. GE's leaders hope that by remaking the company in a high-technology and service mold, they can break the company's traditional image as one that sedately plods along at a rate similar to that of the U.S. gross national product. "The world says we're a GNP-growth company," Carpenter says. "We are in markets which are above-GNP-growth markets. . . . I see the company being a GNP-growth company—plus one, two, or three points."

By making these changes, GE executives hope to turn the company into a more powerful, modern, dynamic entity that will be as much on the leading edge in 1990 as it is today. "We think GE was a step ahead of the environment in 1979," Welch says. "I hope we're a step ahead of the environment today. But clearly, the environment has picked up pace in the last five years. The pace has accelerated. . . . I guess you've got to look back on us and say, are we moving fast enough?"

"The real test of how good and capable we are as a team is how good we look in 1990," Welch says. "One of the things I have to do here is get a company that in 1990 I like a lot more than I like today."

In 1985, Welch commissioned a survey of GE's top managers to find out how they viewed the company and its future. Now, employee surveys are not particularly novel, but it is unusual for a company to query its top 500 managers on their opinions. And GE got some unusual results. Although the managers gave high marks to the company's strategy and leadership, they were more pessimistic about the future. "Forty percent of the people weren't sure that we'd be stronger five years from now than we are today," Welch says. "That disturbed everybody."

But it didn't disturb Welch. "I think that's sensational!" he exults. "Because they are looking outside. They're looking outside at what the Japanese are doing, at what the Koreans are doing, and people are coming at them every day. They're not looking at how powerful they are—they're looking around themselves. . . . My view is, for a company that's looking at competitive forces, that's trying to be global, trying to think about where they're going to go, having people uncertain—liking the strategy, having confidence in the management, but being uncertain about whether or not they're going to win—to me that is constructive."

# 3

## ANTICIPATE AND REACT

### Effective Corporate Change

With the world around them moving at an ever-quickening pace, with competition coming at them from all sides and the next technological leap just around the corner, successful managers today are putting a new emphasis on the environment in which their businesses operate. No longer can companies have the luxury of setting internal goals based on previous years' performance without so much as a nod to what the competition might be doing—the tactic followed for years at many major industrial firms. To stay on the leading edge of their industries, today's managers must be fully cognizant of what their competitors are up to, what their customers need, and what else is happening in the world in which they operate—and then be prepared to act immediately on what they see. Ideally, successful managers must anticipate external developments—or even cause them to happen themselves.

"It seems to me that if you are going to be successful, the key word is 'anticipate'—then comprehend and react," says former General Electric Chairman Reginald H. Jones, one of the business world's most astute philosophers. "You have to be looking out ahead and trying to anticipate what various vectors or forces are going to cause in the business environment that will impact upon you and your corporation."

"I make the argument that 80 to 90 percent of the things that fail are not because people don't execute or implement—it's because they don't read how fast our competition is moving or how fast the market is changing," says Jones' successor, Jack Welch.

"The first thing is to make sure you realistically evaluate the environment you're in—what it really is, not what you wish it to be, or what you conceive it to be," says National Intergroup Chairman Howard M. Love. "You have to make sure you're looking at a real environment, and that means you have to talk to a hell of a lot of people inside and outside your business, you have to get outside your company, travel, and do a hell of a lot of listening."

Under Jones during the 1970s, General Electric turned strategic planning into something of an art form, laying down tenets of planning that have been copied by numerous companies. That planning system, with an emphasis on regular reviews of all businesses and strict financial control, also depended on sophisticated pulse-taking of the world around General Electric. These extended beyond a simple reading of the economic environment and into surveys of the factors that influenced that environment. "We attempt at General Electric at the corporate level to develop, let's say, environmental studies," Jones says. "We try to figure out at a corporate level where the world's economies are going, where the different national economies might be heading, and we look at major societal trends that may impact upon the economy, and so on."

But that doesn't mean you stick your finger in the air and try to make an economic forecast. After all, when was the last time you heard an economic forecast that was correct? What Jones talks about is like the difference between a weather forecast on the 6 o'clock news and a detailed study of a region's climate. "I think it is a great mistake to just try to make economic forecasts," Jones says. "You've got to make these forecasts of these very major waves or trends in public thinking and public demand and so on, so your awareness of what society is looking for is heightened. And you've got to couple all this with the technological forecast, because the technological forecasts impact economic forecasts [which in turn] impact the societal forecasts." In 1976, for instance, GE under Jones convened a panel of technology experts inside and outside the company to prepare what Jones calls a "five-foot shelf" of detailed technological forecasts for the next few years. To use an even more specific example, GE was watching more than just the competition—which was formidable—as it developed the magnetic resonance (MR) body scanner in the late 1970s and early 1980s as a successor to CAT scanners for hospital use. With resistance to health care costs growing around the nation, General Electric was concerned about a backlash that could limit the markets for the extremely expensive MR equipment. So it also kept watch on public opinion on health care costs, prepared to throttle back its MR development program if it appeared that public policy was going to make hospitals reluctant to purchase such expensive equipment. Fortunately for GE, the backlash never materialized, and the company now leads the market for MR technology.

General Electric's current managers have taken Jones' philosophies one step farther. They have revamped GE's planning and management system to make it even more sensitive to the world around it, and put an even greater premium on managers' abilities to anticipate change and stay one step ahead of it. In part, the new philosophy is a reaction to failings in the earlier GE planning system. "The planning system that we had, I will argue, went through the motions, but wasn't as effective at accomplishing the result," says Michael A. Carpenter, the vice president for corporate business development and planning who came to GE in 1983 from the Boston Consulting Group. "When it was set up, it was very useful because it caused people to think about what strategy was, and it caused people to think about competition and the business economics. But as time went by, the process that was put into place to ensure that discipline became a rote process." Too often, Carpenter said, GE managers filled out the complicated forms that were the backbone of the old planning system without giving much thought to what was really going on. "It became bureaucratic, form-filling, non-strategic—planners talking to planners," Carpenter says. "The general manager would say in July, 'Jesus, I've got to prepare my strategic plan.' He'd get through that, and the other 11 months of the year he'd run his business."

Welch charged Carpenter with putting a new vitality into GE's strategic-planning process—restoring creativity and dynamism to the process. Carpenter began by decrying the very term "strategic planning." "I won't use the words 'strategic planning,'" he says. "Strategic thinking, or strategic management, or some other word, is very central to what we do on a day-to-day basis. I think the whole strategic thinking process has more impact right now than it did when we had a strategic-planning system."

To hear Carpenter tell it, thinking strategically, GE-style, is similar to being a successful military planner. It requires an analysis of every possible factor and an attempt to anticipate what the competition will do next—and how to force them to do what GE wants them to do. "Any company you talk·to will tell you about understanding your competition and beating your competition and all that," says Carpenter. "But if you scratch below the surface and you ask how much do they really understand the competition, and you took the general manager of the business and put him in a room and said, all right, in three pages or less, write down [a rival's] competitive strategy, write down how you stack up relative to him, write down what his options are, what his historical behavior patterns are, what he's most likely to do, and what the result of that is going to be—you will get a blank stare 99 times out of 100. . . . Most people aren't brought up to think that way. Most people are brought up in business to think that if you do a good job, you'll do OK."

General Electric wants the managers of its divisions to be able to think differently—to be able to produce answers to all of those questions about their competition, and more, and to be able to act on them. "We do planning today that is exciting," Welch says. "We do planning where we take a company like X—be it Whirlpool, be it Emerson—and we say, if we were running that company . . . the ideal two strategies to get [GE] would be—and we lay out in great detail the other guy's strategy from his perspective."

For example, in a recent review of GE's electric-motor business, division executives prepared a detailed analysis of archrival Emerson Electric, as if they were planning for Emerson rather than GE. "They said, if we were Emerson, this is the product-line strategy we would have, this is the plant-consolidation plan, here's what we would be doing, and therefore, here's what their relative cost position ought to be compared to ours in 1989, if they do everything right," Carpenter says. From that base, the GE managers presented their own strategy—based on what they expected Emerson to be doing several years down the line. "That is the kind of understanding that you've got to have among the business management," Carpenter says. "They've got to be able to put themselves in the seat of the competition, and not only understand what drives their business but understand what the other guy's trying to do."

"It is just another dimension," Welch says. "It's taking his plan and running his business, and not saying, 'Here's where he is today, here's what his costs are, now if I do this, I'll be up so and so'—as if he's going to stay stagnant for the next five years. It's taking his move, it's actually making it, drawing up his plan, giving his plan for the next five years, if he does it right, as best you know it. Now, he may have a better plan than you can devise, but at least it brings it into a much more dynamic fashion."

GE officials admit that this philosophy is still in its infancy, and so far is only used by a handful of the company's divisions. But it's spreading throughout the company, and stimulating the creativity of the company's managers. "It's getting to be who can be most creative about their competitor here," Welch says. "I think we're seeing plan after plan evolving to higher levels of sophistication. We spend the first half hour of every meeting now describing the competitive world."

GE's managers believe the process is beginning to pay off. Carpenter claims the company's Calma interactive graphics division has gotten such a handle on the competition's plans that "we have got . . . all those guys nailed. I don't mean we're going to beat them, but we know what we've got to do to beat them, we think, and we have plans in place that are competitively driven. My experience in Fortune 500 companies is, they talk a lot about competitive analysis, but it's not real. It's 'Competitor A has a good marketplace reputation, they've got good quality products and the distributors love them.' And that's bullshit. Whereas I think we're going down to a level of reality about understanding competition and understanding the economics of our business. It's coming out of this new approach."

One of the key elements to understanding the competition, in the GE scheme of things, is a not-so-new notion—Know Thy Customer. GE managers are urged to maintain close contact with customers, both to be able to assess customer needs and to find out what's going on in the overall marketplace. This relationship with customers is heightened by the planning process—in drawing up Calma's most recent plan, GE planners conducted 70 face-to-face interviews with customers and another 250 telephone interviews, asking them to choose between various product attributes, looking for comparisons between GE and the competition, and seeking other information that might give the company an edge. "I think customers are important. Talking to our customers and understanding what they need is a principal part of our strategy development,"

Carpenter says. "There's a difference between talking to customers, understanding their needs and having a good relationship with them, and understanding in a more fundamental way the changes that are driving them and that are changing their business environment. And that is often a harder thing to understand."

"There are two levels of understanding of customers," Carpenter argues. "One being, what does my customer want from me to allow me to do business with him more effectively, the other being what are the pressures on my customer—or on my customer's customer—that are changing the way he views the world, changing his strategy, and therefore will have an impact on me. Let me give you an example: In the motor business, we sell to a compressor manufacturer, the compressor manufacturer will sell to a room air-conditioner manufacturer or to a central-air-conditioner manufacturer. It's one thing to say, 'Aha, this is an important customer, what have I got to do to serve him better?' It's another thing to say, 'Aha, if I were his customer, the thing I really worry about is the Japanese taking over the air-conditioner business, and my problem is how do I stay competitive as a compressor manufacturer, and what are all my options in thinking that through—and therefore, what are the implications for me as his motor supplier? How can I help him achieve his objective?' " Analyzing such information, GE hopes it can figure out both how to serve its customers better and, by implication, how to steal a march on its competition.

"My view is, you learn more about your competition by talking to your customers," Carpenter says. "If you can understand your customers' needs and how they're changing, your competitors' strategy and how it's evolving, and the economic levels in your business, you've got it made."

Given that kind of knowledge, GE ideally likes to take the process one step further, and try to cause things to happen in the markets in which they compete. The idea is to be able to take steps that force competitors into a defensive position, to make them junk their own plans. Carpenter calls it changing the rules. "One of the things you're always searching for in understanding customers and competitors is, how do I change the rules?" he says. "If you and I are playing chess, and you're a better chess player than I am, I can play chess with you forever, and I can get better and better, but on average you're going to clobber me. On the other hand, if halfway through the game I can change the game to basketball, and you don't figure it out for a while, I have a shot.

"In mature businesses, you've got to figure out ways to change the rules of the game," Carpenter says. "Dishwashers is something of an example of that. . . . In dishwashers, we had a reasonable share of the business, reasonable competitive position in the product and all the rest of it. We decided to go the massive automation route. The massive automation route did a number of things simultaneously—it not only produced a better-quality product at a lower cost, which was the obvious objective—it also raised the stakes in the game for all the other competitors. A number of them couldn't hack it. So we ended up with a 12-point [market-] share increase in that business by making it more difficult for the competitors to continue to play by the old rules. And if you look at that industry right now, you begin to see White Consolidated—which has played the game of minimum investment while Whirlpool and GE have raised the stakes—beginning to look a little sickly."

So not only do you want to plan your competitors' businesses for the next few years—you also want to be able to manage them, in a sense, by forcing them to react to your aggressive moves. "The only way to make money is to manage your competitors," Carpenter says. "It's managing a lot of things. It's not just managing your cost position relative to his—it's also managing the way he thinks about the business, managing the way he thinks about you. . . . The most productive form of competition is where you can convince him, at minimal cost to you, not to take you on, because you scare him to death. He knows every time he puts his hand in the cookie jar—whunk! So I think there's an element of the game that is won not only on the battlefield but in the minds of the enemy."

"One of the challenges that corporate management faces, therefore, is to be able to know enough about the business to be able to spot where there's a chance to change the rules," Carpenter says. "That's a very important part of that strategic-management thinking process—and one of the reasons for getting more into depth in the individual businesses."

One of the most satisfying outcomes for GE of its new attitude toward strategy was its 1984 victory in a battle for military jet-engine business against rival Pratt & Whitney, a division of United Technologies Corp. By analyzing P&W's weak points, GE was able to wrest away a sizeable portion of the military jet engine business, winning a Defense Department contract—potentially worth billions—to supply jet engines for such high-performance military fighters as the F14, F15 and F16. To win the contract, GE took a close look at P&W's military business and identified its competitor's vulnerabilities. One, for instance, was a mounting Pentagon dissatisfaction with the durability of P&W's engines. So, GE, when it presented its bid, emphasized the reliability of its engines—and won the contract.

Anticipating and comprehending changes by competitors and in the marketplace is one thing—acting on them is another. Given the increasing pace of change, the burden is on companies and managers to be as flexible as possible and to be able to react quickly. Fast reaction is particularly important in high-tech fields, where the environment and technologies are changing so quickly that what's new today may be obsolete tomorrow. "In the personal computer business, where you have a product cycle that's maybe a year to a year-and-a-half, you don't have the luxury of being thoughtful," says IBM Chairman John Akers. "You don't have that period of time where you can test and respond and test and talk. You're going to have to make some decisions, cut and run, and see what the market does. Sometimes it will be fabulously successful, hopefully— and sometimes it won't."

In many companies, speeding up reaction time means pushing many decision-making functions farther down the corporate ladder than ever before, giving low-level managers a chance to do the things they see necessary to adjust to market changes without waiting for clearance from above that often can get snarled in bureaucratic red tape. In many technology-driven businesses, particularly, delays in decision-making can leave a company far behind the competition as technologies evolve.

To speed up the decision-making process, Gould Inc. has set up boards of directors at the lower divisional levels to give its fast-moving high-tech businesses the greatest possible autonomy in decision-making and adjustments to market conditions. General Electric now allows the heads of its four major business sectors to approve expenditures as large as $20 million without consulting Welch, and to delegate the approval of expenditures nearly as large to subordinates—something unheard of at most companies. And General Motors Corp. has reorganized its basic corporate structure to give managers of its various automobile divisions a greater ability to react to customer needs and to interact to fill those needs.

By decentralizing the decision-making process, in one sense upper managements are making more time for themselves to worry about planning for businesses rather than running them. "When you get right down to it, my job, and others who are in the corporate office, our fundamental responsibility is to develop a strategy, a long-term strategy for the corporation," Gould Chairman Bill Ylvisaker says. "People who are running those businesses are developing near-term strategies—getting out new products, and developing and marketing technical skills to keep abreast or ahead of the competition."

But that does not mean that top managements of companies decentralizing their decision-making are becoming further and further removed from the operations of their businesses. Quite the contrary—in most cases, the executives say the more thorough planning process requires them to learn more than ever before about what their lower-level operations are doing. "You've got a fine line to walk. The fine line is, the general manager has got to be the guy who runs the business," Carpenter says. "On the other hand, the corporate management has got to know enough to be able to challenge the guy intelligently. . . . If you get to the point where the general manager feels like he's not running the business, then that's another risk—but I think we're a long way away from that. And any general manager who would let you do that you don't want anyway."

"I don't try to tell them how they run their business," RCA Corp. Chairman Thornton Bradshaw says of his subordinates. "But I know how they run it."

"From the ground up, we make sure we understand where each of our businesses is going," RCA President Robert Frederick says. "Each one must understand where its source of earnings is going to come from, and what business it thinks it's in. . . . And then we can look at those in context with an overall corporate direction."

One of the keys to effective decentralization of decision-making is an effective set of checks and balances on lower-level managers. GE officials say they could not have given more responsibility to their lower-level managers and revamped the planning system without the old planning system's legacy of tight corporate auditing and other checks.

In addition, managers must accept their new responsibilities. Some have trouble adapting. Borg-Warner Chairman James Beré says, "Those that want to be decentralized, many of them, say, 'Let me do what I please,' and I say fine, we'll permit you to do that—and then you look in and you find that they're absolute dictators. They won't let anybody else participate." Conversely, Beré says, "Many of the very young [managers] who say, 'I want to be a decision-maker, I want to do it'—basically they've been taught in a culture that they either have to have a database to support what they're doing, or they have to have a consensus of their peers to do what they're doing. They don't have the intestinal fortitude to say, 'This is what I'm going to do.' "

Many of the modern strategic-planning set-ups are geared specifically to the needs of the businesses they affect. No longer do leading-edge companies require their division managers to come in like clockwork once a year to discuss their plans for the coming year. Now, these companies get managers of fast-moving businesses in to discuss strategy every few months—while slower-moving businesses are seen much less frequently. "We've got a process which is very, very sensitive to the timing needs of the business," Carpenter says. "It's a discriminatory process. We will say to some businesses, 'Look, we're very comfortable with everything you're doing, the numbers look good—we don't want to see you. We'll see you in two years. There will be another business—it doesn't have to be in trouble—but a business where there are real strategic issues that we're trying to resolve, [such as] factory automation. Factory automation is a business that's in a very dynamic environment. Our strategy is evolving all the time. We probably meet with those guys every three or four months."

The process Carpenter describes requires a sharp sense of timing, because knowing just when to move is one of the most crucial elements of changing a company. More often than not in American business, managements seem to hang on to old businesses and old ways of doing things, either because they are scared to react to the changes around them or for simple sentimental reasons—and the corporations get left behind as a result. "The idea that you anticipate change, the need to change, and change before things become negative crises, is an important strength of this company," says GE Senior Vice President Frank Doyle. "I think it's one of the toughest jobs to get people to convert and recognize the need to change."

One of the classic recent stories of a company that failed to react to the environment around it and paid the price is International Harvester Co., the Chicago tractor and truck maker that today is just a shell of its former self as a result of years of timid management and unwillingness to make needed changes in its operations. That the company has kept itself out of bankruptcy is a tribute to the management team that took over in 1982 and began cutting away unprofitable operations and inefficient production facilities. Effecting change at Harvester was difficult not just because of management mistakes, but also because of sentimentality—the company could trace its heritage directly to Cyrus Mc-

Cormick's invention of the mechanized reaper in the 19th century, and thus was loath to scrap generations of tradition by shutting down or selling its farm-equipment business. When it finally did sell the agricultural operation, in late 1984, it did so with a great deal of reluctance. But analysts agreed that the move, which left Harvester—now renamed Navistar International Corp.—solely as a manufacturer of heavy trucks, all but guaranteed the company's survival.

Speaking to shareholders at the company's annual meeting that followed the decision to sell the tractor division, IH Chairman Donald D. Lennox touched on some of the concerns that were involved, in the decision: "Management and the board of directors knew the psychological impact that the sale would have on employees, retirees, customers, dealers—in fact, the entire agricultural community. They knew, too, that they were interrupting a long-standing tradition. But there was really no other choice. . . . I know that, deep down, the decision to sell the agricultural business was, under the circumstances, the best decision that could have been made for all concerned." Still, he said, "It was a tremendous price to pay." But it was one Harvester might not have had to pay had it recognized changes in the farm-equipment industry a few years before—principally the effects of an economic downturn that turned its key markets into disaster areas.

The idea, then, is to stay a step ahead of such changes, to anticipate them and react to them in ways that will benefit your company. Sometimes such prescience is hard to rationalize to employees, customers, and others who don't understand the need for change, as GE's Doyle points out. "U.S. Steel closes a plant and everybody knows why U.S. Steel closes a plant," he says. "We close a lighting plant, and I'll tell you, it takes a lot of explanation. Foreign competition hasn't arrived yet, we have the dominant market share and technology . . . we really are a powerful player, we've got the low-cost position, we've got the market presence. It's a business where the world would say, 'Why don't you just leave it alone?'

"We know what happens when you leave it alone. And to start changing the lighting business as radically as they are changing it—taking it from 42 plants to 33 plants, making $300 or $400 million worth of investments—churns up everybody. Everybody says, 'Why? There aren't Japanese lightbulbs on the shelf.' That kind of thing. Getting people to act before they are in a negative crisis, and getting the world to accept that you've had to act, is the tough issue."

But the need to anticipate and react to change, and even to control it, is beginning to catch on throughout American industry, even if it takes a disaster as bad as International Harvester's to get the point across. Says Harvester/Navistar President Neil A. Springer, "Where we were once the victims of change, we now advocate it on a constructive and continuing basis. We firmly believe that the art of progress is to preserve order amid change and to preserve change amid order.

"Our company has experienced and survived a great ordeal," Springer says. "We have learned to accept change—indeed, embrace it. Experience is a tough teacher. It tests you first and then offers the lesson. But because of our experience, we're now a company that knows where it's going and how we intend to get there."

# 4

## MARTIN MARIETTA

### Rebuilding from the Ashes of a Takeover War to Become a High-Tech Leader

Given the merger wars of the past few years, what happened at Martin Marietta was not unique. Set upon by a corporate raider, the company won its freedom only at the cost of a massive amount of debt, a story since repeated at such companies as Phillips Petroleum Co. and Unocal Corp. But Marietta, surprising even its most devoted followers on Wall Street, quickly struggled free of the debt handicap and used the experience as the basis for a major shift in the company's orientation, which has made it much stronger than before its run-in with "mergermania." Even company officials admit that the battle with Bendix Corp. in the summer of 1982 has made Martin Marietta a better company by forcing it to make much-needed changes in its business mix and way of operating.

As a result of the clean-up operation after the merger battle, Martin Marietta has ended its decades of diversified conglomeration to concentrate on its strongest businesses—the defense industry and related government work. And using its considerable expertise as a manager of complicated defense contracts, the company has created a series of lucrative new businesses managing such operations as the Oak Ridge national research laboratory and the Federal Aviation Administration's restructuring of the national air-traffic control system—using its strengths to create new, logical opportunities.

"We're off trying to grow ourselves basically in areas relating somewhat to aerospace, but I guess more broadly in large systems management," says Martin Marietta's president, Laurence J. Adams. "We're good at managing the development of a Pershing II system, we think we're good at managing the development of a data system that gathers all the personnel data and presents it on sailors around the world. Large systems. The perfect example of a new direction using the old talents is the FAA air-traffic control system update program. . . . We aren't making any hardware in that program, but we're doing the systems design, we're helping prepare the specifications for all the elements of the system, we're helping evaluate the proposals that come in to equip the system." The new businesses are giving Martin Marietta a new kind of diversity, making it so strong in a multitude of areas of government work that it will be balanced enough to handle a downturn in defense spending or in a particular large program, such as its MX missile. "To some considerable degree, what we are today was commanded for us by outside forces," says Martin Marietta Chairman Thomas G. Pownall. "What was forced on us resulted in leaving a better foundation than previously."

The story of Martin Marietta's battle with Bendix has been oft-told: Bendix, led by its ambitious chairman, William Agee, mounted a hostile takeover offer for Martin Marietta in August 1982, only to have Marietta quickly retaliate with a takeover bid of its own for Bendix—a tactic known as the "Pac-Man defense," after the videogame in which characters try to gobble up one another. The two companies stalked one another in courtrooms and boardrooms for a month, before a third player entered the fray and put a stop to the circus. Allied Corp. purchased Bendix, swapping Bendix's holdings in Martin Marietta for Marietta's Bendix stock. When the dust settled, Bendix was an Allied subsidiary, Agee was out of a job, and Martin Marietta had remained an independent company—but at a huge price. Allied owned 39 percent of Martin Marietta's stock, and the company had run up a debt of almost $1 billion defending itself, increasing its debt-to-equity ratio to a whopping 70 percent.

The situation forced Martin Marietta's top managers to take a hard look at their company. Even before the Bendix affair, Marietta's leaders had been concerned about the company's business mix. In many ways, the company was an industrial hodge-podge created by excessive conglomeration. Its highly profitable aerospace work, such as the MX and

Pershing missiles, Titan rocket boosters, and a variety of satellite-building contracts, was joined with a host of capital-intensive, cyclical businesses, including cement, aluminum, and construction materials. Martin Marietta's business mix was in part left over from the merger that created the company two decades earlier, the joining of aviation pioneer Glenn L. Martin's aircraft company with American Marietta, a diversified construction- and industrial-products company.

At the time, the combination had made sense, the various businesses balancing one another nicely, keeping the company strong, if not spectacularly so, through all manner of business cycles. But additional acquisitions over the years had made the company ungainly, and the energy crises of the 1970s hit many of the company's nondefense businesses hard—even as defense work was picking up steam in the early 1980s. "It was becoming apparent to us that our commercial businesses were getting into some difficulty," Adams says. Even before Bendix, the company's managers had thought about selling the cement business, but a prospective deal fell through.

The situation was exacerbated by the company's major expansionary investments in the cement and aluminum businesses, which simply weren't paying off as those industries slumped. "Several major investment decisions had been made regarding the aluminum business under the assumption that energy prices would be relatively constant— or at least would not become outrageous, as they did," Adams says. "So we had an awful lot of money committed and being spent on capital expenditures in that business, at the same time that the energy costs were going to hell."

If Martin Marietta officials hadn't quite decided what to do about these problems, the aftermath of the Bendix fracas forced them to make some decisions. "Bendix caused us to expedite these things by maybe a couple of years or longer," Pownall says. With the company staggering under its newly acquired debt load, things didn't look very good. "We were faced with the prospect of going under, if we weren't very careful," Pownall says.

Looking for ways to reduce the mountain of debt, the company began selling off or closing down its nonaerospace businesses. It sold a dye company, some chemical operations, and much of its cement division. But attempts to find a buyer for the aluminum division were initially to no avail. Slumping prices of aluminum made that industry extremely unattractive. "We tried first to sell the aluminum company," Adams says.

"We said, that's the one that's going to be the dog—and it turned out that everybody else knew that too. So there weren't any buyers around." Because the division was fully integrated, involved in all steps of aluminum production, it was difficult to sell piecemeal. In addition, simply closing down the division would have required Marietta to break tangled contractural obligations—at a high penalty price. "The flexibility that we had with that business was almost nil," according to Adams. Finally, in 1984, Martin Marietta sold most of the money-losing aluminum operation to an Australian firm that wanted to enter the American aluminum market. The rest of the division was written off. By 1984, Martin Marietta had worked off much of its debt and bought back the 39 percent block of stock held by Allied—achievements that had many on Wall Street giving high marks to Pownall and Marietta's other managers.

Prior to the battle with Bendix, Pownall had been an unknown quantity, and many—not the least of whom included Bendix's Bill Agee—had expected him to acquiesce to Bendix's merger proposal. But Pownall showed a toughness both in fighting off Bendix and then in picking up the pieces afterward that few outside the company realized he was capable of.

But having made the tough decisions about what to cut away from the company, Pownall and Martin Marietta's other leaders had to plan for the remaining parts. "We really said, we have to decide where we want to take this corporation now, because it's obvious that the conglomerate is gone," Adams says. "There were a couple of ways you could go. You could go out and become another kind of conglomerate, or you could go out and focus."

Martin Marietta's leadership considered resuming the conglomerate route, and looked at a number of potential acquisitions. But the company's buying power was limited and, in any case, the company's engineering-oriented management wasn't comfortable with the idea of running a conglomerate. "We're a hands-on management," Adams says. "That's not the way to run a conglomerate. We aren't smart enough to be good hands-on managers in the world of cement and aluminum and what have you. I didn't feel comfortable, nor does Tom Pownall feel comfortable, in the kind of involvement we had in the decision-making process in some of those things. You'd better know something about the business you're going to be in, if you're going to be involved in making these kinds of decisions. I personally thought that was probably part of our problem in the conglomerate business."

In other words, Marietta's top management—most members of which had come up through the aerospace side of the business—wasn't sure it knew enough to run anything else, and didn't want, out of ignorance, to repeat the company's past diversification mistakes.

Martin Marietta decided to go the other route, and concentrate on what it knew best. "We said, OK, we don't want to be a conglomerate," Adams says. "We want to focus in areas where we have strengths, and we want to use those strengths to expand the markets we were already in and to create new markets which were related. . . . That was a very big change in direction."

But fear about a lack of familiarity with other businesses wasn't the only reason the company decided to focus, according to Adams. "We thought we had established within our aerospace operation some capabilities which could be extended into other kinds of businesses . . . in areas we did know something about, in areas where we did feel more confidence in our decisions."

So in addition to being an aerospace giant—its work for the Pentagon and for commercial aerospace customers accounts for nearly three-quarters of annual revenues—Martin Marietta has taken huge strides into related systems-management and high-technology fields, in most cases entering businesses in which it already had a peripheral interest and knowledge and capitalizing on that entrée to create a whole new line of business for the company.

As a result, businesses grew out of other businesses for Martin Marietta in a real-life example of the "synergy" so many other companies speak of in wishful tones. The company expects such new businesses as the loosely defined information-services field to reduce its reliance on aerospace to about half of revenues in a few years. Pownall defines "information systems" broadly. "I take it to mean communications, generating data, displaying it—in a management sense. . . . That's going to continue to grow markedly, well into the future, and there are parts of that in which we believe we have an opportunity to express ourselves." But, he also says, "We're spending most of our time in this information-systems business still trying to divine where we want to be and sampling some of it as we go along."

One of the best businesses Marietta has sampled and found to its liking is a direct descendant of the defense work it has done for years. Realizing that managing massive defense contracts had given it a unique talent for running government-related operations, the company began seeking out management-services jobs for various government agencies. The contract to run the Department of Energy's 18,000-employee nuclear energy research center in Oak Ridge, Tenn., is worth as much as $20 million a year to the company. And combining its aerospace know-how with its management expertise, the company won a $684 million, 10-year contract to develop a new federal air-traffic control system for the Federal Aviation Administration (FAA). One obvious offshoot is the selling of packaged air-traffic control systems, based on the FAA system, to foreign countries. Similarly, the inclusion in the Oak Ridge contract of the opportunity to fund some start-up businesses in the Oak Ridge area, as well as any technology Marietta can learn from Oak Ridge itself, provide other future opportunities for the company. "There's an immense talent base down there," Pownall says of Oak Ridge. "We've got to learn something."

Another of the company's strongest new business areas is in data-processing. Again putting to work some of its expertise in managing large-scale projects, the company has turned what in many companies is a mundane internal service division into a hot performer. The data-processing division now provides software and services to a variety of outside customers—mostly government agencies—for use in computing and managing payrolls, finances, and personnel matters. The growth has forced Martin Marietta to acquire a software company to keep all those computers humming and a part-interest in a computer-data network to enable it to tie various data systems together—as well as to provide ingredients for new, related business opportunities. Analysts estimate that data processing could triple into a $1 billion business for Martin Marietta before the end of the decade.

From data-processing, Marietta turned to communications and information services, logical offshoots of both its data-processing and aerospace divisions. This business covers a variety of military and commercial fields, including "command, control, communications, and intelligence," the tongue-twisting designation for sophisticated military command systems. The FAA air traffic control system contract is part of this division, and the company is seeking more like it to capitalize on Marietta's strengths in these areas.

In addition, Martin Marietta is trying to grow businesses from its existing work in other fields. After years of building satellites and rockets for others, Marietta now is planning to launch a pair of communications satellites on which it would lease space to others for data, voice, and video transmissions. The satellite program pulls together a wide variety of the company's new and old skills and interests to create a new line of business. And a consortium of Marietta divisions is working on another futuristic endeavor: the design of key components for a manned space station.

The company is also trying to bring technology and its other expertise to bear in creating new business opportunities in the defense sector. "The first thing you need is the technology," Adams says. "You've got to be good at it. You absolutely cannot fake that. Your customers are too smart." But in some new, highly sophisticated defense areas, such technology can take years to develop. So, when necessary, Martin Marietta plans to go outside and acquire needed technology to add to its other defense-contracting strengths to enable it to pursue opportunities in new fields. For instance, the company would like to enter the business of providing anti-submarine-warfare (ASW) equipment—a technology the company does not now possess. Adams says Martin Marietta can save itself years of development work and hasten its entry into the ASW business by acquiring small companies with expertise in such fields as acoustic signal processing. "It's a key technology—a lot of the ASW is based on acoustics," he says. "You can buy that, maybe pay through the nose, look like a dumb investment, but then, put together the technology, and the kind of marketing skills and proposal skills and everything else that we have in that world—I think we can compete."

That was the philosophy followed in the company's acquisition of the software house and the part-interest in the data-transmission network. Company officials say they plan to make other, similar investments. "What we are trying to do when we do that is more than just make an investment—we're trying to make a business arrangement," Adams says. "Even though it may not be specific at that time, we have a general agreement that here are areas in which we will work together." The arrangements have advantages for both companies, providing funds and access to a broad customer base for the small company and technology and other know-how for Martin Marietta. "A number of these companies have some very bright ideas and some very bright people, and then they find out after a while they're undercapitalized," Pownall says. Martin Marietta's investment takes care of that, and meanwhile, the small company is providing the larger one with a short-cut to new technologies and markets. "In some cases, time is a factor," Pownall says. "To get the knowledge they've got . . . is something that's quite valuable."

Martin Marietta officials say they will continue to strike up partnerships as needed to develop new opportunities for their company, and Adams, for one, would like to see more risk-taking injected into the process. "I would be for making some more gamey acquisitions, and taking a little criticism for overpaying," he says. Such risk-taking, Adams argues, would be on a much smaller scale than some of the chances Martin Marietta took in the past, when it spent hundreds of millions of dollars on what it thought were safe bets for capital investments in the aluminum and cement businesses, only to have those businesses go sour. "We really didn't think we were taking big risks when we were investing in these capital-intensive businesses," he says. "We really thought we were putting in good, solid production capacity that would make materials that the world would need—and that didn't seem to be all that risky."

These new enterprises Martin Marietta is seeking to develop, however, entail some risks. In many cases, they involve leading-edge technology that the company is using in an attempt to create a defense product the Pentagon will want to buy—in a sense, creating a market where none existed before. "You create an opportunity to bid," Adams says, "as opposed to waiting for a request for a proposal." It's a highly competitive game, with companies like Hughes Aircraft, E-Systems, and Raytheon vying with Martin Marietta to be in the vanguard. Martin Marietta has recently been locked in a battle, for instance, to develop a new generation of sophisticated radar for the so-called "smart missile." The company is betting on a technology called millimeter-wave radar; competitors are using infrared radar. "It may cost us," says Adams. "Millimeter-wave didn't come along as fast as we had hoped, and IR, although it's not quite as good, is not quite as tough to produce. So we're scrambling a bit."

In making such decisions on technology, Adams says, "You look at where you stand with respect to the rest of those guys out there, and pick out the places where you think you can get ahead of them and beat them, and bet on what's going to happen out there in the market, go out and make it happen . . . and away you go."

Such a philosophy requires a particularly attentive management style. "It's more a bet on the not-sure-of-the-future kind of a business than in the past," Adams says. "It . . . really requires that the senior management people in the operation have a pretty darn good understanding of the area in which we're fooling around, because you are making decisions based on judgments that sometimes don't have such solid financial backing."

Martin Marietta hopes that such expansionary thrusts in the aerospace field and others will create new businesses that will diversify the company within the broad arena of government work. Relying on the government for virtually all of the company's revenues, then, doesn't much bother the managers of Martin Marietta, because they believe they have so many different kinds of government contracts that they are protected against any kind of expiration or suspension of a particular government program in which they are involved.

One advantage is that many of the company's government contracts are fairly open-ended; gone are the days when the end of the life-cycle of a Pentagon or NASA contract would leave a breach for the company. And those projects the company is working on that will terminate someday are, for the most part, still in fairly early stages—such as the MX and Pershing II missile contracts. "We're very, very diversified in the defense business, and then also we're diversifying in the government," Adams says. "We've got the FAA contract; in defense we've got contracts in the administrative side—the business of keeping track of the enlisted men in the Navy, for instance—we have contracts with the Department of Labor. So we have broadened the government part of it.

"I would put it in the context that we don't sit around worrying about the percentage of our business which is government and the percentage which is commercial. If we have an opportunity to expand in the non-government area, then we'll do it. And when we're looking at acquisitions, if a guy has got something good going in a non-government line, that's a plus. But let's face it—one of our major major skills is working with the United States government."

As Martin Marietta follows a strategic plan bent on exploiting that skill, it is writing an ironic postscript to a plan drawn up by the company's previous management in 1975. Back then, still running a conglomerate, the company's leaders envisioned a 1985 version of Martin Marietta engaged primarily in cement and aluminum production, with aerospace and government work a relatively minor part of the company. It took economic forces, the Bendix raid, and a new management philosophy to put a much different—and arguably far more successful—spin on the company. Adams sees that 1975 plan for the company's business mix as an example of why it is difficult to predict too far into the future in a changing world. "That was for 1985. Now, if you look at 1985, we're not in most of those businesses," he says. "Our ability to forecast what's going to happen that far out is nil. We just don't have the slightest idea.

"If there's one thing you know, it is that your forecast of the future is wrong," he adds. "So you have to have a plan which is pretty flexible, something that you can move around in."

# 5

# PLAY TO YOUR STRENGTHS

Martin Marietta's managers found that they could maximize their company's chances by exploiting its strengths in technology and government contracting. Similarly, other companies are surviving today's turbulent world by playing to their strengths.

E. I. du Pont de Nemours & Co. entered the 1980s geared up for the scenarios the 1970s had presented: solid growth, marred primarily by the prospect of continued higher rates of inflation, and the fear of possible renewed energy shortages.

Thus far, the 1980s have been precisely the opposite. And like many other companies with the same expectations, Du Pont has had to pull off a painful mid-course correction to steer its way through an era of slow growth and low energy prices. "In the 35 years following World War II, the chemical and allied industries grew at about double the rate of GNP growth," former Du Pont Chairman Edward G. Jefferson told shareholders at the 1985 annual meeting. "This has changed." From mid-1984 through the middle of 1985, there was no growth in the nation's industrial sector, and a company that managed to keep pace with the economy was hardly growing at all.

As with Martin Marietta, the responses that Du Pont and other companies are making to this new environment are based on a much harder, more critical look at their strengths and weaknesses—not just in terms of current sales and profits, but with an eye toward using traditional strengths as the foundation for future successes.

In Du Pont's case, the search began with a new attempt to understand what made Du Pont different. For most of Jefferson's career, Du Pont was a chemicals and fiber company. But he argues that it has also been a "discovery" company. Although that label smacks of a public relations concoction, in fact it does describe a company that came up with such breakthroughs as nylon, Teflon, and a host of other polymer and synthetic materials through the middle part of this century. And the "discovery" tag also applies to where Du Pont wants to go in coming years—moving away from the commodity chemical businesses that fueled growth for the past couple of decades and more deeply into innovative products that can guarantee the company even more powerful growth.

"If you think about what makes the difference to us, whether it's in extractive industries like coal and petroleum, or coming up with the latest crop-protection chemicals, it's discovery," Jefferson says.

A back-to-basics philosophy like that espoused by Du Pont is a marked change from the corporate philosophies of a decade or two ago, when conglomeration was all the rage. Companies like Teledyne and Norton Simon were managed like stock portfolios, collections of often widely disparate businesses usually run with a highly decentralized form of management—the corporation as holding company, letting managers of the individual businesses pretty much run their own show. At the same time, many companies began diversifying into businesses far removed from their corporate histories. Nowhere was this more prevalent, perhaps, than in the oil industry, where Mobil bought the Montgomery Ward department-store chain and a cardboard-box company and Exxon got into the electronic office-equipment business.

Mobil's and Exxon's ventures proved to be embarrassing underachievers. So were many of the widely diversified conglomerates, which generally found the job of managing many disparate businesses too cumbersome and difficult. As a result, pure conglomerates are no longer much in vogue, and companies are getting back to basics. Companies are simplifying themselves—not necessarily shrinking, but concentrating on the businesses they know best.

"When you talk about changing things, you change the way you do business, you change the way you operate in response to a changed environment, but you really should identify what your values are and the strengths in those values," says Ian Ross, the president of American Telephone & Telegraph Co.'s Bell Labs. "And you don't change those in a hurry." In AT&T's case, that means getting employees and managers to shift to a faster gear required by the competitive telecommunications world AT&T has jumped into—without sacrificing the commitment to high-quality products and service that were key links in the company's ethic for three-quarters of a century.

Sticking to what you do best means, in many cases, looking for businesses that "fit"—in other words, those that will either improve existing lines of business or interact with what's already there to create new opportunities, those providing the elusive "synergy" that has increasingly become both a corporate buzzword and a strategic priority.

Or it can mean branching off from an existing business with a new product or service to carve out a niche—a new corner of a market in which a company can use its technical or cost advantages to prosper. The ability to recognize such advantages and use them, either to find niches or to build the company as a whole, is a key quality of leading-edge companies. "I think we ought to play to our strengths," says GE's Welch. "We're looking for things [on which] we can bring something to the party, that we can add." As an example, he offers GE's $1.1 billion acquisition of Employees Reinsurance Corp. in 1984, which fit neatly into the growing credit and related financial services side of General Electric. "It's a risk-assessment business. That's what credit is all about, that's what we've been in for a couple of years. It's quality, and it fits the strengths that we have. We can add strength to it," Welch says. Ditto GE's $6.3 billion acquisition of RCA. Though some critics have attacked the merger as empire-building, GE and RCA executives see opportunities to combine the strengths of the two companies to build for the future.

The idea of synergy, of bringing together related strengths, is nothing new—companies have been doing it for years. But it often has occurred more by accident than design. What has changed recently is that managements are deliberately trying to assemble companies whose whole is much more powerful than the sum of their parts. On their own, Allstate Insurance, the Coldwell Banker real estate firm, and the Dean Witter brokerage house are all fairly impressive, strong companies. But banded together under the Sears Financial Services umbrella, with access to the giant retailer's customer lists and offices in Sears stores, the three different companies form a potentially powerful network for financial services offerings. Sears thus becomes a sort of financial supermarket in which customers can literally buy, finance, insure, and furnish a house—and play the stock market with whatever money is left over. Each element benefits from the presence of the others, a textbook effort to create synergy.

A strategy of synergy requires a flexible, forthright handling of competing divisions or units within a business. It may be necessary for one division to sacrifice an opportunity to clear the way for another division whose prospects are even better—and it's the job of top management to explain that trade-off to all sides and make certain that managers whose operations are asked to sacrifice aren't penalized because they don't hit their targets, according to Robert Kavner, senior vice president and chief financial officer of AT&T.

It is vital in striving for synergy that the parts actually fit together, that management actually knows the businesses on which it is building. To do otherwise can mean disaster. When Mobil bought Montgomery Ward, it figured it knew the merchandising and retailing businesses from its years of operating a nationwide string of service stations. But it was wrong. Selling clothing and housewares turned out to be a world away from pumping gas, in part because gasoline is more of a commodity business, and had for years been something of an afterthought for Mobil and the other oil companies. Gasoline sold because motorists had to have it. Not so in general retailing, Montgomery Ward-style, in which Mobil discovered what competitiveness and fickle consumers were all about. After years of losses, Mobil now is reconciled to selling Montgomery Ward, which it once figured was a sure thing.

Martin Marietta's example richly illustrates how synergy can be used to create profitable new businesses through permutations of older businesses. "The best way to win business is to grow the business you have—by far," says Norman Augustine, Martin Marietta's vice president in charge of the company's burgeoning information-systems division. "A substantial part of our sales comes from follow-ons to businesses we already have." These follow-ons have led Martin Marietta into fields far removed from the missiles and rockets that have long provided the bulk of the company's revenues. But they all had their start in that business.

Many newer technologies lend themselves to such exploitation. Since they often require far less capital investment than many older industrial lines, it is often easy to clone new high-tech businesses.

A decade or so ago, Martin Marietta began pumping research and development money into the then-developing high-technology electronics side of the aerospace business—lasers, microcircuits, infrared sensors, and other devices. That forced the company to begin developing know-how in computer hardware and software and communications used to control such technology, and gave the company seeds for a variety of wholly new businesses.

"As time went on, the state of the art changed and advanced so fast, in the computer field and in the communications field, that when you put those two together you had a critical mass, or a synergistic effect, if you will, where we felt that computers plus communications could make a whole new business," Augustine says. To all that, the company could also add its expertise in managing large government missile and rocket contracts—complex tasks that require a broad spread of knowledge. "They tend to be skills that require breadth as opposed to depth," Augustine says. "You need both engineers and executives who are able to relate to structural systems, to optical systems, to computer systems, to communications systems, to software—very broad capabilities. And you need experts in each of those disciplines. A lot of other people have those experts, but they don't have the ability to thread them together."

That expertise and the company's technological knowledge combined to generate a stream of new businesses. "The fortunate thing from our standpoint is that the groundwork had been laid over many years," Augustine says. "The pieces were all there. . . . We could see that by combining these things together, we could have the makings of a rather substantial business in the information systems area."

Martin Marietta's Information Systems division, which Augustine heads, is now a fast-growing $750 million-a-year business—still just a fraction of the company's aerospace operations, but catching up quickly. The division has won a variety of contracts to design and assemble computer systems for government agencies and others, including computerized record-keeping systems for the Navy and Labor Department, and the contract from the Federal Aviation Administration to redesign the national air-traffic control system. That in turn will create more business, as the company succeeds in supplying smaller, ready-to-run versions of the air-traffic system to foreign governments. "It's our belief that most countries would want to have a system that has the U.S. Good House-keeping seal on it—a scaled-down version," Augustine says. The air-traffic control contract draws from a variety of Martin Marietta's areas of expertise: computer system design, programming—the company now has a surprising 1,000 software engineers—communications, systems management, and even, peripherally, the company's heritage as a builder of airplanes.

Another broad-based contract that may generate new business for the company is a job doing preliminary development of the electrical-power distribution system for NASA's space station. The company hopes that the contract will give it a look at many other areas of the space-station project it might want to bid on. "It permeates the whole spacecraft," Augustine says of the power system. "It's a very appealing thing, because you've got to know a little bit about everything that uses power. So it sort of gives you the ubiquitous element of the system."

The idea of developing new businesses out of old also permeates Martin Marietta—from the way in which it has evolved the Titan rocket booster over more than a quarter century from a simple missile launcher, the Titan I, to a sophisticated space launcher, the Titan 34D, still one of the company's best sellers. And many different areas of the company are working together on another project, Martin Marietta's planned entry into the satellite communications business. The company has the ability to build the satellites and the boosters to launch them, to manage the launch, to develop computer systems to control the satellites, and even to use them as the anchors of a communication network set up by Equatorial Communications, a telecommunications company in which Martin Marietta owns a 25 percent interest.

Augustine emphasizes, however, that Martin Marietta could not evolve businesses in as bold a manner without satisfying customers along the way. "The key to the follow-on market is happy customers, because if they didn't like the Titan I, they aren't going to buy the Titan II and so on. So the absolute key is what we call 'mission success,' which means quality," he says. "If you don't have that, then the whole strategy of expanding the business you have stepwise, by evolution rather than revolution, goes out the window."

Martin Marietta's experience is also an example of careful selection of business niches to exploit, Augustine says. Many of the company's new businesses have little competition, allowing the company to build a

dominant position. The company calls it a question of finding "discriminators"—qualities that give Marietta an edge over its competitors.

"We list all of our competitors, we list ourselves, and we list each of
our discriminators as objectively as we can," Augustine says. "We assign
our marketing department to play the part of the enemy and to take their
side, present their case, so we try not to pick fights we don't think we
can win." Martin Marietta picks its fights well—it claims to win twice
as many contracts it bids on as its competitors. "Part of that is not that
we're so much better than anybody else," Augustine says. "We're just
very careful about what we get into. . . . We don't get into something
unless we think we can win it."

Increasingly, companies are looking for niches that will protect them
from tough, cost-cutting foreign competitors. That's one of the reasons
why Gould is in the business of customized computer design and engineering systems, in which its relationship with customers is key, rather
than in the more general business of providing generic computer and
control equipment to the industrial market—an arena in which aggressive
cost-cutting such as that practiced by Japanese manufacturers could prove
devastating. The Japanese themselves have been the masters of capitalizing on market niches. One of their crucial initial footholds in the U.S.
consumer electronics market came from introduction of small black-and-
white televisions into this country—a product that their American rivals
had overlooked.

Knowing your company and deciding what businesses to move into
also means knowing when to stay out of a business. RCA Corp. Chairman
Thornton Bradshaw, who for almost two decades was a top executive at
Atlantic Richfield Co., is a firm believer that a company should not go
into a business it doesn't know. He came by that belief the hard way.
"I've had too much experience in the past, at Atlantic Richfield and here,
with these developments that come out of our labs that are unrelated to
anything we do and we think are absolutely great—and we go into it and
we make an utter hash of it," he says. In one case at Arco, he says, the
company's research and development center came up with a promising
new technology to toughen wood by irradiating it; in another instance,
the company labs developed a longer-lasting heart pacemaker. Neither
technology had anything to do with Arco's primary business of pumping,
refining, and selling oil, but the company plunged in nonetheless—and
got clobbered. There was nothing wrong with the technologies; Arco
simply didn't know the ins and outs of the new industries it had entered.

It eventually sold both businesses. Having learned its lesson, Arco's ambitious forays into biotechnology in the 1980s have been grounded in the company's basic understanding of petrochemicals.

As a result of his experience at Arco, Bradshaw believes that if corporate labs develop a technology that doesn't logically fit or extend a company's business mix, the company is best off selling or licensing the technology to someone else to develop.

The priority that today's companies give to building on their strengths is forcing a change in American management theory. Years ago, the axiom was that a good manager can manage anything, and many companies switched managers around from business to business at a dizzying pace in the name of "broadening" them. Not for nothing was it kidded that IBM stood for "I've Been Moved" and GE for "Gone Everywhere." Managers at those and other companies barely had time to learn a job and a business before they were shifted to the next challenge.

That's changing today. The implied superficiality of knowledge involved in those quick shifts is now seen as a detriment by many top executives. Companies now are moving managers around much less frequently than before. Instead, they're leaving managers in place to thoroughly learn their jobs and businesses, on the theory that a manager with greater experience in a business will have a better grasp of its subtleties and undercurrents—enabling that manager to run the business better. This change is making companies more stable—and better able to compete in a changing world.

"I'm a believer in less movement and more vertical work," says GE Chairman Jack Welch, who wants managers to have a feeling of "ownership" about their businesses. "I don't like the idea that a manager can manage and manage anything," he says. "The expertise, the fingertip knowledge, the understanding of the competitive environment, the inner workings of how customers buy, why they buy, and why they don't buy are far more important than a 'manager' with a financial sheet in front of him rather than a business," Welch says. "So I believe any manager has to know the inner workings of his business, or her business, has to have done it for a period of time—and is better equipped to compete in the exterior world having done that."

Rather than training "managers," Welch wants GE to create "businessmen." The difference is subtle, yet profound. A manager, as defined somewhat derisively by Welch, can "sit here and pull off financial reports, have an orderly in-basket and an orderly out-basket, and have the day wrapped up if he answers all his phone calls that day." But a "business-man," as defined by Welch, "can probe and dig and question and be curious and go visit customers and talk to more people, talk to people on the plant floor, and get a better feeling for it." Thus equipped, that "businessman"—or woman—is in a better position to make decisions for the business than a more traditional, less-involved manager, who might go by the book rather than by the gut.

# 6

## RCA

## Restructuring a Troubled Company around Its Strengths

What makes a corporate marriage? In these days of megamergers, why does one company decide to pay billions of dollars for another corporation, buying weaknesses as well as strengths, taking on the difficult task of melding two corporate entities into one?

And why does a company agree to be bought? Why do the executives of a company with a rich corporate history agree to fold it into another company, sometimes eliminating thousands of jobs?

Those questions faced the leaders of General Electric Co. and RCA Corp. in late 1985 when they began negotiations on what was to become the largest non-oil merger up to that time. The answers they found were that the possible wrenching changes the merger could bring might be no worse than what the companies would face on their own in the hard business world of the next few years. Together, the executives of GE and RCA decided, the companies could be stronger than they were apart.

For GE Chairman Jack Welch, the deal's matchmaker, a union with RCA promises to give GE a rich infusion of talent, technology, market strength, and cash. GE's top management, which prides itself on an

ability to pick winners from out of an array of business opportunities, is
licking its chops over the stable of prospects RCA presents.

Welch says that adding RCA to GE produces a strong new company
better able to compete in the toughening international business environment. "We need all of the resources we have here to support us as we
move around the world to win in world markets," Welch says. "Getting
stronger to compete in world markets is the only way we're going to have
an increased standard of living."

On the other side of the question is RCA Chairman Thornton Bradshaw, now destined to be the last man through RCA's revolving-door
executive suite of the past few years—but the man who, it could be
argued, did the best job of managing the company. Such a good job that
it was attractive to GE to pay $66.50 a share—$6.4 billion in all—to
buy it.

As a consequence of the merger, Bradshaw is assured $7 million in
pre-tax profits from the sale of RCA stock, which has caused some grum-
bling farther down in RCA's management ranks where such golden par-
achutes were not provided. But Bradshaw, whose long commitment to
RCA as CEO and director has been deeply personal, says his eye was on
RCA's future, not his own.

"The one thing that has been keeping me awake at night is, did RCA
have sufficient financial strength to carry out what it has to carry out?"
Bradshaw said after the merger was announced in late 1985. "Do we
have the patience of shareholders during periods of time when . . . earnings
might not be as high" because of investments needed to turn businesses
into winners? "Those are the things that kept me awake at night. Now
that, in my opinion, is what General Electric has solved."

For the past few years, it has been Bradshaw who has done much of
the problem-solving at RCA—and it has been no easy task. Indeed, what
he has done to revamp RCA is almost as dramatic as Welch's restructuring
at GE, something that appealed to GE's executives when they decided
to bid for the company. "RCA has been on the same strategy of focusing
where [it] can win and extricating [itself] from where [it] can't, or where
winning doesn't have any value," says Michael Carpenter, GE's chief
strategist.

But where Welch was able to refit GE using the advantages of time
and money, Bradshaw had no such luxury. His job at RCA was more
akin to raising the *Titanic*.

Chief executives came and went at RCA through the decades of the

1970s, and it could be argued that each left the company worse off than it was when he arrived. By the time Bradshaw took over in 1981—the fourth CEO in seven years—RCA was in a pretty bad way. It was in the process of eking out a meager profit for the year, its worst performance in ages, while revenues had actually dropped slightly from the year before to $7.8 billion. By almost any measure, RCA was a bloated casualty of the pell-mell rush for diversification that had infected American business in the 1960s and 1970s. From its base as a maker of home-entertainment equipment and products and owner of the NBC radio and television networks, RCA had over the years added such diverse and unrelated businesses as Hertz rent-a-car, Banquet frozen foods, a greeting-card company, a huge financial services firm, and even a carpet maker.

"The company had lost its way," says Bradshaw, an RCA director brought in to try to clean up the mess after 17 years as president of oil giant Atlantic Richfield Co. "RCA was in extraordinary businesses, and yet somehow or another during the 1960s and 1970s, I guess other fields looked greener and it went into some ill-advised diversification efforts that didn't work out particularly well for themselves."

Under Bradshaw, RCA got back on track—mostly by getting rid of those various offshoots. He strengthened the company's existing businesses, moving RCA back to the fore in consumer electronics and breathing new life into the NBC television and radio operation by stabilizing its traditionally topsy-turvy management and giving the network the time to regain its health. NBC's prime-time television schedule, the most important part of the network, has climbed back on top in the industry ratings after years as a weak third to rivals CBS and ABC. So successful was Bradshaw in his rebuilding job that by 1985 he was able to oversee the first orderly transfer of power at the top of RCA in a decade, handing the chief executive's reins over to President Robert R. Frederick, with Bradshaw remaining as chairman. The company Frederick took over was a throwback to the RCA of a decade before: a company built around a strong technological base, with extensive interests in broadcasting, military and private communications, and consumer electronics equipment—all areas that made it attractive to GE.

"If RCA had never lost its faith in its stake in electronics and communications and entertainment, I don't think it would ever have gotten into any trouble, because although there were certainly ups and downs in those businesses, as there are in all businesses, certainly those three comprise the biggest new industrial revolution that's taking place," Bradshaw says. "We had been heavily involved in those three core businesses, each one of which had a great future. Not only had we been in some of those businesses, we had started some of those businesses. RCA was associated with the start of networks, and the start of the electronics business, in the 1920s—radio broadcasting and the manufacture of radio sets and television sets and so forth. We've been involved in all of these things. RCA had been in satellites about as early as anybody else in the world. So that was strength No. 1—it was in the right businesses. . . . Today, everything is built on electronics, or will be in the future, and everything will be dependent on communications."

When RCA decided to accept GE's offer for the company, Bradshaw wasn't the only one worried about RCA's ability to keep up with the tough competition in the years ahead, even in its newly strengthened condition. Some analysts were also questioning whether RCA could truly compete, especially in light of the beating it took in the 1970s and the scars left from Bradshaw's overhaul of the company in the past few years. But just about everybody agrees that the company might have been all but dead without the steps taken by Bradshaw.

When Bradshaw took over RCA, he was no stranger to the company. He had been a director of RCA since 1972—through the three previous, increasingly disastrous regimes. Robert Sarnoff, son of RCA's founder, was eased out of the chairmanship in 1975 because of philosophical differences with the board after adding Hertz and Random House publishing to RCA's portfolio. His successor, Anthony Conrad, lasted 10 months before being forced out after it was revealed that he had neglected to file income-tax returns for five years. And Conrad was replaced by Edgar H. Griffiths, whose six years on the job were rife with disagreements with the board over the company's direction—or lack of it. Griffiths seemed obsessed with getting "quarter-by-quarter" earnings improvements at the expense of long-range performance, and shuffled acquisitions in and out of RCA to give the illusion of increasing profits for a company whose performance was essentially flat. The board finally threw out Griffiths and replaced him with one of their own: Bradshaw.

But Bradshaw says his time on the board did not prepare him for what he found when he began running the company on a day-to-day basis. "The first year," he remembers, "I'd go home at night and say, 'My God, look what I found today,' and I'd tell [my wife] about some problem that would be a terrible problem. And she would say, 'But you were a director. Why would this problem come as a surprise to you?'

"It was a perfectly reasonable question," Bradshaw concedes with a laugh. "The answer undoubtedly is that almost all directors are very busy at their own businesses. . . . They know what the management basically chooses to let them know, frankly. They don't know enough. I didn't know enough. We knew enough, though, during that period of time to get rid of three chief executives, and that, after all, is the primary function of a board. We certainly didn't know enough, any of us—certainly I didn't know enough—to pinpoint what the real problems were. I don't think you get at those problems until you get your hands dirty on a hands-on management basis."

Bradshaw had to get his hands very dirty. Arco had been a solid, growing entity when he left it after 17 years as president. RCA, by contrast, was a disaster area. The company, once one of the most respected in American business, was suffering from high debt, low morale, and a bad reputation on Wall Street. "It was in a very bad way," Bradshaw says. "The diversification that had gone on in the 1960s and 1970s was an overdiversification by any standards, and it had created an almost impossible management task to oversee the operations of frozen foods, a book company, a real estate company, an electronics company, etc."

Bradshaw says that while RCA had diversified, it had never set up a management structure to deal with that diversification. While some classic conglomerates, like Teledyne and Gulf & Western, had been successful in setting up a lean, decentralized holding-company sort of management structure to oversee their far-flung interests, RCA still had a top-heavy management chart that seemed bent on trying to run all of its disparate businesses from corporate headquarters. "If you had assumed that RCA was, in truth, a conglomerate, you had to manage it a different way," Bradshaw says. "No one ever assumed it was really a conglomerate. So therefore they tried to run it as though it were a unified company that made sense. And that was an almost impossible thing to do.

"I don't want to in any way downgrade conglomerates," he adds. "If you've got a good conglomerate, and you run it as a conglomerate, you can do very well indeed."

But Bradshaw didn't envision RCA as a conglomerate. So he had to clean house. "That was one of the things that had to be done over this period of time—cleaning out the overdiversification, coming back to a core company that made sense," he says. "This is what we've been trying to get at over these past years—trying to clean out the things we should not be in, trying to make sense of what remains, trying to concentrate on it, so we can get to be known as an electronics, communications, and entertainment company. We've put all our best efforts in that area, all our funds, all our best people. Therefore you run it in a very different way. You run it as a company that is an integrated company, that makes sense, where one part, in general, relates to another."

In many ways, Bradshaw found, the acquisitions of the previous decade had sapped the company's strength. "The crucial outcome of those was a diversion of effort and money during a time when RCA should have been building up its base in its core businesses," Bradshaw says. "I think that sort of in a nutshell is what had gone wrong. And then of course there was a severe loss of morale during that time. I think people throughout the organization knew that RCA was in some very basic important businesses and they were being neglected. It sort of shattered the morale and the cultural unity that this company had had at one time. So really the job wasn't all that hard coming in here. There had to be an affirmation of faith that those core areas were what RCA knew how to do, first, and second, that those core areas were explosive and growing areas in the future. If you put those two together I think you've got a company with extraordinary growth potential."

Bradshaw's vision for RCA, then, was to return it to its strengths, to build it around the businesses in which it had long been successful. "We had to reaffirm the faith, we had to very clearly set forth what the objectives were, what the businesses were that RCA would be in. We had to define the company, what it was, what we hoped it would be five or ten years from now, we had to clear the decks financially, particularly, or else we wouldn't be able to move or take advantage of the skills within the company, and we had to regain the credibility with the outside world. . . . And finally, I think we had to restructure the top management." Bradshaw juggled the names on the doors throughout the executive floors of RCA's Rockefeller Center headquarters tower in Manhattan. By the time the company was sold to General Electric, more than two-thirds of RCA's top 60 managers were either in new jobs or new to the company. "I don't think there was ever a real loss of highly capable, competent people at the middle management levels," Bradshaw says. "I think it was the top management that lost its way."

Bradshaw also had to restore the company's financial health, sagging under a boatload of debt run up by the company in making many of its acquisitions. "Over the years, the company had just bought too much and found itself in a real financial bind. . . . It was very difficult to raise funds for the company. We had no financial flexibility." So Bradshaw began selling off his predecessors' prized diversification attempts. The biggest piece he divested was CIT Financial, a financial-services business acquired by Griffiths in 1980 for $1.2 billion. The $1.5 billion brought in by the sale of CIT restored RCA's financial flexibility, and the sale of some other subsidiaries—most notably Hertz—provided the company with nearly $2 billion in cash. "So therefore, getting rid of the overdiversification, the companies that didn't fit, the parts that didn't fit, really accomplished two goals—it started to make sense out of the company, through what was left, and it relieved the financial pressure," Bradshaw says. That pot of cash, incidentally, was part of what made RCA attractive to GE, providing the combined company with additional cash to pour into technology investments (or for paying off the merger costs).

In pruning the company, Bradshaw was also able to redirect its resources to the areas in which he believed it was strongest, by getting rid of businesses that, while attractive, were diverting the company's attention. "Some of the things we shed not because we didn't think there was growth in them, but because they took away from our opportunities in [other] fields," he says. "By having to support those businesses, we were unable to do right by the businesses we thought were going to grow faster."

As he cleared away the debris of the acquisition binge, Bradshaw uncovered one of the key elements of the company he wanted to build on—its strong technological base. RCA's research and development arm had long been one of the best in the nation, in a class with GE's R&D Center and AT&T's Bell Labs. The R&D base had been a little out of place in the diversified RCA—its electronics engineers had little to add to the frozen food business, for instance—but its skills had never atrophied.

"RCA had, right from the beginning, appreciated the fact that [its traditional] businesses depended upon research advances, and so therefore it had built research laboratories and had a great research tradition," Bradshaw says. "And it always poured money into R&D. No matter how badly we were doing in the past three years, for instance, or in the first two years when I got here, we increased the R&D expenditures each year. RCA has always had a commitment to that absolutely essential research and development. Without that, certainly the communications business and the electronics businesses cannot exist. I think even in 1982, RCA had the second largest number of patents of any company in the

United States, second only to General Electric. We were even ahead of Bell Laboratories. That's a hell of a strength."

The technology base gave RCA an ability to carve out major shares in new businesses related to the old skills. For example, RCA's expertise in television picture tubes—it is the nation's leading maker of color televisions—led the company into the fast-growing computer-monitor business. And its television-camera technology could allow it to create new lines of products—such as high-quality cameras used for security and industrial surveillance. "If we can't leverage our considerable skills in the whole area of video, and where it's going, and win in this one, then we've got trouble. And we think we can win," Frederick says. "That's an important growth business for us. . . . It's merely an illustration of where you can have a strength and leverage that strength rather than trying to go outside and diversify and buy earnings someplace else." Similarly, the company's technology opens possibilities for expansion of its already strong satellite communications and defense electronics businesses. The company is the leading owner and manager of commercial satellites, having built and launched more than 80. "We are in a leading position, we have the advantage of building them ourselves, and we have the experience of running them ourselves," Frederick says. "So it's a good business for us to invest in." But RCA also knows that the satellite business is a risky game: The loss of its Satcom III satellite shortly after launch a few years ago was a major blow to the company's satellite business, and seemed in many ways at the time to symbolize the company's ongoing problems and frustrations.

Under Bradshaw, RCA tried to stay away from developing new businesses that strayed too far from the company's basic product lines, sales abilities, and other objectives—a strategy that will fit in nicely at General Electric, with its similar strategy of playing to existing strengths.

One of the most attractive parts of RCA to General Electric was the company's defense-contracting work. Both companies were already huge defense contractors, but where GE's work was primarily in industrial hardware like jet-fighter engines, RCA's has been primarily in electronics and communications fields. As the military weds more and more electronics technology to old-fashioned hardware, GE-RCA could be an unbeatable defense-contracting combination.

Under Bradshaw, RCA worked hard to build up its defense business. The company used its strengths in communications and electronics technology to win contracts in such areas as military communications and electronic surveillance and defense—notably the Navy's AEGIS system. Government business rose to 15 percent of the company's annual revenues. RCA had another reason for beefing up its defense-contracting business—it knew it could transfer some of the know-how from its government work in such basic areas as silicon-chip circuitry into commercial businesses. "That's one of the reasons that the government business is important to our strategy," Frederick says. "The product doesn't itself just transfer over, but what you learn about manufacturing chips, what you learn about the capabilities of the chips, certainly is transferable."

Like other highly technology-oriented companies, RCA has faced the pressures of getting products using sophisticated technology onto the market fast enough to gain a competitive edge—and to not get left behind as technologies change. Here it had an edge in a cache of consumer and industrial marketing ability that Bradshaw judged to be first-rate once he took over the company and could see it up close. "The surprising strength to me was its strength in merchandising and marketing," he says. "Over the years they had built up a marketing structure, and people who understand marketing, who understand merchandising. I hadn't realized that—as a director I hadn't realized that. . . . It came out of the consumer electronics business. It came out of the necessity of producing millions of television sets, merchandising them, selling them, and beating the competition in one of the most highly competitive markets of any kind there is."

But RCA knew the pitfalls of misreading consumer demand and bringing new technology to market too quickly. It learned the hard way, through a debacle in videodisk players that finally resulted in a $175 million write-off in 1984. The company came to market with a technology for playing back movies and other programming on disks that got high technical marks —but was blown out of the water by the explosive growth of the competing videotape technology. What happened was almost the quintessential example of how a company can misjudge technological and marketing changes.

Bradshaw calls the videodisk escapade an example of what was wrong with RCA's old management style: The company plunged ahead into the field despite some clear warnings and a misreading of the market, failing to anticipate that the competing videotape-player industry would simply overwhelm RCA's effort. Too, the company's failure to persuade other consumer-electronics firms to jump onto the videodisk bandwagon left RCA without any allies to share the risk of the new technology.

"You can look back and you can write a pretty good case history of a whole series of management errors," Bradshaw says. "The manufacturers did their job, the marketers did their job—and they did it extraordinarily well. There were just some basic tactical errors that were made, which can happen in any risk business. I don't make any apologies for those. . . . There was just a mistake in timing—we came in late. There was a mistake in the appraisal of what would happen to the tape market— no one called that. . . . We thought that as long as we could put out a machine that would sell for half of what a tape machine would cost, and we could sell our videodisks for one-half of what the tape would cost, that we'd have a vast market—even though we knew that we could not record as the tape deck can record. We thought there would be a mass market for that sort of thing. Well, that mass market just evaporated when the tape decks came down in price at an extraordinary rate, and when you didn't have to buy the tape—you could rent the tape. Put those two things together, and that advantage we had disappeared. That I think was basically it."

Although the videodisk experience was a disaster, Bradshaw was able to reverse the slide in an even more important area of RCA's business. After years of poor performance, the NBC broadcasting network seems to have returned to the health it last knew a decade ago. "NBC is coming along very nicely, thank you," Frederick said in 1985. Industry analysts credit the turnaround to former independent television producer Grant Tinker, brought in by Bradshaw to steady NBC after a roller-coaster performance during the 1970s resulting from the machinations of mercurial television programmer Fred Silverman and a series of other gurus. "We're very pleased with the things Grant has done there," Frederick says. NBC's overall radio and television operations are stronger, but the key measure has been its improvement in the prime-time television ratings race. Although the network has not yet established a firm hold on the overall No. 1 spot in the crucial prime-time ratings derby, shows such as *Cheers*, *The Cosby Show*, and *Miami Vice* gave it a strong position among young, upscale viewers coveted by advertisers that NBC was able to parlay into the No. 1 position overall. "We're very pleased with the progress," Frederick says, "and have to be constantly wary that ABC will turn it around and find the magic solution and knock us off. That's competition."

Having rebuilt RCA, Bradshaw had no compunction about agreeing to merge it with General Electric. In fact, he says, GE made such a perfect fit with RCA that he was willing to recommend that the board accept a price that he might have considered too low coming from another company. For one thing, Bradshaw was confident that under GE's ownership, RCA would not be broken up and sold willy-nilly, as it might have been by another suitor (although GE will likely have to sell some parts of the combined company for reasons of regulatory compliance and efficiency). Having so carefully sculpted RCA into a healthy company, Bradshaw did not want to see it shattered.

Such pride and belief in the best arrangement for a company raises another question that a CEO is forced to answer when it comes time to consider merging with another company. The best answer to that question, Bradshaw believes, was a merger with GE.

"We have been so determined that we will not be broken up," Bradshaw says. "I think the grouping of businesses RCA finally came down to in the last year or so is a very important grouping of products insofar as America's competitiveness throughout the world is concerned. And just to break them up into little pieces and parcel them out to high bidders here and there, I think you lose the thrust, the real importance that RCA can contribute."

# 7

# GOULD

## An Industrial Company Becomes a
## Purveyor of High-Tech Electronics

It is perhaps every chief executive's dream to shape and mold his company into something he can point to as his creation. By that measure, William T. Ylvisaker may be unique: He's gotten to direct such a makeover twice—with the same company.

Gould Inc., the company Ylvisaker chairs, got its start as a maker of batteries and other mundane products. When Ylvisaker took over as CEO nearly two decades ago, he began changing Gould into a go-go maker of electrical equipment and auto parts, pushing annual revenues past the $2 billion level in the process.

Then he tore it apart and started all over again.

In its latest incarnation—after the sale of $1 billion in assets—Gould is a high-technology company with interests in semiconductors, micro-computers, factory automation, and sophisticated electronics equipment used in the medical and defense fields. Revenues are running at more than $1.3 billion annually, and while some critics are skeptical, Ylvisaker is convinced he has positioned the company in businesses that will grow faster than the economy as a whole—and much faster than Gould would have expanded had it remained in its earlier form.

"It wasn't a partial change," Ylvisaker says. "It was really a total change of the company. . . . Certainly we're far better off than we would have been if we'd left it where it was."

The change did not come easily. No matter who is managing it, such a drastic makeover of a company—once, much less twice—has wrenching effects on corporate culture, personnel, and finances. Ylvisaker, who always had a reputation as an autocratic manager, has been portrayed as reaching new depths of ruthlessness as he transformed the company to meet his vision. Eventually, even Ylvisaker became a casualty of the changes at Gould. Its directors, while endorsing the vision, concluded late last year that the management of a high-tech company required a more subtle, supportive touch than Ylvisaker had employed when Gould was a more conventional industrial firm. So Ylvisaker was eased out as chief executive officer in favor of Gould President James F. McDonald, the youthful former IBM executive whom Ylvisaker had hand-picked as his eventual successor.

Still, Ylvisaker seems to resent suggestions that he softened his management style over the years. "I don't think I've mellowed or changed, as some people might suggest," he says. "You just adapt your style to the needs of the business or industry that you're in."

Surely, the businesses in which Gould now operates are much different from the company he headed in 1968. Known as Gould-National, it was at that time a $124 million-a-year maker of car batteries for customers like Chrysler and Ford. Its earnings were slumping, and revenues seemed to be in danger of stagnation as technical improvements—many of them Gould's own—extended battery life and reduced the replacement market.

Ylvisaker immediately set about to change the company. "We wanted to build a company that had better balance than just being in the battery business, which has its ups and downs depending on the automotive industry and the weather and price conditions," Ylvisaker says. "There was foreign competition coming in, so we were looking for a better balance of businesses where the technologies could overlap."

Ylvisaker first tightened up and modernized the company's battery-making operations, and then went looking for new businesses. In 1969, he merged Gould-National into Clevite Corp., a Cleveland-based industrial conglomerate with interests in auto parts, batteries, and electrical equipment. Ylvisaker saw this version of Gould as an electrical and electronics company supplying industrial markets, and made further acquisitions to fulfill that vision. In 1976, he added I-T-E Imperial Corp., a major maker of electrical equipment. Now the company's business mix was 55 percent electrical/electronic, 30 percent industrial, and 15 percent batteries. By 1980, Gould was turning over $2.2 billion a year.

But Ylvisaker wasn't satisfied. "As we approached the 1980s, we started to look out at the changes that were taking place in the worldwide business economy," he says. "I think we recognized quite clearly that the automotive industry and the electrical industry—especially the high-voltage electrical industry—were going to suffer severe setbacks, declines in opportunity both here and in Europe, which was where our major investments were, as well as a decline in the marketplace in terms of market share. Realizing that, and saying, well, if that's a fact, what were we going to do?"

The answer to that question could be found in analysis of the company's financial figures. In its electronics technology divisions, the revenues had tripled and profits quintupled in the years from 1975 to 1980. The rest of the company was, at best, just barely keeping up with the growth in the economy. The primary market for Gould's products was still the automobile industry, and with Detroit under siege, Ylvisaker expected severe setbacks and declines in opportunity. "While our electronics operations would prosper and grow at above-average rates in the 1980s and 1990s, our other businesses were headed for difficulties," Gould Vice Chairman David Simpson summarizes.

Ylvisaker says, "We took the four segments of the business, looked at their return on investment, their future outlook, the profit margins, and the growth—and the battery, the industrial, and the electrical [businesses] were all flat-to-down. But in the electronic and defense side of the business, the outlook was strong in terms of the future, the return on investment was high, the growth was high, the margins were high, and the profit opportunities had been exceeding everything else we were doing. And the outlook was good. So we said to ourselves—and it's not an easy thing—if we take 75 percent of the company and turn those assets into an electronics base, and into high-technology, we were convinced that the growth would be strong through the 1980s, the 1990s and on into the next century. We had a real opportunity to build a high-growth company."

The solution, in other words, was to bet the company on its fastest-growing part. In doing so, Ylvisaker believed, he would be adapting the company to the changing economic and technical environment, putting

Gould into businesses that were technologically hot and whose growth would likely outstrip that of the general economy in coming years. "We were fortunate to recognize well enough in advance the changes that were coming in the U.S. industry, as well as, to some degree, in the European economy," he says. His vision proved clear—Gould's more traditional businesses have since been disappointing. "If we had remained in those businesses, we'd be a marginal or loss company today," Ylvisaker says.

Deciding to jump into high technology is one thing, but knowing where to jump is another. High-tech is a fast-moving stream, and many industrial companies have stuck their corporate toes into new technologies and been swept away. The classic example, perhaps, is Exxon, which poured more than $1 billion into trying to get a foothold in the market for electronic office equipment and came away with nothing, unable to translate its expertise in management of the relatively slow-moving oil industry into the faster-paced high-technology electronics market.

Ylvisaker's strategy was to focus Gould on areas of technology in which it could establish business and market niches, hold some sort of technological advantage, avoid competition—particularly from abroad—and interact with the company's other high-tech strengths. "We didn't just want to get into high-tech electronics businesses," he says. "We had a more specific idea. We wanted to be selling products to the engineering community, products that would not be subject to major foreign competition, and also ones that would service similar marketplaces."

In particular, the company wanted no part of the consumer-electronics field. "We don't think we know the consumer business," Ylvisaker says. "That's an area that is dominated by distribution and price, neither of which we have the capability of being competitive in. If you look at the major electronic companies that have tried it, they've all been hurt badly. You're seeing it happen in PCs today, you saw it happen in watches, you saw it happen in calculators—anything where there's high volume that goes to the consumer." To avoid that trap, Ylvisaker decided, the new Gould would continue serving its traditional industrial customers, but with entirely new types of products.

So Gould identified its potential markets: industrial automation, high-speed information processing, test and measurement instruments, medical electronics applications, defense work, and selected electronic components. All had one crucial thing in common—they relied on some form of computer data-processing technology for control. "Fundamentally, we said that the computer, in terms of all forms of instrumentation, whether it be in the factory, on an engineer's desk, in the scientific area, in a military use, is going to control everything that happens. So we thought that we had to be in that," Ylvisaker says. "We looked at that sort of as the core to attach everything to."

There were other criteria, as well. Gould wanted to have the No. 1 or No. 2 position in technology and marketing in all the markets it chose. It searched out business niches that would prove difficult for other competitors to enter. And it put an emphasis on customer service—the ability to tailor products directly to a specific customer's needs. Gould products, therefore, are things like custom-designed and built computer-based testing and measurement equipment, computer-aided design and manufacturing systems, and factory robots. All are designed by Gould to fit specific customer needs.

"We're solving customer problems, whether it be on the factory floor, the research center, the design area, whatever," Ylvisaker says. By concentrating on service and customer needs, Gould freezes out the foreign competition and floods of cheap imports in its chosen markets that have plagued other electronics companies. While foreign competitors have had great success in commodity-type equipment fields that put a premium on price and supply, it has been difficult for them to gain a foothold in service-oriented corners of the electronics industry.

"It's more of an application and engineering product, and it has to be sold as such," Ylvisaker says of Gould's emphasis. "The service is very important, the engineering sale itself is very important, and if you look at foreign competition—I'm not worried about the U.S. competition, because in most places we're right on top—but for the foreign competition, they've never been very successful against the whole U.S. base in engineering sales, because they don't have the service, and they can't go to the customer and say, what are your problems, how do I solve this problem—which is what we're really selling."

In addition, by finding niches and keeping to them, Gould not only avoids foreign competition, Ylvisaker believes; but also stays out of the sights of some of its larger potential competitors at home. "We're not competing with IBM," he says. "And we don't want to."

Once his plan for the company was complete, Ylvisaker went about shuffling Gould's assets. Within three years, beginning in 1980, he had sold $1 billion worth of assets and acquired as much. He didn't make the acquisitions willy-nilly. All of Gould's potential purchases were subject to much scrutiny, including the formation of "pro" and "con" teams of Gould managers who argued both sides of a possible acquisition with Ylvisaker. The first to pass muster was Systems Engineering Laboratories, a maker of 32-bit minicomputers that gave the company the base for many of its other acquisitions—the computers that Ylvisaker felt had to be the core of most of the company's products. That acquisition was followed by all manner of testing and measurement companies, solid-state power supply and component companies, an integrated circuit maker, a transistor maker, and software technology.

The acquisitions put Gould into a variety of hot businesses. It has carved out a niche for itself in the programmable controllers segment of the office automation market, offering products based on its 32-bit mini-computer that can monitor and control all aspects of factory automation. Gould also relies on minicomputers as the backbone of a variety of other products in fields such as seismic analysis, computer-aided engineering, and laboratory computation. Additionally, Gould computers are the brains for more than half of the flight simulators being made today. In the test and measurement field, Gould makes logic analyzers, oscilloscopes, and waveform recorders used in a variety of applications, including the testing of new computer equipment. The company has carved out lucrative niches in the medical instrumentation business as well, making such products as sophisticated blood-pressure measurement systems, cardio-pulmonary diagnostic systems, and other monitoring and diagnostic products. On the defense side, Gould is a leading maker of torpedoes and sonar arrays, and also produces avionics components and simulators and trainers. And with so many of its products relying on computer chips, Gould has become a major maker—for its own use and for outside sale—of such components as custom and very-large-scale integrated (VLSI) circuits and of the ultra-thin copper foil used in the manufacture of printed circuit boards. The company also produces software for use in controlling its own computer-system products and for such fields as computer-aided design.

Because of this variety, Ylvisaker jokes that Gould "is referred to in some offices on Wall Street as a $1.5 billion start-up company." Indeed, while it may be too early to tell whether Gould can maintain its lead in the many high-technology businesses in which it competes, the company's financial results have lately begun tracking upward after some early setbacks. Still, the transition has not been without its problems.

"The three years of transition were really very difficult in bringing these diverse businesses together and maximizing the benefits of their working together," Ylvisaker says. "We needed somebody who could pull that all together." Gould hopes that somebody is McDonald, hired in 1984 by Ylvisaker to oversee the integration of the various parts of the company.

McDonald's background at IBM—in his last job he ran that company's manufacturing systems division, with additional responsibility for IBM's technology center—indicates he understands the directions in which Gould is headed. McDonald—still in his mid-40s—also demonstrates the trend toward selection of younger CEOs, whose age permits them to give their companies longer-running leadership and strategic continuity. "We need somebody who can be making decisions for the long term that can impact the company," says Ylvisaker—who it should be noted, had driven a number of previous heirs apparent from the company.

Ylvisaker's history as a tough, do-it-my-way chief executive would indeed seem unsuited to the participatory management culture associated with successful Silicon Valley firms like Hewlett-Packard Co., with their strong emphasis on individual expression and creativity. There are countless examples of industrial companies that have plunged into high-technology fields, buying up a number of small start-up firms, only to have the new acquisitions sour when the heavy-handed corporate bureaucracy drove off the creative entrepreneurs who came with those firms. "Older and larger corporations typically have cumbersome review processes for new ideas, and people work in divisions isolated from the rest of the company, so they lose a sense of identity with the company at large," Simpson says. "[High-tech] companies tend to be small, loosely organized and characterized by fast decision-making, open to new ideas and employee understanding of the whole company and where he or she fits in. . . . What we had to do was define an organization consistent with our size but responsive to the needs of this new employee population."

So Gould's, and Ylvisaker's, management styles had to change. Ylvisaker freely admits that he used to be a tough taskmaster; but he says that was the only way to effectively run Gould's previous industrial businesses, which required tight controls to maximize their slim profit margins. This holds true in industries "like the battery business and the automotive-parts business, because the innovative opportunities by comparison are relatively small to build profit margins. The difference between success and failure is really very tight controls," he says. Ylvisaker also believes that some of his reputation as a tough manager has come from disgruntled former Gould executives who were forced to leave the company because they were unable to change their own styles to fit the company's changes. "When we made the decision in 1980, we had quite a few managers here who were unhappy about it," he says. "They were fundamentally unhappy because they didn't have the technical back-ground to be able to understand and cope with the new businesses. . . . I think that's the biggest bridge to cross." Mainly, Ylvisaker says, his tough reputation was forged by a need for tough management of the businesses Gould was in.

Gould's new high-tech businesses, he agrees, require a much different style of management—one belying Ylvisaker's dictatorial reputation. "You look at the electronics industry," he says, "and the difference between success and failure boils down to two things. First is creativity and product development, and second is distribution. . . . It's a case of creating an atmosphere for those people where they have the freedom and the op-portunity and the excitement of innovating, of getting those new products out, because product obsolescence in the business is anywhere from six months to two years today. So you've already got to be doing something new, and you can't legislate that. You've got to provide much higher incentives, greater freedom." And Ylvisaker argues that he and Gould were no strangers to this type of management when they made the shift from industrial-products businesses to high-tech—because the company already had high-tech interests. "We had 25 percent of our business in electronics, and I think we learned how to run that," he says.

To meet the needs of its new businesses most efficiently, Gould's new management structure relies a great deal on decentralization. The company has set up separate operating boards of directors for each of the company's four main divisions—electronic components, industrial au-tomation systems, instrument systems, and defense systems—consisting of both Gould executives and outside experts in those particular fields. These boards provide perspective on the company's operations and co-ordination between divisions, whose executives serve on each others' operating boards.

With the decentralization, Gould's corporate headquarters now func-tions as more of a coordinating organization, Ylvisaker says, keeping constant tabs on divisional strategies. "We're constantly reviewing," he says. "We used to do it once a year; we're doing it four times a year now, because of the product obsolescence and the market changes. We're always analyzing competitive products, to know where you stand, so that you make sure that you have a product coming into the market that's going to be better. The change is so rapid that you're always adjusting your strategic thinking to take that into account."

Keeping top corporate management out of the hair of divisional managers, pushing decision-making as far down the organizational chart as possible, and emphasizing corporate entrepreneurship were central to Gould's new management philosophy. "It became clear that our success as an electronics company was going to be a function of the people we attracted or retained to manage these businesses," Simpson says. "We spent a considerable amount of time discussing the forms of organization that would be hospitable to the electronics industry. In fact, creating such an environment was the only choice we had, for two reasons: Anybody with a good idea in electronics doesn't need to work for a company—he can raise all the capital needed to start one—[and] we had acquired several such young companies and would surely acquire others."

Gould's system is designed to encourage an interchange of ideas between the company's various divisions. This system also makes managers of the other divisions, top management, and the outside experts—through the divisional operating boards—freely available to consult with each division's managers. Gould also has put a premium on marketing and on getting products from the laboratory to the marketplace in the shortest time possible, again to keep up with the fast-moving competitive environment. "Fundamentally, it comes from the customer," Ylvisaker says. "You've got to go to the customer and say, 'What are you going to be needing three to five years from now? What are your plans? What are your problems, and what can we do to solve those?' That's our fundamental approach. We take that back, and the marketing people are always meeting with the product development people. It's a constant interchange between the customer, the marketing people and the product-development people to solve the problems. It just never stops."

Gould has also taken steps to build up its sales muscle by consolidating the sales organizations of its diverse operations. "The fact that we're combining all of our sales organizations, all our sales offices, gives us a lot of strength out there in the marketplace," Ylvisaker says. "We've got 21 divisions, really, that have been consolidated into six businesses, which in our judgment gives us a lot of presence in front of the customer. We get consolidation of our efforts at trade shows. . . . Instead of having a little booth with one product in the corner, you've got a huge Gould booth with all the products there."

In addition, McDonald has begun meeting with top executives of companies that are key customers—a touch that reflects the increased competitiveness of the company's new markets versus those for its former industrial products. By paying that kind of close attention to customers at all levels, Gould believes it can keep abreast of customer demands in the fields served by its products and minimize competitive surprises. Firsthand knowledge of customer needs, communicated quickly to the laboratory, Ylvisaker believes, can give the company a handle on one to three years worth of business. "Then what you've got to do is design it and make it at the lowest possible cost," he says—in that respect a philosophy not much different from Gould's industrial-products days.

Its second makeover just about complete, Gould believes it has positioned itself for annual growth rates in the neighborhood of 20 percent over the next few years—a good deal better than it might have expected from its old businesses. Others are not so sure, suggesting that the jury is still out on whether Gould has correctly identified the markets it has gone into and adequately protected itself from debilitating competitive pressures. They point to the company's mid-1985 write-off of $150 million to cover problems in its semiconductor business as evidence that Gould remains in a state of flux, still trying to find the most effective mix of businesses for future growth.

Whether it is successful or not, Gould's latest incarnation represents a change in the company that Ylvisaker might be talking about when he describes the difference between the pace of change in Gould's old businesses and in its adopted high-tech fields. "They were kind of creeping advances," Ylvisaker says of the old days. "You were trying to create ideas, but they were not the sweeping changes you have now. I guess you could say one was an area of product improvement and manufacturing efficiency, and the electronics industry is one of product obsolescence. You rarely improve a product—you build a totally new one and make the other one obsolete. It's very exciting."

# 8

# THE HIGH-TECH
# REVOLUTION

## Opportunities and Caveats

Gould's new directions show how technology is a powerful weapon for corporate change, both as a source of new products and services and as a way of dramatically increasing productivity. The technological revolution, then, is not limited to Silicon Valley and other well-known battlefields. Increasingly, technology is becoming a powerful engine of change for many American corporations, transforming many old-line industrial companies into new economic forces which are applying technology to existing businesses or using it to create new ventures.

For all industrial societies, and the United States in particular, technology has become an essential component of economic competitiveness and thus of a healthy, rising standard of living.

But technology has never been so hard to manage. The waves of change are rolling in faster and more unpredictably than ever, making it the best of times for managers and companies that can catch the crests and ride them—and the worst of times for those that can't.

There's a joke making the rounds of executive suites these days about the difference between high technology and low technology: If you can understand it, it's not high technology. As American business moves farther out into the reaches of technology, that jibe has a certain ring of truth to it—indeed, few top executives truly understand the technologies with which their companies are involved. But even if they don't quite understand how it works, the best managers do know how important technology is to their corporations' success, either by creating new products or services to sell or—perhaps even more importantly—providing more efficient, more productive ways to manufacture more traditional products. In this sense, technology is by no means limited to the development of exciting, advanced new products—it is also an increasingly important way of keeping older businesses on the leading edge.

"Don't give me this thing about high-tech, low-tech," says GE Chairman Jack Welch. "Technology is right in the belly of every business."

But if a company is going to go out and make those high-tech widgets, it had better know what it is doing. Most areas classified as high technology are fast-moving, very competitive games, where the environments and rules can change in a matter of months or even weeks as new developments and products hit the marketplace. Silicon Valley is littered with the carcasses of companies that came up with one good idea—only to have the market rush past them a few months later behind somebody else's brainstorm. If you're going to play in high-tech, you have to be prepared to move quickly and nimbly.

"I think it's important for every single person, manager, and non-manager to understand the nature of the business," says Morris Tanenbaum, vice chairman of American Telephone & Telegraph Co. "There was a period of time when a craftsman could go into a building and spend the greater part of his career fine-tuning a piece of machinery. It became very, very familiar to him. We put a central office in, and it could be in service for 20 or 30 years." But not any more. It's been 20 years since AT&T put in its first electronic switching equipment, and in that time, the technology has evolved rapidly and continuously, with each breakthrough in the technology of high-speed telecommunications switching requiring an update of the company's equipment. "If you walked into one of those offices [today], you wouldn't see a single piece of machinery that you'd recognize from 1965," Tanenbaum says, "because two or three years after the first one was put in, we changed the memory technology." In the years since, he says, the switching machinery has gone through three more evolutions to keep up with rapidly advancing electronics technology. "Every single piece of that machinery has changed," Tanenbaum says. "So the craftsman is in a period of continuing reeducation."

"You cannot fall asleep in our high-tech industries," says RCA President Robert Frederick. "You've just got to keep going forward. You've got to make investments, you've got to make investments in people, you've got to be creative in what's coming next, because it's moving very fast. . . . Success is not easy, but complacency is a big risk."

Different companies are handling the high-tech revolution in different ways. At Gould, it has meant shifting the company out of its old-line industrial businesses and betting the farm on high-tech fields. At General Electric, it involves attempts to inject high technology into all areas and all levels of the company's businesses—from diving into computer-aided design, silicon-chip technology, and other high-tech products to attempting to apply technology to increase the efficiency and productivity of older products and their production lines.

Technology has insinuated itself into American society in so many subtle ways that it is sometimes difficult for Americans to realize just how pervasive the technological revolution has become. To gain some perspective, says Bruce Merrifield, an assistant Secretary of Commerce, one need only realize that nine out of every ten scientists who have ever walked on the planet are alive and working today. The impact of this outpouring of science is awesome, coming in units as large as the space shuttle or home and office computers, and as small as fingernail-size silicon chips capable of storing a million bits of information or equally tiny integrated circuits that can perform 90 billion operations per second. In 1970, points out John Young, president of Hewlett-Packard Co., the mainframe computers that handled the huge mathematical problems of space flight—capable of carrying out one million calculations per second—cost $1 million each and took up several hundred feet of floor space. Ten years later, a computer with that same power cost $50,000 and could sit on a desk. By the year 2000 it will cost $30. And it will be small enough to fit inside a brief case.

The geometric progression of that example illustrates the ever-quickening pace of technological change. Each permutation of technology seems to come quicker—and often cheaper—than the one that preceded it. That pace is causing radical change in how new products relying on technology are developed and marketed. "Where product life cycles used

to be ten or more years, we now have cycles of six months," says Robert
Kavner, senior vice president and chief financial officer of AT&T. "Three
years is wonderful. Five years and you're in heaven." General Electric,
which developed X-ray machines, enjoyed the benefits of that technology
for decades. The next advance, computer tomography (CAT or CT)
scanners, were on the market for just a few years before they were superseded
by the magnetic-resonance imaging (MR) device, which uses a powerful
magnetic field to align the nuclei of certain cells in a patient and then
bounces a radio pulse off those cells to measure their position, providing
sharp images of a patient's organs and bones. "We were No. 1 in the X-
ray business. If we stayed at that pace and didn't adapt to CTs, we wouldn't
have been No. 1 in diagnostic imaging any more," GE's Welch says.
"And if we didn't move faster even still in MR, we would have lost our
No. 1 in the combined [CT and MR market]. That's a perfect example
of a company trying to adapt to change that's increased in its business."

To keep up with such rapid change, GE and other companies are
putting a premium both on developing new technologies and in getting
them to the marketplace as quickly as possible. "We've got to get from
laboratory to marketplace faster," Welch says. For GE, as others, this
means sinking huge amounts of money into research and development—
a couple billion dollars a year in GE's case. And while companies in
trouble once cut back on R&D spending as a way to cut corners, many
prescient managers today are finding money to maintain or increase
corporate lab work regardless of a company's financial condition. Even
as RCA was financially on the rocks in the early 1980s, Chairman Thornton Bradshaw kept pouring money into R&D. And International Harvester, perhaps the most cash-strapped company ever to survive without
bankruptcy, never totally gave up on its research and development efforts
in hard times—IH maintained market share in part by continuing to
build technologically superior tractors and trucks even as it was losing
hundreds of millions of dollars, and the first thing the company's management did when Harvester's financial condition stabilized was to order
a hefty increase in R&D spending.

The key, then, is to use technology to wheedle out more and more
improvements for existing products and to develop new products to stay
ahead of the competition. GE planning chief Mike Carpenter sees technology as one of the most potent weapons a company can have against
its competitor, because it allows a firm to tip the competitive balance in

its favor by stealing a march on the competition. "Technology is one of the levers to change the rules of the game against competition that isn't able to do that," Carpenter says.

At GE, division managers are urged to keep in close touch with the company's top-flight corporate laboratory complex in Schenectady, N.Y., to keep tabs on any improvements the scientists and researchers there have to offer—an example set by Welch, who was a frequent visitor to the Schenectady labs when he was managing the company's fast-moving plastics division a decade or so ago. "He one time made the comment that he wanted to see the automobiles of every general manager in the company up here in the parking lot," says Roland W. Schmitt, head of the GE lab complex and senior vice president for corporate research and development. "So we expanded the parking lot." Now, hundreds of GE managers trek to Schenectady to see what the labs can do for their businesses. Sometimes, even when they get there, it's too late. When the GE labs developed a new product called Comband, which allowed cable television broadcasters to inexpensively double their programming output on a single channel, the GE division manager to whom it was offered was singularly ungrateful—despite the fact that it had made it from conception to market in just two years. "The general manager whose business this went into, I thought, would be bowled over with gratitude," says Kenneth A. Pickar, manager of GE's electronics laboratories. "He came here and said, 'Well, it was okay, but you didn't get it fast enough. I'm not sure how long the market is going to be open, and you guys are going to have to work a lot faster.' "

Technological change is moving so fast that even a company with a revolutionary new product often can't keep it to itself for very long. As soon as it hits the market, it often seems, somebody is copying it—and making it more cheaply overseas. That rapid transfer of technology frustrates many companies. But others try to maximize the technology edge by trying to get a new technology to market as quickly and as early as possible, to take advantage of every last minute of time before the competition shows up. "Not only is the technology progressing very rapidly, but also the transfer, domestically and internationally, is very, very rapid," says Ian Ross, president of Bell Labs. "I was interested in reading a history of clocks a while back, and I hadn't realized that one of the early clock industries was in England, and over a period of over 100 years, that technology got transferred to Switzerland. It took that period of time. How long does it take to transfer the one-megabit chip technology into

Korea or Japan or Hong Kong? You're talking these days about a couple of years.

"So your transfer of technology is very much more rapid than it was before. If you are putting your technology into product, you've got to move rapidly these days, and as soon as that technology is in your product, it's available to your customers, so they know what it is. As soon as you sell something, you reveal your technology," Ross says. "If you're talking about something that's going to impact the business five to ten years out, you can't hold that a secret for ten years. Never could, never will. One reason less enlightened companies don't do as much research as they should is that you don't have a proprietary lock on your research because of its long horizon. But the enlightened company says, 'That's OK. If I get first crack at it, that's all I need in a fast-moving market.'"

Not only does technology transfer rapidly from country to country, it often seems to be improved with each step, putting additional pressure on the originating company or country to keep improving its discovery. RCA's Bradshaw observes that we don't have "the kind of monopoly that we once thought, where if you had a big educational base, if you had a great cadre of engineers in the United States, if you had the world's greatest record for innovation, then you'd keep an edge. That isn't so. It travels around the world much faster than anyone would have considered."

Keeping up with, or better yet ahead of, that pace is an expensive game. It demands players willing and able to make almost continuous investments in research and development and new production equipment to manufacture products based on the latest technological breakthroughs. For that reason, many experts believe that large companies will continue to be the major locomotives of technological change—although small, entrepreneurial companies will continue to get a fair share of technological "wins."

Says AT&T's Ross, "It takes $100 million to build a silicon line— one fabrication line—and it takes several of them [to be competitive]. It takes a comparable sum of money to develop the next generation of technology that feeds that line. That says we're going to have some big companies at the leading edge of this. The Japanese have them, we need them. That doesn't say there isn't a place for small companies that can do very important niche kinds of things using other people's silicon and tailoring their own software. But in order to really drive that technology, you're going to need big companies, companies that can afford to invest in the R&D, can afford the factory facilities that will make this go, and the kinds of companies that have the values, the cultures that say, 'We are willing to invest for the long term'—which isn't very long when the technology is doubling every year."

Most important, however, is getting technology out into the market, selling it to end users, and finding out what customers will want the labs to come up with next. "You need a good marketing activity which is sensing what the customer thinks he or she needs," Ross says. "You need a good systems engineering activity which is analyzing how much you can match the technology that exists or will exist to what the perceived market needs are. . . . I see the technology and the marketing and the systems engineering as an interactive process."

"Many products get to the end of the assembly line and somebody's forgotten to find out if anybody can sell them," says RCA's Frederick. "So your marketing and distributing strengths are very often as important as your ability to conceive, develop, and produce. So we have to make sure that we match these. Our very bright people in the laboratories and in advanced engineering organizations can think up a lot of things that we can't sell. Our job is to match the capabilities with the market—on a timely basis. If you're too early, you spend a lot of money; if you're too late, forget it. So our job is to match the market with the product."

For some companies, the fruits of technology do not show up in new products. It's much easier to use technology to come up with a fundamental redesign of a piece of electronic system, say, than to use it to improve on the design of a simple steel bar. Still, the manufacturer of that bar can apply new materials technology or production know-how to make that bar stronger or to cast it more efficiently.

These are the more subtle uses of technology that, perhaps even more so than new products, can revolutionize American industry. The basic design of a farm tractor has not changed for decades. But John Deere is making them more efficiently than ever by manufacturing them in a highly automated plant. Similarly, Timken Co. has greatly improved the quality of its steel, while making it at a much lower cost, by building a state-of-the-art steel mill in Canton, Ohio—an example of how technology is affecting basic industries far removed from the so-called American technological centers of Silicon Valley or Boston's Route 128.

In many cases, however, American industry has been slow to apply technology to its production lines. The reasons for that failure are manifold. During the 1970s sharp fluctuations in interest rates discouraged

capital investments in new manufacturing equipment. And while the
1980s brought lower inflation and strong tax incentives for business investment, many companies had to strain to afford the equipment they
needed to keep pace with accelerating changes in technology. Some
observers have blamed it on complacency of managements that failed to
move soon enough to modernize aging plants: "We thought somewhat
restrictively for a while, because we were getting all the business anyway,"
says former General Motors Vice President Alex Mair. "So when somebody came forth with a new plan with some numbers that showed how
great it was, it was very difficult to get that through."

As a result, many companies, especially in older industries such as
autos and steel, find themselves today playing catch-up in process technology, trying to modernize manufacturing operations—from parts and
order control to production lines—as quickly as possible to improve
productivity and restore profitability. "If you look at autos and steel—
what's left of it in this country—and agricultural machinery and you go
on down the list, you begin to see that effectively, their fundamental
technology is on the wane and they're looking for another means to be
competitive," says AT&T Senior Vice President John Segall. At first,
many companies tried shifting manufacturing operations overseas, Segall
says, before trying to apply manufacturing technology to the problem.
"Now, I think, a lot of them realize—certainly GM does—[that] the
answer to their problem is to manage their information better and thereby
get the kinds of gains they can't get by making workers work harder or
faster or things like that. It manifests itself in things like robots [and]
sophisticated ways of linking the factory floor to [management informa-
tion] systems."

In short, says GE's Carpenter, "One of the biggest hits, particularly
for a company like GE, is to apply high-tech to boring low-tech." You
might not think of dishwashers or locomotive engines as the epitome of
high technology, but GE's facilities for making those products are among
the most advanced manufacturing plants in the world, using all manner
of robotics, inventory control, and computerized monitoring systems.

The ripple effect through the economy of such modernization programs is far-reaching—particularly if the alternative is losing the business
altogether. Take GE's modernization of its railroad locomotive plant in
Erie, Pa., for instance. "Several years ago, we reached the moment of
truth in Erie," Welch says. "Either invest to become more productive
and achieve higher quality, or fold the tent." By updating its production

technology, GE has turned the ancient plant into a highly competitive factor in an industry nobody would immediately label high-tech. It cost the company hundreds of millions of dollars, but it saved the plant and the businesses in Erie that serve the facility and its workers. "I'm certain the department stores and supermarkets in Erie understand the linkage between investment in manufacturing—a $180 million payroll—and the survival of a service business," Welch says. "Every time we create a good manufacturing job, we win, the service industry wins, and the U.S. Treasury wins. In the same three-year period that GE paid no income tax"—while taking advantage of tax credits that helped pay for Erie and other manufacturing-modernization projects—"our employees paid about $5 billion in federal income taxes, and the company paid another $4.5 billion in state, local, and other federal taxes, none of which would have been paid if the Eries of our world didn't win."

"Now an old locomotive factory, complete with smokestacks, is not what is envisioned on the high-tech and services dreamscape," Welch says. "But we couldn't be more proud of it. Because if you walk through the final assembly building in that plant you return to the golden era of American competitiveness."

Thus is technology revolutionizing GE's older "core" businesses. "The technology investments are the only way the core can survive," Welch says. "And we can't have anything in our core, in GE, that doesn't require, or doesn't have the opportunity for, technological leap-frogs, process-technology wins, and investments."

General Motors has also modernized and automated its production facilities, and its acquisitions of Electronic Data Systems and Hughes Aircraft are intended to inject still more technology into GM products and processes. "What we have to do is manage much more with the idea in mind that we'd better not have any old machinery or equipment that isn't as good or better than the rest of the world is planning," GM's Mair says. "In order to lead, you'd better have something that's better than what exists. The key to managing technology is to have an absolute freedom to develop technologies and use them."

Mair believes that applying technology to gain an edge in production efficiency is even more crucial and effective than developing new products based on advanced technology. "Most product advantages only carry you for a few years anyway, because you can copy those," he says. "Whereas the manufacturing processes are harder for people to find out about. Your efficiencies are much more difficult to discover." These technology-based productivity advances, he believes, are far greater than those that can be achieved through the more traditional productivity-boosting trick of driving people harder. "Those are going to be modest compared with the changes in the technology of manufacturing in which we are able to form things faster, machine things faster, manufacture and design machinery that stays running longer [and] doesn't break down. . . . That's where the gains are going to be made—in the management of the technology and allowing the technology to run free, to inspire it and provide a freedom for the transfer of that technology into our plants and products."

John Sculley, the chairman and president of Apple Computer, sees manufacturing technology as one of the best ways to stay ahead of the ever-mounting competition from abroad. "Their advantage is manufacturing," he says. "We have to be as good as the best Japanese companies will be three years from now. It's like shooting ducks: You have to aim at where they are going to be." To that end, Apple did something highly unusual when it built its revolutionary $20 million factory to produce Macintosh computers in 1984: It wrote off the costs of building the plant as fast as it legally could, so that the factory's financial base would not be a consideration in deciding when to replace it. "With the Mac factory, we did something that American industry never has done. If they did, we wouldn't be in the trouble we're in with automobiles," Sculley says. "That is, instead of waiting until we run out of capacity, or letting the business-school strategic planners tell us what the discounted cash flow investment model says and when we should cut over to a new factory based on when the return curves cross, we've said we want to write off our first factory as rapidly as the FASB [Financial Accounting Standards Boards] accounting rules will allow us to, which looks like two years. We'd like to write it all off in one year, if we could—a $20 million factory—because we know we'll probably build three generations of these factories in the next three years, if we're going to be as good as the best Japanese companies are in three years—because the technology is changing that rapidly.

"The conventional wisdom is you don't write a factory off in two years," he adds. "But we think the conventional wisdom is wrong. That's what got the steel industry into the situation where it didn't modernize."

Applying technology to the manufacturing process does not just mean automating the assembly line. It also means adopting sophisticated control and monitoring systems, usually computerized, to run that production line as well as other aspects of the business. AT&T's Kavner says that one of the most subtle competitive factors "is the strategic advantage inherent in a management process that provides timely, relevant, and reliable financial information to our market-oriented management. AT&T's success depends on developing such a process to identify accurate cost data. It depends on that process to furnish marketing and sales management with insightful analysis of gross margins and pricing alternatives. It depends on that process to yield relevant forecast data to orchestrate production so that we do not prepare for demand that fails to materialize or for demand that exhausts our proposed resources. It depends on that process to prepare precise breakeven comparisons—the tools needed to ensure we are the low-cost producer. It depends on that process to put together business plans that will use our resources optimally—plans that will build on actual commitments, not fond hopes or expectations."

"Every company in our industry—information management and high technology—is wrestling with how to do this effectively," Kavner adds. "Those that don't will lose. More companies have died because of inappropriate internal controls and bad data than from bad R&D and bad production."

All good managers, it would seem then, are singing the praises of technology. But there are a couple of caveats. One is the danger of standing still in the technology race, adopting an attitude of satisfaction and complacency—while the competition streaks by. Another danger is quite the opposite—plunging deeply into high-technology products or processes just for the sake of it, without an understanding of how the high-tech game is played or what the stakes are. Many companies have invested quickly and with indequate preparation in high tech and wound up with little to show for it. Gould Chairman William Ylvisaker believes that such a company will end up managing its old and new businesses so differently that it will cause divisiveness within the company and result in ineffective management. GE's Welch, who is attempting just such a grafting of high-tech businesses and processes onto an old-line company, disagrees, but has another warning about high-tech acquisitions. "Quickly implementing high-technology business new to you is a difficult task," Welch says. "As you graft these things on . . . the assimilation time to execute just the simple stuff is longer than one anticipates."

Still, the warnings about possible perils associated with the adoption of high technology are more common sense than anything else—and it is perhaps even more a reflection of common sense to utilize technology in the first place. For today's technological advances are providing the leverage for the improvement and expansion of all facets of business, and players in few industries can do without a technological injection—lest they find the competition leaving them behind. "The tremendous change in competition has caused the world to rise to a new level of forcing new technology," Mair says. "It is the second industrial revolution—and it dwarfs the first one."

# 9

## SEEK ALLIANCES AT HOME AND ABROAD

The IBM personal computer occupies a special place in the history of International Business Machines Corp. It quickly catapulted a late-starting IBM into the lead of the office-automation market, one of the most important markets in the computer and electronics field. The Charlie Chaplin figure that danced and skated across IBM's television spots for the PC created a new public image for IBM as a company that could solve the everyday problems of business managers as well as the huge number-crunching tasks of business.

But there was something else about the IBM PC that made it a symbol of the times. In a sharp break with tradition at IBM, only about half of the machine and its components came from the company's plants. The rest—including the monochrome monitor, keyboard, graphics printer, and a large share of the semiconductor chips—came from abroad: Japan, Singapore, and Korea. That mighty IBM should look to foreign sources for key components of one of its most visible products was not so startling. Other American electronics firms had been doing that for two decades. But when RCA, General Electric, and other companies went offshore for television components in the 1960s, they were simply trying to cut costs. The IBM PC, on the other hand, symbolized a new kind of business alliance for the 1980s—alliances not among allies, but among competitors, in the interest of expediency and competitive advantage.

The rising competitive pressures on American companies and their foreign rivals have sent them all looking for help from one another—help in the form of a missing product or technology, help in entering new markets, and help in sharing the financial risks of major ventures.

Domestically, a historic shift in antitrust doctrine under the Reagan administration has opened the door to corporate mergers and joint ventures among competitors on a scale that would have been unthinkable even 10 years ago. "I grew up in a world where the antitrust laws were used as a political instrument to prevent these kinds of things from happening," says Irving S. Shapiro, the former chairman of E. I. du Pont de Nemours & Co. and an authority on corporate law. That is no longer the case, and it means a far different, far more open environment for mergers and joint ventures now.

Internationally, the trend is the same. At a time when trade tensions between the United States and its major trading rivals in Asia and Europe are at their most antagonistic pitch since before World War II, the alliances and interconnections between these rivals are spreading rapidly. The semiconductor industry is one prime example. The cutthroat trade in semiconductor chips—the brain cells of the computer age—has become a major source of economic conflict between the United States and Japan. American firms accuse Japanese competitors of predatory price cutting in violation of trade laws, while an increasingly resentful Japanese business leadership says Americans are being poor losers and making unreasonable trade demands upon Japan. But that confrontation hasn't slowed the spreading commercial and technological partnerships.

"There's more bilateral collaboration between corporations than there used to be—as well as more competitiveness," says Andrew S. Grove, president of Intel Corp., one of the leading U.S. semiconductor companies. "Our most feared competitor, NEC, with whom we are in deadly litigation—NEC is our largest customer in Japan." The legal conflict between the two companies involves a make-or-break issue—Intel's right to maintain copyright protection over the instructions in two of its leading microprocessor products, thus blocking NEC from marketing competing products with similar instructions. But Intel and NEC don't let that dispute mar their commercial friendship in other areas where they can buy, sell, compete, and collaborate, Grove says. "You have to make sure you don't spill over, but since you're dealing with different people, it isn't too hard," he says. NEC's computer division, thus, is a customer of Intel's at the same time that its semiconductor division is dedicated to replacing Intel's products.

John Young, president of Hewlett-Packard Co., says the trend is unavoidable. "It's a direction we're going in. We have joint ventures with Samsung in Korea, with the Chinese government. Five years ago, if you'd have said we'd have a business partnership with a communist government, I'd have said you were crazy, but there we are, and it's working better than some of the others we have, as a matter of fact.

"And there are more and more of these coming up," Young says. "It's not just foreign relationships. There are so many complicated things to do today at a system level where your own expertise is even short of what's required. Even IBM—when they're doing it, there's something to it. If they don't have the resources, clearly that's a signal to most everyone else."

The complexity of today's technology demands collaboration, Young says. "We just do not have enough expertise to deal with these issues—automating a General Motors plant, for example. You have to work together with a whole series of people . . . a legion of very sophisticated new technologies that have to work together at once. There are a lot of drivers like that adding to the trend."

The most powerful driving force is competition, and it is creating unusual alliances of competitors and former adversaries in this country. One example is a research venture in the apparel industry, which has produced a robotic system for sewing garments—and an unprecedented degree of cooperation within that industry, according to its organizer, Harvard University professor and former Secretary of Labor John T. Dunlop. The sewing system is a flexible, programmable machine with deft mechanical fingers that can pick and fold limp pieces of fabric to make sleeves, the backs of suit coats and vests. It uses a camera eye to locate pieces of material and guide a sewing head to the proper place for stitching. Developed by the Charles Stark Draper Labs in Cambridge, Mass., where guidance systems for NASA's space shuttle and nuclear missiles are designed, the sewing system is touted by its backers as the most advanced in the world. It operates with a speed and precision that few humans can match, industry officials say.

It is the product of an alliance between leading apparel firms such as Hartmarx Corp., textile and synthetic fiber companies such as Burlington Industries Inc., J.P. Stevens & Co. Inc., and DuPont, and a labor union that has had its battles with the clothing industry before, the Amalgamated Clothing and Textile Workers. The final partner is the Commerce Department, which has committed nearly $8 million since 1980 to help fund the research, roughly matching the private contributions by the partners in the venture, which is called the Tailored Clothing Technology Corp., or (TC)². The companies that took part are the powers in the industry, and their backing for such a research venture was essential, because the small apparel companies that populate the clothing industry could not have raised the money to finance development and production of the technology and equipment.

The ability of these large firms to unite on a research venture is an indication of the relaxation of antitrust policy under the Reagan administration. "The ones who can do the research are the biggest," says Jeffrey Arpan, a professor with the International Business Program at the University of South Carolina. "If Burlington, Milliken [& Co. Inc.], and J.P. Stevens get together, it would probably raise eyebrows. Throw in Levi Strauss and DuPont. . . ."

The union joined in despite the obvious impact the robotic sewing system would have as a replacement for some of the union's members. The machine can do one-quarter of the sewing required on a suit coat, replacing perhaps one-fifth of the ACTWU workers who are now required to do that job. "If that's all that happens, we'll have 15 or 20 percent less people," says Murray Finley, president of the ACTWU. However, he adds, "if it enables us to become more competitive, to substitute what we make for imports, we could make up for that loss in jobs. If we don't do it, I'm convinced we'll lose the jobs anyway." An identical reaction came from the workers at Genesco Inc.'s Greif clothing plant in economically distressed Allentown, Pa., where the sewing system got its field trials. The clothing workers here "see it as the salvation of the industry," says Mauro DeFazio, an ACTWU manager for eastern Pennsylvania. "If we don't start competing, we won't have an industry."

The goal of the joint research venture was the equivalent of a "moon shot," its developers say—an attempt to leapfrog existing technology to create a strong advantage for the participants. Whether that comes in time for a textile industry that is being hammered by imports remains to be seen. But whatever its immediate impact on the industry's competitiveness, the venture has already succeeded, says William A. Klopman, chairman of Burlington Industries and chief executive of (TC)². "We have clearly demonstrated that automation of garment making is technically feasible, something not everyone was willing to believe," Klopman says. "We have spread an awareness that conditions affecting any one sector of our industry affect us all—unions and industry; fiber, textile, and apparel alike. We're all in the same leaky boat, and we've all got to bail and row."

"The adjustments are very widespread," says RCA Chairman Thornton F. Bradshaw. "Some companies go out of business. That's an adjustment. Other companies change their product line, so that they avoid the direct confrontation of trying to compete in a world where in some areas it's almost impossible to compete internationally. Other companies do their manufacturing offshore—that's RCA to a large extent. Other companies team up with some of the foreign competition—that's [also] RCA to a large extent. . . . If you can't lick 'em, join 'em."

Coalition-building has become an imperative, and not only for domestic industries like the textile and apparel makers, seeking to share the costs and spread the risks of new technologies. It is also essential for many manufacturing and service companies that must compete in global markets. The heavy costs of technological competition and the uncertainties imposed by shorter product and process life cycles push more and more companies toward partnerships. So do governmental regulations that severely restrict the ability of American companies to acquire companies directly in many foreign countries. And there may be important opportunities legally to shape the course of competition by allying with a foreign rival.

Although coalitions are hardly new, their fundamental nature is evolving into new forms in response to the growth of global markets, as Harvard Business School professor Michael E. Porter and colleagues recently have documented. Traditional coalitions were tactical and limited in scope, involving quick and inexpensive access to markets or technologies. The new partnerships are strategic, often linking major competitors in fundamental ways, Porter and co-author Mark B. Fuller note in *Competition in Global Industries,* published by the Harvard Business School Press.

These mixed corporate marriages are typically hard to manage and frequently disruptive to a firm's overall strategy. Coalitions "have a greater likelihood of creating a competitor or eroding industry structure when competition is global than if it is multidomestic and the coalition partner is a foreign firm," Porter and Fuller advise in the Harvard study. "We believe that coalitions in the most vital activities of a firm's value chain should be resorted to only rarely," they add. "A firm must ultimately master such activities itself if it is to sustain a competitive advantage in its industry. . . . However, coalitions can be a valuable tool in many aspects of global strategy and the ability to exploit them will be an important and probably growing source of international competitive advantage," Porter and Fuller say.

On one level, the expanding commercial alliances among the world's leading companies is a positive thing, strengthening as it does the economic ties and personal contacts among major trading nations. But there is another side to it. To a large extent, U.S. firms are obliged by other nations' laws to seek foreign partners in order to be allowed into those markets. Only IBM, it appears, has the power to demand the right to establish manufacturing operations overseas on essentially its own terms, as it demonstrated in Mexico. And even IBM has to establish extensive manufacturing operations in foreign countries to maintain a hospitable climate in the overseas markets in which it does business. "You see, every country is interested in world trade," says John Akers, chairman of IBM. "But what they mean by that is exports. People have these very sophisticated terms about the world economy and world trade and so forth and what they really care about is export. And if the IBM company is a significant negative influence in their balance of trade there's going to be a lot of discussion about that. So you can't be a world-class competitor in this industry without manufacturing around the world. It just can't be."

For most everyone else but IBM, manufacturing around the world requires some significant foreign participation. Hewlett-Packard President John Young, speaking about his company's foreign partnerships, says, "It would be nice to say I'm doing this because I want to, not because I have to because I'm denied market access. Right now it's mixed. . . . It's a real issue in many countries."

In large part, the alliances between American and foreign firms are marriages of convenience, permitting an exchange of technology for technology, or technology for capital. In Intel's case, for example, it licensed

NEC to make some of its chips in order to get access to some of NEC's important technology—in particular, a chip that governs displays on computer screens. One could run down the list of leading American, Japanese, and European manufacturers and discover a cat's cradle of interconnections: American Telephone & Telegraph Co. and Italy's Olivetti; GM and a long list that includes Toyota, Isuzu, Suzuki, and Fanuc Ltd., the robotics company; Ford and Toyo Kogyo (Mazda); Chrysler and Mitsubishi; General Electric and Rolls-Royce; Volvo and Renault; and Eastman Kodak and Matsushita. In the telecommunications world, there are clear signs of a polarization of companies toward two of the technological superpowers, AT&T and IBM, as each seeks to fill gaps in its competitive armor. In the former's camp are Amdahl and Nippon Electric Co., while IBM's entente includes MCI Communications Corp., Mitsubishi Electric, and Nippon Telephone and Telegraph Co.

Such alliances can be—and should be—templates for economic relationships among industrial companies, says Kenichi Ohmae, manager of the Tokyo office of the consulting firm McKinsey & Co. Ohmae's book *Triad Power* argues that the successful competitors in the 1980s and 1990s will be the companies from the triad of leading industrial societies—America, Japan, and the European nations—who are able to form the most effective partnerships.

How the benefits from these alliances are divided among the partners depends on their relative competitive strengths. In the case of rough equals like Olivetti and AT&T, the alliance serves to provide the companies with an immediate position in the others' markets. AT&T, which became a major investor in Olivetti, was able to turn to its Italian partner for the personal computers it needed when it entered the U.S. computer market in 1984. In return, Olivetti sells AT&T's telecommunications products in European markets. A different relationship has developed between the American steel industry and Japan's, the technological leader, which is providing equipment and expertise to help the American companies bring their quality and production yields closer to the best in the world. National Steel's relationship with Nippon Kokan K.K. has grown into an expanded partnership which includes Japanese trading companies. These companies have channeled capital into National and will distribute finished steel to National's customers. And the ties are not just with Japan: United States Steel has struck an agreement with South Korean competitor Pohang Iron and Steel to modernize a U.S. Steel plant in Pittsburg, Cal.

For U.S. Steel, the pact brings money, up-to-date steel-making technology, and cheap raw steel from Pohang to a 75-year-old plant; for Pohang, the payoff is a foothold in the American market, as well as a new American customer for its raw steel.

But for each such example, there are countless others where the technology flows the other way, as the history of the young U.S. biotechnology industry demonstrates.

Although the industry was born with federal assistance and nursed with venture capital, a new source of financial aid has become increasingly important as the industry readies its first biotech products for commercial sale. These partnerships involve foreign capital, notably from Japan and Europe, which has been invested in the American companies by their overseas rivals who are anxious to share in the latest biotech discoveries. "It is necessary for start-up companies to fund operations from sources other than sales revenue," says Thomas D. Kiley, a vice president of Genentech Inc. "It often means trading future rights to moneyed organizations with a lesser grasp on the technology. We are technology-rich, but less well-heeled." Genentech has about a dozen contracts with prominent U.S. and foreign firms, which have helped it remain financially solid for its first six years even though none of its products had been cleared for sale in this country. "These arrangements are vital to our growth," Kiley says. Although most of Genentech's contracts provide for the manufacture of the products here for overseas sale, other biotech companies have or will be transferring important technology abroad as their contribution to their international partners.

"Most observers would agree that currently the new flow of biotechnology transfer is outward from the United States," the U.S. Office of Technology Assessment has concluded. One of the vital, unmeasurable issues is where to strike a proper balance between relatively free access to U.S. technology and the protection of discoveries that could be the foundation of a leading American position in biotechnology. An open door will hasten the growth of the industry the world over, in which American biotech firms would share, bringing the benefits of this new science to more people more rapidly. But it will be a haunting irony if American biotech firms discover 15 years from now that the technology they shared came back to ruin them. The American companies need the money right now, to assure a chance at a strong future, and their foreign rivals are happy to provide it.

The same conflict is emerging in many other industries. Take as an example Eastman Kodak Co.'s decision to pioneer in the market for 8-mm camcorders provided by Matsushita. The cameras and film will be cheaper than the equipment used for standard videocassette taping, and Kodak hopes that will encourage use of the 8-mm format by amateurs and professionals. If so, Kodak will be on the ground floor. The risk to Kodak from this partnership, however, is that one day the American company will discover that it has blazed a path for Matsushita, enabling it to test the market before it jumps in with its own product line, undercutting Kodak, its former partner.

As the trend toward partnerships grows, then, the question American companies must ask is whether they are using the alliances to cure short-term problems, while neglecting the truly vital longer-term considerations. Foreign ventures can be band-aids, allowing a company to fix a problem without really addressing what caused it—buying a technology, for instance, while neglecting the reasons that it was unable to come up with the technology itself.

The case of Control Data Corp. is illustrative. Under its founder and former chairman William C. Norris, Control Data became a leading proponent of technology-sharing ventures. Norris was the creator of the Microelectronics and Computer Technology Corp. (MCC), in which a score of leading American computer companies are pooling research on supercomputers, artificial intelligence, and other frontier problems of computer science. But as the joint ventures and partnerships proliferated, Control Data found it had so many irons in the fire, it almost put the fire out. It was so busy pushing various computer-peripheral products out the door that it lost sight of the fact that it was losing ground to competitors in such key areas as manufacturing costs and quality—thus dulling whatever competitive edge the ventures were providing. Norris faults himself for not forcing Control Data to defend itself sooner against the intensified competition in computer peripherals from American and foreign companies. "The fact is that peripherals had been making good money," he says. "The people then running it just couldn't perceive what happened and simply didn't move fast enough. And I'm chief executive officer and I'll take responsibility for that," he said in 1985, shortly before his retirement.

With the company in default on nearly $300 million in bank debt in 1985, Control Data was forced to undertake a traumatic, overdue cutback and to focus on the technologies and markets where its prospects were strongest. Control Data is still pursuing alliances, but it's picking its shots more carefully. "We are not in the process of changing the focus of Control Data Corp.; we are in the process of narrowing the focus," says Norris' successor as chairman, Robert Price. "The thing that is true is that we have been trying to do too many things. Very simply, we do not have the resources, in people, talent, time, or money, to do so many things. So we must do fewer."

# 10

# NATIONAL INTERGROUP

## The Metamorphosis of an Old-Line Steel Company

Throughout the first three-quarters of this century, the monuments in the business world were raised to the builders of the great industrial and marketing empires, men like Sloan at General Motors, Wood at Sears, and Watson at IBM.

But this decade of sudden, destructive shifts in the competitive winds has produced a different breed: chief executives whose role is taking apart and reassembling the companies they head, selling failing or unprofitable parts, adding to others, in hopes that a stronger business will emerge. The history of National Intergroup Inc. is the story of just such radical surgery.

Howard M. Love joined National Steel Corp. in 1956 with a Harvard MBA, and began a traditional—and in his case highly successful—march up the corporate ladder. At any point along that way, if you had asked "Pete" Love what business he was in, he would have said, without hesitation, the steel business.

Yet since 1980, Love has led the transformation of National Steel from a company that looked, thought, and acted like a traditional steel producer into a hybrid holding company called National Intergroup Inc., which Love has tried to tailor for the difficult business conditions of the 1980s and 1990s.

Its steelmaking operations have been heavily pared back. A large plant was spun off to employee ownership, and the remaining steel business was turned into a stand-alone subsidiary jointly owned by National and a powerful new partner, Japan's No. 2 steel company, Nippon Kokan K.K. In 1989, as soon as the contract with NKK permits, Love intends to sell National Intergroup's remaining share of the steel business to the highest bidder.

The new National Intergroup will be formed around two recently purchased enterprises, a crude-oil shipping company and a wholesaler of pharmaceutical products—fulfilling Love's plan to turn National away from its 50-year heritage toward a new base in the faster-growing, healthier service economy. For National, the service sector beckons as a refuge from the pressures of imports, heavy investment requirements, and high labor costs that now bear down on manufacturing.

It is a performance that dramatizes the singular role of the chief executive of a major American corporation in the1980s. Although he was responsible to a board of directors and surrounded by strong-minded senior executives, Love's position as National's chairman and chief executive enabled him to be the catalyst for the changes that would completely restructure the company. Unlike any of his predecessors, who assumed that National's future would follow its steelmaking past, Love raised the fundamental question of the corporation's identity, setting in motion the process of transformation.

What was National? Was it the sum of its assets, the steel mills, office buildings, and the rest? Or was National really its employees? Or their families and communities? Or its shareholders? If it was all of these, how would Love weigh the conflicting interests in choosing a course for the company?

The answers required radical change on two fronts. At the corporate level was Love's campaign to hammer out a new vision of National's future and then win the support of managers and employees for this revised mission. And in National's steel mills, a second campaign is underway to make National's steel operations world-class in quality and productivity once again, with the help of NKK.

There has been no shortage of criticism as Love has found his answers. The change has come too fast for many whose loyalty is to the steelmaking business, and too slowly for some institutional stockholders focused on dividend and earnings growth. Some of the losers in this transformation have resented the picture of Love and his top associates sitting secure and highly paid, while they shuffled National's operations and assets like properties on a board game. But the image is false. As long as the United States' trade policy permitted lower-cost foreign steel to enter the country, National's old steelmaking culture could not survive. The upheaval could not have been avoided.

When Love took over, the steel industry had come out of a sharp downturn in the late 1970s that triggered a severe round of plant closings and layoffs. Just ahead lay the back-to-back recessions of the early 1980s, the worst the steel industry had suffered through since the Great Depression of the 1930s. As a long line of critics has spelled out, it was an old industry that had been too fat, dumb, and happy for too long, comfortable in the gentleman's competition that traditionally prevailed in the American steel market until the mid-1970s.

There was plenty of blame to go around: The industry's executives had been far too slow to spot the competitive threat posed by foreign steelmakers, equipped with more modern, productive facilities and backed by the export promotion policies of their governments. They were blindsided at home by the success of small mini-mills, which relied on scrap steel and efficient furnaces to make premium-priced specialty steel products, taking business away from big steel producers.

Its planners had given too little thought to a third threat, coming from the steady development of new materials that would in time replace steel for many uses in building, packaging, transportation, and defense-contracting.

The steelworkers' union didn't catch on to the changing competitive position of the industry in time, either. It used its bargaining leverage to push labor costs far above the average for U.S. manufacturing industries, adding to the load American steel producers had to carry. The steel producers, anxious for labor peace that would prevent disruptive strikes, signed a no-strike agreement with the union, which also contributed to the rapidly rising cost of labor. Among steelworkers and management alike, there was a careless confidence that whatever the industry made, however it was made, there would be buyers. The prevailing attitude was, "If Pete won't buy it, Joe will," says Ed Sambuchi, vice president and general manager of National's Great Lakes plant near Detroit. "But now Pete's broke and Joe's out of business." And, he might have added, Tom's buying from Brazil and Bill's getting his steel from South Korea.

National was still flying its familiar colors as a steel company when Love took charge in 1980. Steel operations accounted for 80 percent of its $3.7 billion in sales and 38,800 employees, far outpacing its other businesses—aluminum and the financial services operations of its California-based savings and loan subsidiary. Its massive tinplate plant in Weirton, W.Va., enabled the town to boast of being the tin-can capital of the world. Elsewhere, its plants were an important source of sheet metal for the auto industry. National was the seventh-largest producer of steel in the United States.

But if you looked hard at National, if you turned away from the strong sentimental pull of its steelmaking history, it appeared that the company was crumbling too fast, in too many places, for any patch-up operation to fix, according to Love. He and a handful of executives began meeting in secret in 1980 to share that hard look at the company's future. Somebody, noting the headcount of 13 executives, dubbed them the Last Supper sessions.

"You have to look at your place in the industry and within business in general, because you're competing for capital and people," Love says. "You have to ask, do you continue to put money into businesses that aren't paying back? That doesn't take a masters degree." On that basis, National's steel business looked increasingly like a loser to Love. It had too much capacity and too many obsolete mills, coke batteries, and furnaces that had not been kept up to date and would take reams of money to restore. The analysis showed that even if National could afford the capital, the steel market wasn't likely to be strong enough to give National the businesses it would need to repay a higher level of debt. "You have to evaluate all that and maybe say, 'Gee, this isn't the world I grew up in,' " Love says.

He concluded that it would take decisive government intervention to put the company's older operations back on their feet, and he wasn't willing to gamble on that.

"I knew it had to be done," Love says. "But we had to get everybody on board to understand," he adds, speaking of the small group of top management. "That started the thought process of everybody . . . I felt I wanted to run a profitable company. That ensures the long-term success of employees and everyone. . . . I knew where I wanted to go. I was looking for help on the road to take."

A dilemma over National's Weirton plant crystallized the issue. The city of Weirton lies along a river in the thin finger of West Virginia that pokes up between the steelmaking valleys of Ohio and Pennsylvania. In the past five years, many of the steel plants and mills in those valleys have been shut down and now stand empty.

Weirton was in trouble then, too. The plant's chief product, the tin can, had been steadily losing out to aluminum and plastic containers, and the Weirton plant faced an uphill struggle merely to hold its ground. By 1980, one of the plant's major facilities, its battery of coke ovens, was in urgent need of reconstruction. Not many years earlier, the decision would have been automatic. Coke is one of the essential ingredients for steelmaking, and the accepted, efficient strategy is to make it at the plant site and sell the byproducts (e.g., natural gas) that are created in the process. "That's better than buying the coke you need," Love says. As long as everyone assumed that Weirton was an indispensible part of National, the answer was obvious: rebuild the coke ovens.

But now Love and National's top management had begun asking the unthinkable questions. Once rebuilt, the coke-oven battery would last 15 years or so. But did the tin can have that kind of future? Was there any point in competing with aluminum cans—or those made out of some new, as yet unforeseen material? Would the product of the mill still produce the kinds of profits National's management wanted? Were there better ways for National to spend the money?

"We wrestled with it," Love says. National's management finally concluded that as a long-term investment, rebuilding the coke ovens didn't make sense. "We'd spent $1 billion in the late 1970s [on capital investment throughout National] and didn't have much to show for it."

In 1982, the decision was made. After nearly two more years of negotiations, National sold Weirton to the plant's management and steel-workers, making it the largest employee-owned corporation in the nation. As part of National, there would be no hope for Weirton's long-term prosperity, even with the reductions in labor costs that the United Steel-workers agreed to. But as an independent, employee-owned company, Weirton was able to lower its overhead and labor costs dramatically and concentrate the full attention of management and steelworkers on the plant's survival.

With the Weirton decision behind them, Love and the rest of National's top management turned to the larger question of National's future. In September 1983, the company changed its name and became National

Intergroup Inc., with its steel operations just one of six operating divisions, no longer the heartbeat of the company. Its statement of purpose that year expressed the significance of the shift: "No longer could one group [within National] look to another group either to make a profit or as an excuse for not making a profit [a not-so-veiled reference to the steel business]. . . . In the past, we had basically a steel culture [and] managed to emphasize production. Today, we are attempting to develop a culture that emphasizes marketing, risk-taking, participation [and] product excellence."

When the new mission statement was issued, many did not rise to salute. But Love did not try to impose it on the company. The statement became, instead, the starting point for a freewheeling debate about National's future that spread deeper and deeper into the company's ranks.

Even without Weirton, National's remaining steel businesses didn't look strong enough to keep up with the rest of the company, not without some help. The help came from NKK, the Japanese steelmaker, which bought the half-interest in National's steel operations for $273 million in 1984.

For National, the partnership offered a double benefit: a new partner with the commitment and capital required to succeed in the steel business, as well as first-class technology in the steelmaking areas most important to National. "I don't think we would have had the staying power that we'll have with the Japanese," Love said at the time of the NKK announcement. "The Japanese have a technological expertise that simply is not available domestically," National executive vice president Fred E. Tucker says. "We have not done a good job funding research and development over the years," Love adds. "They say research companies spent 4 to 8 percent of sales dollars on research, and we've been zinging along at about two-tenths of a percent. We're trying to get that up to 1 percent."

The test of that proposition came with the opening by National of a new $110 million electrogalvanizing line at the Great Lakes plant in 1986. National's engineers believe that the process for bonding a microscopic protective layer of zinc on the sheet steel will make it as good as or better than any in the world.

Much of the technology and expertise is coming from NKK. The precision of the electrogalvanizing line will permit thin coatings using new alloys that will reduce the weight of steel products without sacrificing strength. It is this kind of specialized, high-value product that will provide the biggest rewards for the company and the best chance for survival in the steel industry's fight to the finish. But the new technology and Japanese capital was not sufficient. There had to be a fundamental change in attitude toward steelmaking, by managers, supervisors, and steelworkers, if National was to close the quality and productivity advantage enjoyed by Japanese competitors. "It's not just the equipment. It's employee attitudes, management attitudes, a combination of things, " Love says. "It's thinking, 'Let's do it right the first time.' "

Inside the plant, a gradual intertwining of the American and Japanese steelmaking cultures is proceeding, Sambuchi says. "They've given us a different point of view," he says, describing the painstaking search by Japanese engineers and technicians for ways to improve the efficiency of the plant and the quality of the steel.

The immediate impact of National's Japanese partnership has shown up in the details of the steelmaking. Early in the process, a team of inspectors from NKK went through the Great Lakes plant on hands and knees, looking for problems. They found 160 different opportunities, large and small, for improvements—like changing the size of a pump, replacing a piece of equipment, or building storage racks for finished coils of steel so they won't sit on the plant floor picking up debris before they're shipped. But there has been a substantial impact on attitudes, too, Sambuchi says. "Their philosophy is that an idea is not great until it's implemented and you get the benefit back," he says. "Sometimes, we put an idea on paper, but getting it implemented is painfully slow. They say when you've got a good idea, you don't stop until you get a benefit from it. . . . And it works. Things are getting done. Their presence has encouraged us to be religious about it." "Everything they do is centered on reducing waste," says William Wright, manager of technical problem-solving at the plant. "We've been into that for some time, but it's something we have to expand on. Our potential there is tremendous. We're astounded by the little things they do."

The Japanese insistence on writing down and documenting every step of the steelmaking process seemed at first to threaten the much looser American style, which relies much more on the eyeball judgment and ingenuity of experienced steelmakers, who have their own individual tricks and techniques. And the American steelworkers would have resented it if a new technique had been forced on them, Wright says. Instead, they were asked to help prepare new standard procedures for steelmaking, spelling out the tricks and know-how in writing, and in detail. That involvement made it the workers', not the managers', standard, Wright says. And prompted by what they've learned from the Japanese, National's managers emphasize that while there is one best way of making steel at any one time, that method isn't static. It can always be improved.

The plant also is a test site for an experiment in labor-management relations. The steelworkers who volunteered to work on the production line have been trained in the new process for more than a year at their regular pay, and are guaranteed at least one year of employment. National and the United Steelworkers union are trying to work out a novel pay system that gives the steelworkers greater responsibility and provides rewards for achieving quality goals. Terry Seabolt, director of human relations at the plant, says, "We're talking with employees about pay based on the quality of the product, [with] more self-direction of employees and fewer supervisors. We'd like to have a big premium for quality. If we're going to survive, we have to be on the leading edge of employee cooperation."

The change from an authoritarian management demanding high-volume production to one that asks for quality first, then production—while at the same time stressing steelworker participation—is a big leap. It's too far for some, Sambuchi says. "We've got pockets of declining morale because [some employees] haven't bought it," he says. "The rest of the people are leaving them behind."

With the proceeds from the NKK investment in hand, Love began National's second move—a run to daylight away from the steel business into services. His initial thrust caught many by surprise—an attempt at a $700 million merger that would combine National with Bergen Brunswig Corp., a Los Angeles-based distributor of drugs, healthcare, and consumer electronics products. In many ways, Bergen Brunswig was the exact opposite of National—a young company that had taken a fast ride up the ladder along with the rest of the growing services and technology economy.

But in Love's eyes, it was a case of opposites attracting. National had a pile of cash in its pocket thanks to the $273 million NKK invested in the steel venture and National's own unused tax credits. And the steel company could count on its remaining businesses to keep the cash flowing, even if the profits remained disappointing. Bergen Brunswig, a high-growth company with a strong profit record, was well along on a continuing expansion program and needed National's cash. Like other service companies that lack the huge capital investments found in businesses like the steel industry, Bergen Brunswig also had a relatively high effective tax rate. National's deductions would take care of that. Combined, the two would create a company with $4 billion in sales—only one quarter of it coming from steelmaking.

Love won shareholder approval for the merger, after a bruising proxy fight. But in April 1985, Bergen Brunswig got cold feet and pulled out of the merger, citing an unexpected setback in National's aluminum business. "Their unease had built up," Love says. "It was a way out." The setback was temporary, and in 1986, Love made the investments that will provide the core of National's future operations, buying the Permian Corp., a crude oil shipping company based in Houston, and FoxMeyer Corp., a Denver-based drug wholesaler. In completing the restructuring of National, Love has put its steelmaking business in new hands, assuring a long-term commitment from a strong backer, and he has put National's cash to work in the more promising services sector.

National is close to the point where the transformation must be concluded, Love acknowledges. The uncertainty about the future has exacted a toll on the morale of employees and managers, and some valuable leaders have been lost to other firms as a consequence. Change and adaptation work best coming from a stable foundation. "You can't be in transition your whole career," Love says. "You have to say, 'This is where we're going,' and settle it down. You have to have a career roadmap. You go through an initial stage [saying], 'This isn't right.' You define what has to be done. But at some point you have to put a stop to it. We have to get on a schedule so the employees and investing public can see where we're going and how we're getting there."

# 11

# A NEW ALLIANCE

## Management and Labor

Throughout American industry, companies and employees are struggling to create partnerships, and nowhere are the stakes higher than at National Steel. To deal with the relentless pressures from import competition and low profits, National must find new ways to reduce costs and improve productivity dramatically. Pete Love, chairman of National Intergroup, warns that if steel prices don't improve, National will be hard put to raise capital from its Japanese partners. "The owners," he says, "are going to take a hard look at that business and wonder whether or not it's worth investing additional funding in."

National's laboratory for experiments in building closer relationships is its Great Lakes plant outside Detroit, where National has built a $110 million steel-finishing line with the help of its Japanese partner, Nippon Kokan K.K. Called an electrogalvanizing line (EGL), the new facility offers National state-of-the-art techniques to produce rustproof body panels for the auto industry.

As Stanley Ellspermann, National's vice president for human resources, describes it, a key to building the EGL line was a precedent-breaking agreement between the United Steel Workers union and National management over how the new line would be operated. The company provided training for steelworkers who would work on the line, including trips to Japan to see NKK's technology. The union, in turn, agreed to eliminate rigid job classification to create a more flexible, productive team.

"Before the board even improved the investment, we had a memorandum of understanding with the union that talked about basically treating these people as salaried employees, to pay them for the quality of the output of the line, to train them so they were capable of doing each other's job, to allow maintenance people to do operating work and operating people to do maintenance," Ellspermann says. "That commitment from the union to work with us was in large part responsible for us going ahead with that thing." In return, National has promised to offer a profit-sharing plan for the steelworkers. "Our concept is to allow the employees to participate in the success of the company," Ellspermann says. "If we expect dramatic increases in productivity, we ought to be prepared to reward that."

"Our approach is not one of adversary with the union, which doesn't mean we pussyfoot around or lay down for them. It's communications," says former National Steel President Robert D. McBride. For several years, National executives and counterparts in the steelworkers union leadership have been meeting regularly to dicuss problems and solutions. "We've faced off on some very hairy, sensitive issues. Each side laid the problems out . . . and as Buddy Davis of the steelworkers said, when you put together the two lists, it's amazing that 80 percent of them are the same," McBride says. "That has put us in a position where we clearly understand where the steelworkers stand and they understand where we're coming from. They understand *in toto* the details of our financial situation and how we're projecting the future, and we've invited them to the table to help us project that future. If they think we're full of crap, then what's their idea?"

"We made a statement, we wanted to encourage employees to participate in this business," says Ed Sambuchi, general manager of the plant. "But we had to be listeners, which was probably the hardest thing for any of us to do. My version of listening was, I'd wait for a pause so I could jump in."

"When we did listen," Sambuchi says, "we learned a lot."

With the help of their Japanese partners, the National steelmakers are improving the communications throughout the plant, according to

McBride and other executives. "We build too many walls: 'This is my turf—stay the hell out,' " McBride says. But the Japanese, with their culture of consensus-building, take naturally to strong horizontal communication among peers, and the Americans have much to learn on that score, McBride says. "Breaking down those walls is the biggest challenge we have," he says, whether the walls divide union and management or managers with different responsibilities. And McBride believes that American steelmakers, raised in a culture of individualism, should be able to build a better top-to-bottom communications process than the Japanese. "Obviously, somewhere the decisions have to be made, but we're more participative now," he says. "It means a lot of listening and taking more time in the decision-making."

"Historically, we've had very much of an adversarial relationship with the union," Ellspermann says. The attitude, he says, was, "Bring your guns and knives, and we'll talk about this problem." Now the goal is to involve the work force, to give them a reason to want to make the company successful—to provide the security that they need. "Our answer to rewarding employees in the past has been, give me an idea on how to eliminate your job and I'll lay you off," Ellspermann says. "It took us a long time to realize that doesn't work. That's not exactly a proper incentive for people."

There are no magic formulas for writing such new agreements blending profit-sharing and job security with cost savings and wage modernization, as the traumatic contract negotiations between Eastern Airlines and the machinists union in the 1980s demonstrated. In exchange for wage cuts, the machinists gained a large block of Eastern stock and seats on Eastern's board of directors. But once they got into the boardroom, the machinists, rather than sharing with management an understanding of Eastern's financial condition, got an inside look at the companies' books that only heightened their suspicions of management.

But difficult though they are to create, healthy partnerships built on trust, respect, and communication are essential for companies that seek to meet the challenges of today's changing environment. The key is creating a corporate culture built on respect, candor, and trust.

When H. Ross Perot showed up at General Motors in 1984, he must have looked as foreign as Marco Polo arriving at the court of Kublai Khan. The culture of Electronic Data Services, the quick-hitting computer-services firm Perot had founded, was in most ways the opposite of what he found in GM's sprawling empire after GM took over EDS. (Perot quips that a gunner's command at GM goes, "Ready, aim, aim, aim, aim. . . .") So as Perot traveled through that empire, he saw it with a discoverer's fresh eye for the auto company's peculiar lifestyle and rituals. After two years of exploration, Perot concludes that GM's success rests not on robots or computers or horsepower or slick designs. To succeed, he believes, GM must build a better partnership with its people.

The Japanese automakers are not ahead of General Motors in automation or engineering, Perot says. "They're ahead in human relations." The Japanese car and truck plants in this country hire American assembly line workers and use assembly methods and technologies that are no more advanced than those possessed by the American car companies. "But they build a better car for lower cost than the U.S. manufacturers," Perot says. "And it comes down to how you treat people. That's got to change. It's happening now."

"The talent in the company is enormous," Perot says of GM. "The people are a lot better than the cars. That means you have the potential to make a wonderful car if you ever tap the potential of the people."

Respect for colleagues and co-workers is so important at EDS that Perot makes it his personal business to see that that value is ingrained and kept alive. "Is it better for me to work with you or for you?" he asks. "Is it better for you to make me enjoy my work or hate my work? The answer is simple. Yet all over corporate America, we've got guys who show up every morning and make people just as miserable as they can." At EDS, "they understand I will kill a manager who violates our management philosophies," Perot says. "If we have a manager who looks down on someone else, we fire him." The same thing happens, he adds, "if we have a manager that is intimidating . . . if I have a manager that won't listen to other people. So these are things that they hear a lot of from me."

It is one thing to instill and preserve values in a company as young as EDS, whose senior key managers were personally picked by Perot, and where all employees at all levels are chosen because of their ability to fit in with the EDS philosophy. It is an altogether different problem at companies like GM and National, where the products are created by employees who are members of unions with their own philosophies and priorities.

The message Perot is carrying everywhere he goes in GM is that the company and the United Auto Workers must become one organization sharing priorities without losing their separate identities. "We've got to win together or we'll lose together," Perot says. "We're stuck with one another." A partnership between management and labor is possible, based upon a mutual recognition of what has to be done to survive and win, he says. "I believe we're starting down that trail," Perot says. "There are a lot of old wounds. If we [EDS] worked on the factory floor at General Motors 20 years ago, and nobody else had organized them, we would have organized them. Because [GM] didn't treat people right. It's that simple."

Perot recounts a speech given to GM's directors last year by Donald Ephlin, a United Auto Workers' vice president who heads the union's GM members. Ephlin's message was on the treatment of people. "He talked about the hard choices you have to make in business, but if and when you have to make them, there is a sensitive and human way to handle it, and there is a cold, hard, pink-slip way," Perot says. The choice seems simple. It's perhaps no coincidence that unions have had a hard time organizing workers in Silicon Valley, where corporate cultures are based on a much more humanistic style of management centered on employee participation in decision-making and profits.

Jerome Rosow, the head of the Work in America Institute and a top-level consultant to some of America's largest corporations, says the partnership with workers is essential. "If people feel secure, they're going to accept change," he adds. But if they are not secure, they'll fight it, understandably.

Some of the companies in this book have accepted this responsibility to those who lie in the path of change. When Du Pont, for instance, had to make major cuts in its payroll to shrink the company to a more manageable, efficient size, it did not do it, as many other companies have, through wholesale layoffs. Instead, it accomplished a significant part of the manpower reductions through voluntary retirement programs and offers of up to $4,000 per employee to move displaced workers from a shutdown plant to a new job elsewhere in the company. "We try and do those things in ways that are considerate," says Edward Jefferson, Du Pont's recently retired chairman. "It's a bottom-line orientation, but it has a substantial element of consideration of people. . . . We'll slim down the operations, but we're going to run it safely. We'll slim it down, but we're going to have a considerate treatment of people."

"There are enormous dislocations in any given company situation," says Irving Shapiro, Jefferson's predecessor at Du Pont. "Managements are threatened and displaced. Plants are closed in communities. Workers

are displaced. Economics becomes the driving force and other considerations tend to be submerged, and that's troublesome, because as important as economics is, it's not the only issue that one has to deal with.
I quickly concede if you don't have earnings you don't have a business
and nothing plays. But having earnings is not the final answer either.
They are a means to an end."

GE saw the necessity of deep cuts in its ranks during the recessions
earlier in this decade to make its costs competitive with its rivals. It set
the stage for those cuts with a new labor agreement that included substantial plant-closing benefits. "From a social strategy point of view, we
know that we weren't going to be permitted to [close plants] unless we
eased the transition," says Frank Doyle, GE's senior vice president.

"We told the union that we saw a need to exit marginal businesses,
to substantially invest to improve productivity in existing businesses, and
the inevitable cost of that was going to be fewer people in fewer plants,"
Doyle says. "So what we did was, we nailed home our right to do it, in
exchange for some cutting-edge benefits on how we treated people" as
well as a "very early notice strategy" on plant closings. "Given enough
time, people and communities can adjust to that kind of change," Doyle
says—and in GE's case, "enough time" has ranged from a minimum of
six months up to one to three years' warning of plant closings.

"You let it be known that no community is going to lose its GE plant
without plenty of notice," Doyle says. "You let your salaried employees
know that they may lose their job. . . . They know that. But they also
know that they get plenty of notice, they get good benefits, they get plenty
of help, and they probably won't get nailed by the whole experience."
When it has closed plants, GE has put into place retraining programs,
employee-transfer options, job-placement services, and other benefits to
cushion the blow—and in the process the company has even managed
to get editorial commendations from plant-town newspapers for its handling of the closings.

"You really cannot in an economic way replace a job," Doyle says.
"But you can certainly create an environment in which people view the
loss of a job as being handled fairly and openly and constructively, and
I think that's what we've done. You cannot effect cultural change unless
you've dealt with the underlying security concerns of people and communities and the institutions. And you can't deal with those purely through
communications. You've got to alter the way you act."

The changes required to keep American corporations competitive in the next decade and beyond will require such attention to the human side of managing change. As GE's Jack Welch has noted, the corporation is no more than the sum of its human parts, which includes not just employees but their families, customers, suppliers, and the surrounding community that in some way is affected by the corporation's actions.

"One has to be concerned with some of the dislocations that occur and the fact that we haven't yet faced up to that as a society and tried to ameliorate some of the pain," Shapiro says. "But I think on balance, it's a positive development. A lot of dislocation, a lot of pain, but I think a lot of sleepy companies are waking up."

The changes needed to put American companies on the leading edge of the competitive world will not come without pain, but that pain can be minimized through sensitive management and attention to the human details. There is no way to eliminate all of the human hardship of change, but the pain of not making the needed required corporate and management changes to adapt to the new environment is likely to be much greater.

The bottom line for this worker-management partnership, then, is communications. The relationship must be built on a solid, factual understanding about the company's position. "We overcommunicate," Welch says. "I have roundtables here once a month, with 25 employees, secretaries, maintenance people. . . . You know, 'What's happening with the company?' " Welch wants plant managers to do the same thing, "Have roundtable lunches with a broad section of employees—tell them what's happening and don't color it. Candor, candor, candor."

# 12

# AMERICAN TELEPHONE
# & TELEGRAPH

## Learning a New Corporate Culture
## in the Heat of the Technology Wars

The New Year's Day 1984 breakup of the world's largest company, American Telephone & Telegraph Co., was one of the great cataclysms in this nation's business history.

More than two years later, the aftershocks are still rattling the telephone system, as consumers encounter rising monthly phone bills and service charges and struggle with the bewildering marketing battle between AT&T and its long-distance rivals. But the cloud of confusion thrown into the air by this upheaval, costly and aggravating as it is, obscures another change of long-lasting significance. That change is AT&T's attempt to transform itself from a staid, all-powerful telephone monopoly into an agile, aggressive leader in the merging businesses of computers, telecommunications, and electronic information.

Simultaneously, AT&T must turn fast-changing technologies into strong new products and services while it teaches itself how to compete. How well it handles—or fumbles—this unique challenge in the years ahead will fill textbooks for managers in other competitive industries where technology and innovation are the driving forces.

The outlines of AT&T's battleground, the new information age, already are forming, in the steady infiltration of personal computers and word processors into offices and in the beginnings of electronic mail. The stage is being set as well by the steady spread of·electronic libraries accessible through computer terminals in homes or offices and the rapid computer-controlled automation of factories.

And that is just the beginning.

The utopian vision that AT&T promises is an information age built upon a "global network that would permit anyone, anywhere, and at any time to send or receive information without technical or economic barriers," as Ian M. Ross, president of AT&T Bell Labs, puts it.

What AT&T wants to do—and must do—is become a leader in the design and sale of the machines and communications networks that carry out this exchange of information. The market is not only in the United States, but in all of the major industrial nations. "The dawning of the Information Age is bringing about dramatic changes in the fundamental fabric of our civilization," AT&T's Nobel laureate and research chief Arno A. Penzias has written. "Just as the fabric of the nineteenth century was iron and that of the twentieth petroleum, the essential fabric of the twenty-first century will likely be information."

The information market—as Penzias defines it—may well be the most demanding, unpredictable, and competitive of any commercial battleground in the world. Waiting for AT&T are International Business Machines Corp., other established rivals in this country and abroad, and a host of new, nimble high-tech companies.

Although AT&T is blessed with an advantage its rivals lack—a deep pocket of cash flowing from its long-distance business in the United States—it must succeed on three separate fronts to achieve the place it wants in the information age.

First, it needs a product line—computers of all sizes, word-processors, terminals, and semiconductor chips. Although AT&T has been a major manufacturer of products ranging from telephones to complex computerized call-switching systems, it has had to adapt most of its machines and acquire others to create a line of commercial computer products. "Our biggest gamble is a necessity," says Morris Tanenbaum, AT&T's vice chairman. "It is the decision to become recognized as someone who can provide corporations with the basic infrastructure of information movement and management [and] to demonstrate we can really generate systems and equipment." That's not where AT&T's reputation lies now, but "it's where we're putting our chips," he says.

AT&T had the bad luck to enter the battle just as the computer industry was falling into a deep slump and thus far, its efforts to match the sales firepower of IBM and other established computer firms have been awkward and disappointing.

AT&T also has struggled to stay on track towards a second goal of establishing its network technology—the electronics language created for its computer and communications systems—as a recognized standard for the industry. As AT&T's new chairman, James Olson, says, the two goals are intertwined: AT&T cannot succeed in the computer market unless it can take advantage of its communications expertise to link computers into information networks speaking the AT&T "language." Here too, AT&T and IBM are the giant competitors, two huge bodies that are pulling smaller companies into their gravitational fields as they form alliances for the showdown. Whether they will co-exist or collide head-on is not yet clear.

And there is a third, equally important goal that is the key to the first two. AT&T must create a new, competitive culture with its sprawling work force of one-third of a million people, most of whom have grown up in the quieter, more orderly world of the telephone business. The success of its product development and marketing strategies depends upon infusing its employees with stronger competitive instincts and marketing skills, a much closer understanding of new business opportunities, a willingness to take risks, and a stomach for the fight ahead. And it must make this transformation without dissolving the parts of the old AT&T culture that helped hold the company together in the past.

"What AT&T had and has is all the pieces to fill the recipe," says Robert Kavner, AT&T's senior vice president and chief financial officer. "We have development, we have manufacturing, we have young, aggressive marketing . . . enough calories to burn in this management team to compete against anyone. The real issue is the cultural change that had to occur." The challenge is to turn those resources into a unified whole.

The notion that a corporation can develop a "culture"—a deep-felt set of shared values among a majority of its managers and employees—may seem farfetched, particularly when the corporation has 365,000 employees with vastly different jobs, from long-distance operators and linemen to computer programmers and accountants.

But there clearly was such a culture in AT&T before the breakup, even though there were 1 million employees then, says W. Brooke Tun-

stall, a retired AT&T vice president who has studied and written exten-
sively about the impact of the breakup on AT&T.

"I've come to believe that every corporation has a culture, some much
stronger than others," Tunstall says. "People do behave just like nations.
Some nations have stronger cultures because they're older and have greater
traditions and much stronger belief systems. I happen to believe that
AT&T had some of the strongest glue and cultural values of all—things
that its people believed about their customers, managers, and fellow
employees. After all, we had a 100-year experience," Tunstall says. "It
was kind of a close-knit family."

Not everyone called it a culture, but that's a good word for the beliefs
about the Bell System that were carefully passed along to new employees.
Both the mission and the payoff were understood, Tunstall says. "There
was an unwritten social contract [among employees] that they would be
treated fairly, paid according to the marketplace, and if they performed
well, they would have lifetime jobs," he says. "It's hard to believe you
can have a family of 1 million. There was an openness and a pride that's
hard to describe."

Most of the members of that extended AT&T family were lightning-
struck by management's announcement on January 8, 1982, that the
company had agreed to settle the Justice Department's antitrust case
against AT&T—a settlement that split apart AT&T's huge local telephone
business, ending its monopoly over the combined long-distance and local
telephone network. "You wake up one day and find three-quarters of the
company is gone," Tunstall says. "It's like finding out that everything
west of the Mississippi is now in another country."

The loss of the local phone operations was one jolt. It has been
followed by many others as AT&T Chairman Charles Brown and the
company's top management began a transformation of the remaining
AT&T operations, freezing salaries, and then instituting new compensation schemes based on executives' performances, encouraging early
retirement for thousands of veteran employees, and juggling divisions.

The old structure, like the old culture, had been tailor-made for the
kind of business chartered for AT&T three-quarters of a century ago by
Theodore Vail, the founder of the Bell System. Vail's vision, affirmed
by three generations of government regulators, was the management of
a nationwide telephone monopoly. The telephone company would be
private rather than government-controlled, as Europe's systems were,
giving the American version the efficiency and profitability of a private

enterprise. But as a national monopoly regulated—and protected—by
the government, it would be able to provide a reliable service throughout
the entire country at a cost that most people could afford. "Our business
was pretty much a single function of letting people talk to each other,"
Tanenbaum says.

"Vail said, 'We will give a telephone to every American at a low
price. That's your mission. . . . You're part of that mission. And we
won't accomplish it in our lifetime. Now go ahead and do it,' " Kavner
says. "That had an incredible binding power."

But the old culture wasn't matched to the new world that grew up
around AT&T, beginning in the 1970s, that led to the decision by AT&T
and the Justice Department to break up the Bell System. New technologies
such as microwave transmission and computerized phone-switching made
it possible for much smaller companies to compete with AT&T in long-
distance transmission. When it became clear that Congress, the courts,
and many of AT&T's customers liked this competition, the breakup was
inevitable, Tanenbaum says.

"What we have—and what we are—is not merely the residue of what
was once the world's largest company," Brown told AT&T employees as
the breakup neared. "We are, in reality, a new business—with new
freedoms, new opportunities and, yes, new risks. . . . If we are able to
adapt our marvelous culture to a different environment—and if we remember that the business in the 80s cannot be run by memory—we can
set the course for the next century."

AT&T faces a fundamental question as it starts out on that course,
Tanenbaum says—determining what business it is in. "It's a business
decision we never used to have to make"—because Vail had already
made the decision, 75 years before, in laying down the mission of AT&T.

"It seemed complex to us back then, but as you look at it today, it
was relatively simple: people talking to people," Tanenbaum says. "That
was what most of telecommunications was used for and that was where
most of our effort went. The applications [of telecommunications] today
cover the full span of business and private existence."

AT&T's future, its leaders have concluded, depends on establishing
a new, far more complex network that would not only permit people to
talk, but would open a virtually unlimited pipeline to every imaginable
kind of communication: high-quality television pictures, color, animation, bank balances, invoices and purchase orders, high-fidelity music.
Even heartbeats would travel over the network, says Brown, with doctors

reading the electrocardiograms of a patient in a far-away clinic and observing the patient over an interconnected television hookup.

"My guess," says AT&T senior vice president and strategic planner John Segall, "is that the world we're looking at is going to be successful or be improved upon from a standpoint of getting improvements in the systems for managing information. . . . Citibank wants to look like a little bank, so they get a system when you call in and want to know about your mortgage, they can get you credit-card information without having to shift you to 35 places. That's what Sears wants to do. That's what all the brokerage firms want to do." The business world will first use this power to utilize and control information, Segall says. "It's all kinds of information . . . and all the steps of management from the very simple to the very complex." Later on, the benefits of the information age will spread far more widely, to schools and households, from the wealthiest societies to the simplest, according to Brown's vision. "It's everybody's opportunity. That's why there are so many people in it," Segall says. It is a course full of unknowns—about the potential of new technology, about the growth and development of new markets, and the responses and strengths of competitors. But it is the only course for AT&T, Segall says. AT&T set its sights on new information networks for the same reason Willie Sutton called on banks—that was where the money was.

AT&T is hardly a stranger to computers. William Shockley, John Bardeen, and Walter Brattain, inventors of the basic transistor in 1948—the discovery that led to the development of computer chips—were part of an imposing lineup of Nobel Prize winners at Bell Labs. But AT&T had been forbidden in 1956 to market general-purpose computers under a court agreement sought by government antitrust lawyers who feared AT&T's potential power over the then-infant industry. AT&T has been building computers for its own use since the early 1960s—a highly specialized kind used in its complex telephone-switching equipment. The break-up freed AT&T to make and market any kind of computer it chose.

In 1984, its first year of operations, AT&T's Computer Systems division hustled out with a wide variety of machines. There were personal computers, lookalikes of the IBM PC, which AT&T obtained from its Italian partner Olivetti. And for more demanding business uses, AT&T introduced a family of larger computers, based on its telecommunications-switching technology, and manufactured in its own factories, including $10,000 workstations and $300,000 mainframes.

The new machines caused barely a ripple in the computer market, which was entering a painful shakeout period in 1984. But the machines were not an end in themselves—they were an essential part of a broader AT&T strategy to establish its telecommunications technology as a rival to IBM.

To do their magic, computers depend upon a complex set of instructions called an operating system, which translates a human operator's commands into the electronic language recognized by the computer's processing and memory chips. IBM personal computers "speak" an IBM operating language, and so do the IBM-compatible machines made by other companies. By the mid-1980s, IBM had made its language the dominant one in office automation. To play in that game, AT&T had to introduce a line of IBM-compatible products, and it did.

That is really just a nip at IBM's heels, however. AT&T's main thrust is a crucial flanking maneuver designed to make AT&T's UNIX operating system a second, vital industry standard for the non-IBM world, and then to extend that AT&T standard into the new territories of information technology before IBM can get there. Like the Catholic and Protestant missionaries whose exploratory zeal divided the New World into opposing spheres of influence, the battle over telecommunications, operating, and programming standards will divide the information age.

IBM is a computer company, whose strengths in the development, manufacture, and marketing of hardware put it far ahead of AT&T in that field. AT&T enjoys a formidable lead over IBM in telecommunications, but IBM is closing the gap. Its 1985 cooperative agreement with MCI Communications Corp., as well as other, more modest forays into the communications field, make it highly competitive in AT&T's own traditional markets at the same time AT&T is trying to break into IBM's fields.

Kavner is a good symbol of the change underway at AT&T. To begin with, he is an outsider, brought into AT&T from its principal accounting firm, Coopers & Lybrand, after a decade of working on parts of AT&T's accounting business. With an eye on the storms just over the horizon, AT&T asked Coopers & Lybrand to make Kavner the new senior partner on the AT&T account in 1982, despite his relative youth, because of his experience both with AT&T and with other companies that were up to their necks in tough, competitive markets. At first, the AT&T assignment looked like an accountant's Nirvana. "I was destined to be the partner in the largest enterprise in the world," Kavner says. "Highly prestigious.

No risk. I was heading off to a professional career of beauty, real beauty. And then boom. They agreed to do the divestiture." With no regrets, he wound up as part of the surgical team of senior AT&T officials responsible for designing a new structure for the company after divestiture. That led to AT&T's invitation to Kavner to become chief financial officer in 1984.

"There are four movements of change occurring simultaneously that any company in high technology, the information industries, or financial services will have to wrestle with," Kavner says. One is rapid expansion of trade, spilling over national boundaries to create a global market in many high-technology products and services. The second factor is the shortening of product life cycles. Third, market definitions are no longer dependable, because the technology of computers and communications is changing so rapidly, Kavner says. "That creates a level of anxiety that managements never had to deal with before." You go to work one day understanding very well that you're selling communications switching terminals and you know who your competitors are. Then a computer company you've never been up against suddenly announces a joint venture with a terminal company, and now they're your competitors too. Is your market terminals, computers, or both?

"You find a leapfrogging of the applications of technology. If you're making these cups," Kavner says, fingering the styrofoam coffee cup on his office coffee table, "you pretty much know your market, you know your market share, you know the technological threats you might face. You know your competitors. And it must be a wonderful feeling to be in this business." AT&T doesn't have that luxury.

The fourth and last factor of change, he says, is the blurring of battle lines—AT&T's customers and suppliers are becoming its competitors to an unprecedented extent. AT&T has always thought of banks and publishers as customers or potential customers for its products and services. Now companies in those fields are emerging as potential rivals of AT&T, interested in establishing and selling their own communications or information services. Today, General Motors Corp. is a vital AT&T customer as the two companies work at the automation of GM's far-flung businesses. Yet in the future, GM—thanks to its Electronic Data Systems division—is certain to become a supplier of communications services to others, thus putting itself directly into competition with AT&T. "The relationships in business are much more difficult than any time in the past," Kavner says. "When you deal with a customer, you don't know where they're coming from." AT&T's managers now must recognize these changes and react to them very rapidly.

The new environment has created an urgent need for a new kind of manager within AT&T. "Managers throughout the business at all levels must realize this," Brown says. "There is no oasis of stability and serenity just over the horizon. . . . We need managers who are neither becalmed nor rattled into precipitous action in the face of less-than-total information. We need managers who can act—and act effectively—in the face of uncertainty, who understand that today's right decision might be tomorrow's wrong decision, who don't try to manage by memory but by what the situation requires."

Uncertainty, imperfect information, and risk are the new facts of life, and scores of senior AT&T officials have tried to explain to their management troops how these uncertainties are to be approached. It has not been an easy lesson to absorb, as one of AT&T's corporate psychologists explains. "Our studies have found that many AT&T managers are uncomfortable with ambiguity," Dr. Joel L. Moses has written. "Traditionally, our people are logical; they rely on numbers and data-collection techniques to solve problems, while shying away from an intuitive approach that might sometimes be more appropriate. At some other companies, particularly those that have operated in a competitive environment for a longer time than we have, managers are more likely to accept ambiguity as a normal state, neither good nor bad. For them, ambiguity simply is, and it can present opportunities for innovative approaches."

William Stritzler is the AT&T vice president charged with seeding an entrepreneurial, risk-taking culture within AT&T by sponsoring new ventures proposed by the employees or acquired from outside. "If there's anything we'd like to turn the clock back on, I would say that it's that we over-practiced ourselves," he says. "We wrote too many practices in too much detail and they became the way we thought. . . . I suppose most of the senior managers would agree we overdid it."

Before he started his assignment, Stritzler traveled around the country interviewing experts in the venture capital and entrepreneuring fields. Typically, their advice was, "Save your energy." He simply wasn't going to find entrepreneurs inside AT&T, they told him. "It had been bred out of us."

That turned out not to be entirely true. Although Stritzler has not been flattened by a rush of AT&T entrepreneurs seeking money to fund their projects, there are plenty of good ideas. "We don't have to rekindle it," he says. "We did have to nurture it."

The creation and development of new ventures is one kind of risk-taking. But more important to AT&T in the short run is the creation of a workable risk-taking, entrepreneurial spirit among managers of its existing business. If AT&T is to be the "adaptive corporation," in author Alvin Toffler's words, it must create an adaptive management.

One definition of that was promulgated by M. D. Baker, vice president of AT&T Consumer Sales & Services, in a letter to his division's managers. "We must become more accustomed to working from common sense and understanding than from detailed practices," he wrote. Another version comes from AT&T executive Charles Thornton, writing in the company's employee magazine: "I think we'll find that managers will develop a sharper facility for financial decisions that affect not only what they do, but also the larger context. For example, we're becoming skilled now in making back-of-the-envelope estimates or feasibility studies of the revenues and costs involved in any undertaking. We just can't wait the weeks—and sometimes months—it would take to get economic studies in the traditional fashion."

"It's safe to assume from all this that the manager also has to have a good deal of tolerance for uncertainty and ambiguity" he wrote. "Not a passive kind of tolerance, though. Matters are sometimes shrouded in uncertainty because the information flow is less than perfect. And so we have to construct our own little networks, especially wherever our operations may be affected. In short, we're a new company facing competitive challenges wherever we turn. In all our markets, in everything we do, the bureaucratic approach won't work."

It's not so much the replacement of the old culture as it is an adaptation of it. "It's an add-on," Stritzler says. "There are many things about our culture that I pound into people—like a high focus on quality of production. We want to keep the best parts." But AT&T does need a different approach to the way it lets managers move and act. It needs to allow big decisions to be made at much lower levels and to permit new kinds of solutions to be tried, even if that causes pain or discomfort elsewhere in the company—as long as the pain is tolerable, Stritzler says.

But it won't be done simply and neatly in directives from the top, Kavner says. "I don't believe you set out the management style with rules. You set it out with carrots. You set incentives, rewards, accountability systems," he says. "You stimulate healthy behavior, and unhealthy behavior you quickly cut off and display as being unhealthy. . . . If they take a risk and do it responsibly, reward them when they don't achieve it and give them advice to do it again. If they're irresponsible, get rid of them. It's been a massive change."

AT&T can talk forever about cultural change. But Stritzler says, "Our problem is getting that translated from the head to the heart—and eventually to the stomach, into a gut feeling that pushes the manager to act."

# 13

# ENCOURAGE RISK-TAKING

Alan Wlasuk and Carl Calabria would fit most anyone's definition of entrepreneurs—two go-getters with a good idea for an invention they wanted to build and bring to market. But unlike the stereotype of entrepreneurs, they weren't a couple of guys working out of a garage. The two computer scientists just happened to be buried deep within the skyscraping bureaucracy called American Telephone & Telegraph Co.

In the spring of 1983, Wlasuk and Calabria were working around the clock on one of the most exciting consumer products ever conceived of at AT&T. It was to be a low-cost home computer that could do all the customary tricks, plus one thing more, a feature that promised to set it apart from every other home computer. It contained an inexpensive technology for adapting images from a television screen or TV camera so that they could be piped into the computer, altered or redrawn, and then sent back to a TV screen for viewing. With this technology, the simple, cartoon-like color schemes of computer graphics could be replaced by elaborate, multicolored pictures with the photographic quality of color television. The computer could display retailers' full-color catalogs on the screen for at-home shopping. A plastic surgeon could show

patients how they would look after surgery. And an artist could take a
TV picture of the Mona Lisa and change the color of her eyes—or redraw
the curve of her smile.

As entrepreneurs, Wlasuk and Calabria had a fierce commitment to
their idea and a quick impatience for those who didn't share their vision—
which included some key higher-ups at AT&T. "We never doubted what
we had," Wlasuk says, "but like many large companies, [AT&T] could
not get its act together." From AT&T's perspective, the home computer
venture was costly, full of risks, and highly visible if it failed. What
Wlasuk heard from marketing executives up the line were the reasons
why their idea couldn't work, he says. "I was getting jerked around. People
had difficulties making decisions," Wlasuk says. "Nobody said, 'Stop this
shit,' but we realized the company was just not going to make it happen."

To Wlasuk, it was not just an exciting, but abstract, new forward step
in the technology of computers. It was the opportunity for which he had
been waiting for eight years as an AT&T researcher. "I went to Bell Labs
to do great technological things," he says—but in time, he became
frustrated with the focus and tempo of AT&T's magnificent research
community. The technological concept that made their idea possible had
been pinned down and patented by two other AT&T scientists 10 years
before, but because AT&T was a phone company then, not the high-
technology information company it is now, the idea sat on the shelf.

Wlasuk was hooked on the magic of color painting on computer
screens. Computer graphics was a hobby of his—when he had time for
hobbies—and he desperately wanted to do something with the technology
he had uncovered. "I wanted to do products that people wanted and
would use and enjoy," he says. The emergence of a new, post-divestiture
AT&T, hungry for new markets, made that theoretically possible. But it
still wasn't going to happen with the home computer. "I think the whole
thing was born out of frustration—good people doing good work and that
work not getting out the door," says Calabria, the computer hardware
genius on the team. So the two did what any real entrepreneur would
do in their place—they decided to quit AT&T and use their know-how
to start a new company.

But to their surprise, and perhaps the company's as well, AT&T didn't
let them go. Instead, Wlasuk and Calabria became part of a small development team of AT&T entrepreneurs set up outside the corporation's
normal channels, lodged in a converted private home in an Indianapolis
suburb and given the chance to develop a smaller version of the product

and bring it to market. It is the first such new venture team ever created by AT&T—an unconventional experiment that left bruises on parts of the AT&T establishment as the Indianapolis team pushed on toward its goals. But bruises or no, it is an experience that every established American company will have to master to be competitive in the years to come.

The entrepreneurial inspiration, impatience, and drive that burns inside people like Wlasuk and Calabria is perhaps the unique competitive advantage enjoyed by the United States in the arena of international economic competition. The popular business heroes of the 1980s are not the leaders of big corporations. They are the iconoclastic inventor/developers like Steve Jobs and Steve Wozniak, founders of Apple Computer, and Nolan Bushnell, creator of Atari and the videogame boom, whose imaginative genius creates companies and sometimes industries from scratch. President Reagan calls this the "age of the entrepreneur." Peter Drucker, the guru of American management, sees the country on the threshold of a new era—"the Entrepreneurial Society."

The entrepreneur is the key to both the creation of the small, start-up companies that energize the economy and the rejuvenation of the established businesses that make up the economy's structure. There is a temptation to conclude that the constant creation of new businesses assures a strong economy and a steadily rising standard of living for Americans, but that conclusion overlooks the crucial role played by large companies in generating and sustaining new technology. The bulk of the most important technological peaks on the horizon will be scaled by large companies that possess the critical mass of scientific talent, experience, and money to carry out the long-term research and development campaigns that are required, according to Ian Ross, president of AT&T's Bell Labs. However, those campaigns won't succeed unless the major American companies in manufacturing and technology-based service industries can develop an entrepreneurial culture within their own ranks.

"It's all the entrepreneur," says Borg-Warner Chairman Jim Beré. "They want to be in the area where they can see a quick reaction to their talents. They do not want to be part of the bureaucratic system. . . . We have to find a way to engender, to delegate this entrepreneurial spirit and permit it to exist."

"In big companies, we talk about risk-reward," says GE Chairman Jack Welch. "We shouldn't talk about risk-reward, because the risk in a big company isn't anything like you have in Silicon Valley or elsewhere, where you bet your house, your wife, your car, and everything else, and you go out and have to stay up all night and try to make it happen. We've got to get people who feel it's worth taking the swing, because the safe person in the big company is sometimes one who keeps his head down. . . . The risk isn't betting the company," Welch says. "The only risk is that they won't do something."

Nowhere is the creation of such a culture more important than at the new AT&T. And there probably are not many U.S. companies where this transition will be more difficult, because of the distance AT&T must come from its long history as a regulated, conservative, and cost-conscious telephone monopoly. Risk was contradictory to what AT&T was all about, but within the company, a few officials were willing to do something about that. Wlasuk and Calabria went to Hans Mattes, director of the Bell Labs Indianapolis facility, who had recruited Wlasuk for the abortive home computer product. "I said it was time to move on," Wlasuk says. "He said, 'No, let's try to get the company to commit to a venture.'"

There was, then, a way to bring Wlasuk and Calabria's pet project to fruition. Instead of trying to design and build an entire personal computer, the heart of the video-adaption technology could be embedded in semiconductor chips and wired onto a computer circuit board at a much lower cost and risk. AT&T would find all the business it could want selling the boards to the rapidly growing legion of IBM personal computer owners. Mattes and Victor Pelson, the president of AT&T's consumer products division, were willing to risk rocking a very big boat to fight for Wlasuk and Calabria. "They put a great deal of their credibility on the line," Wlasuk says.

And they won. In June 1984, AT&T gave Wlasuk, Calabria, and their small team the green light to try to develop the product, setting them up as a separate venture called Epicenter. They had satisfied the three conditions of "intrapreneuring," as Gifford Pinchot calls the creative process inside large companies: They had the idea, the entrepreneurs willing to fight for it, and Mattes, the sponsor willing to fight for the entrepreneurs.

To handle marketing, they added Joseph Haaf, who had run his own consulting business before joining AT&T's business development staff. And to get the business savvy the project required, they recruited Kathleen Asch, another member of AT&T's development staff. The message to AT&T was, "We feel there's a viable product here and we want to bet our careers on that. We want to push the corporation to the limit to allow us to set this up because we believe that firmly in what we personally can do and what the product can do for the market," Asch says. "The corporation said, 'OK, we believe you.' " "The hard thing for us was that AT&T had never done anything like this," Haaf says. And Calabria says, "Almost everything we did was against the grain."

Although its final chapter has not yet been written, the story of the Epicenter venture demonstrates some fundamental keys to making innovation work within the largest corporations, members of the project team say. First was a competitive drive, almost a fury, that kept the founders climbing over obstacles, backed up by their willingness to leave the company if it wouldn't give them a chance.

Second, once AT&T agreed to let the project go forward, a solid dollars-and-cents understanding had to be hammered out between the corporation and the small venture team about goals, budgets, and time-tables. "The key in this whole area is no ambiguity," Asch says. AT&T and the team members spent "a lot of time setting up financial goals, market goals, product goals. There was a lot of effort up front to define success so there's no ambiguity and so the venture could go forward unfettered until there's a clearly defined point where the [budget] boundary has been breached," she says. "The corporation still measures success by profitability."

The clarity on financial goals was essential because of another unique feature of the operation. The original members of Epicenter put substantial parts of their paychecks—up to 25 percent— into the pot to help finance the venture, with the rest coming from AT&T. If they failed, the money was gone. If they succeeded, they would share in the profits, recovering as much as eight times their contributions.

The Epicenter group collaborated closely with AT&T in setting overall goals for the project—but insisted on and got wide lattitude to solve problems their own way, even if it meant going outside AT&T for help. "You can easily get lost trying to deal internally with AT&T," Haaf says. "You have to make decisions." When a vital issue of product design rears up, you can't wait three months for market research. "You have to go on what you've read, what you've heard, what your guts tell you," he says. "I have to admit we didn't always know what we were doing." But they didn't let the grass grow under them. Although the Epicenter team owes a large debt to Bell Labs for its technology, that was not the only source; some of the key chips came from Texas Instruments. The circuit boards were built by a small Indianapolis company. And while the Epicenter team relied on AT&T's legal staff for help, it went outside for its ad campaign.

At the same time, the members of the team could never forget they were a part of AT&T. "It's obviously very complex. It's not just risk-taking," says Robert Kavner, AT&T's senior vice president and chief financial officer. "Many entrepreneurs disdain being a member of a family. But you've got to be a member of a family here. We have to find a risk-taker who has healthy collaborative capabilities, whose ego is not so fixated on self that he loses the whole, yet who is not so selfless that he won't fight for what he believes in." The AT&T sponsorship paid off in a number of ways, in addition to the funding Epicenter received. The AT&T connection meant faster call-backs on phone calls to potential customers, and an immediate cachet of quality once the AT&T logo went on their product.

Another advantage of the arrangement was that key decisions were in the hands of a small team of people, all within reach of each other, not separated over two or three bureaucratic layers in a large organization. "Sometimes large organizations get frozen into inaction because people at key points are afraid to make decisions," Haaf says. The larger the team, the more the key actors lose contact with decision-making and the easier procrastination and buck-passing become. "That was a big advantage for us," Haaf says. "We could turn on a dime."

That gave the team the chance to connect closely with potential users of the video display adapter and get their reactions and suggestions for the product. "It's because we can control all aspects of the business. Marketing, technical, financial—all those things. We don't have to go ask anyone else," Asch says.

"There's a problem with any large company where the planners are four steps removed from the purchasers," says Asch, a veteran of more than five years' work in new product development. "At AT&T you weren't allowed to go speak to the customer until you had an approved business plan . . . and people were always questioning the numbers in the business plan because you didn't have any market input." The result was a vicious cycle, she says: "We spent a lot of time looking at market research but we never got to the market."

But Epicenter has products. "It's alive, it's real, and customers love it," Asch says. A delighted Stritzler crows, "They brought the product to market in the shortest time imaginable. . . . They conceived it, designed it, got it spec-ed for manufacturing, manufactured, and distributed 1,500 units within about nine months. It's unheard of." And they did it for about one-third the cost of any competing product. *Computer & Electronics* magazine called it one of the more significant microcomputer products of 1985.

The revenue from the $700 Video Display Adapter and the half-dozen related products that have followed in rapid succession from the Indianapolis team are microscopic inside a company the size of AT&T. But the project's biggest value to AT&T isn't financial. It is a living, breathing example of a new competitive strain that must be spliced inside the corporate DNA of the parent company and many other giant American companies.

The innovative chemistry within the Indianapolis group is the product of two different kinds of people—innovators like Wlasuk and Calabria and managers like Asch and Haaf. A company begins by trying to find the entrepreneurs who may already be in a company, create outlets for them, and hope that they can help spawn a new culture for the company—because the evidence is that they're born, not made. It involves "a drive to make things happen which comes out of a person's soul," says Gilbert R. Whitaker Jr., dean of the School of Business Administration at the University of Michigan. "There are lots of students who are committed to an entrepreneurial approach, but the question is, could we develop that spark in people who don't have it? I don't believe we've found the way."

But companies like AT&T have found that there are people in their organizations—some of them working without much notice for years—who have a creative overdrive and can turn it on if the right conditions are established. Companies must create a conduit for ideas—from product proposals to suggestions for smaller improvements—that allows innovation to surface easily, without having to battle up through the layers of the existing bureaucracy. That's Stritzler's job at AT&T. "We need to open the avenues of communication for projects that may sound far-fetched and be slightly outside the corporate culture," he says—projects that may look too small to bother with, or may seem to threaten an existing line of business. There is a lot of evidence that ventures that start inside large corporations take six to seven years to begin to return a profit, while those that begin life on their own as small independent businesses become profitable in half that time. The obvious conclusion: new ventures begun within a large company have to be protected from the bureaucracy.

It is not a new problem nor an original insight. Most of the major U.S. companies have tried, in one fashion or another, to create a better environment for recognizing and rewarding good ideas. AT&T's efforts are worth studying because the company is starting with an almost clean slate—prior to the series of events that turned AT&T from a regulated telephone monopoly into a competitive information company, the corporation had no real need for entrepreneurs. But it needs them now.

Before he took charge of AT&T's venture program, Stritzler spent three months traveling around the United States, talking to the most famous entrepreneurs and the leading industrial technologists, and picking their brains about how to create a hothouse environment to foster entrepreneurialism. The system Stritzler worked out begins with an open door to proposals from inside the organization. But there is no strict strategic plan into which the proposals must fit. "If there is any thread that runs through our ventures, it's that they [tie into] an observable strength in our business system today," he says. One example is the Epicenter computer circuit board, which is based on a Bell Labs patent that is more than a decade old. Another is a venture to develop an information management system to provide greater productivity and cost controls in hospitals.

Stritzler is looking for people with the right entrpreneurial stuff—those with the combination of brilliance and enthusiasm who want to make things happen within AT&T. He has an annual budget of $20 million to support venture projects in their development stage, but isn't spending it all. "I could spend it," he says. "It's not that there aren't enough ideas out there. But we're learning that in the early stages of these ventures, you're a little better off not giving them so much money. I can't explain it exactly, but the people who do best are the ones who are squeezed for funds. . . . Maybe it's a sense of urgency that takes over.

"When I was wandering around the country [looking at other venture operations] there seemed to be two approaches. . . . One was as they did at Xerox, to give you $10 million, send you off to some remote place and say, 'Come back in five years and let us know how you did.' It doesn't seem to work very well. The other is to give you $10 million and look over your shoulder and ask you questions every day," a pattern he attributed to Exxon Corp.'s disappointing new venture efforts. "And that doesn't seem to work very well. Somewhere in between those two is a balance I'm still trying to define. But it appears that if you get right at the comfort level of the person who's seeking the funds, they don't seem to do as well as the people that you drop below the comfort level who are still willing to try."

Another refinement in Stritzler's approach becomes apparent as soon as a project is selected. "We take an idea and get a prototype as fast as we can, and then they go out and get customers and let them work with the prototype. We don't spend a lot of time doing market analyses. The guy comes in, shows it to me in my office, and in the hour we're here we can decide to let 'er rip. . . . What we insist on is that they get close to their customers right away."

The funds in Stritzler's program can carry a venture far enough so that a prototype can be built, and perhaps even support some initial sales. After that, he wants the entrepreneur to cede the venture to one of AT&T's existing lines of business for full-scale production. "It's a very painful way to do the process because it means you have to taint the ventures just a little with the bureaucracy," Stritzler says. But bringing the ventures into the fold offers the best hope of having the entrepreneur's culture rub off on others within AT&T, he says—and that is a basic goal of the whole process.

One of the companies with the greatest success in uncovering entrepreneurs in its own ranks is Minnesota Mining & Manufacturing Co., whose record of new ventures in one recent two-year period includes a suntan lotion that won't wash off, a stapler used in surgery to close incisions, a film for offset printing that works without silver, "and a potion that makes the grass grow shorter," as *Fortune* magazine put it. "Management needs to be aware of these people and be listening to them," says Lewis Lehr, 3M's former chairman. "Some managers have an inherent ability to kill entrepreneurship and innovation. To me, the most important skill is managing, recognizing, and helping the development of the innovators. . . . I guess the secret is to make people constantly aware—managers and supervisors—that one of their jobs is to manage innovation positively. When a person over here has an idea and wants to carry it through an organization, it's very difficult because the organization says, 'Ah, we've got more important things to do.' So someplace in the company there has to be a sponsor at a higher level, someone who can work with the innovator. We're pushing to develop that—to get people to sponsor, recognize, and reward the innovators."

Ross Perot, founder of Electronic Data Systems, says he is constantly telling his people, "Look around. Everything you see was once somebody's idea, because 23 years ago we were not here. And most of these ideas were not my ideas. Somebody had an idea that turned into a big piece of this business. And for God's sake, don't crush your people's ideas. Few things are more fragile than ideas."

Another example from the Gospel According to Perot: "We don't do anything at EDS without talking about it. When we got ready to go public we got everybody in the room and said, 'What do you think of this?' I mean literally everybody."

Walt Disney Chairman Michael D. Eisner says: "You've got to gather people together, and then you've got to get them all excited and come up with ideas—you say black and they say brown, and you say brown, black, and yellow." Eisner's point is that it isn't enough for management to open its ears. It must unlock ideas and stimulate decision-making at much lower levels in the organization. And that requires a willingness on the part of middle-management and rank-and-file employees to speak up, take stands—and accept the chance of being wrong.

"Our whole philosophy at EDS, that we preach from Day One, is that honest mistakes are like skinned knees; they're painful, they're superficial, they heal quickly, and it's all part of the learning process," Perot says.

"Most people do not want to take the risk of failure," Borg-Warner Chairman James Beré says, "and therefore they do not want their people to make mistakes. And I say it's the absolute reverse. You do not develop a quality person without making mistakes. What you ought to do is give them the latitude, and when they make a mistake, you talk to them about it, say, 'It may not be your mistake, it's mine, but that is not what I intended.' Now, what do most people do? Most people—and some young people as well as old—are still in this old nonsense of pleasing the boss. They go to work and put all types of controls up so they don't want the boss to see anything until it's perfect. Well, I laugh, and I laugh so hard, because they can put it through seven screens and it still won't be an any higher percentage of perfection than if you just let people do it. . . . That, I think, is something that's very, very hard in changing. People have the perception that a mistake, one mistake, means a demerit, whereas I look upon a mistake as a growing experience.

"We need younger managers to think this way," Beré says. "When you get over 50 years old you do funny things. . . . I had a lot more courage, I think, when I was 30 and 35. I can see my bosses saying to me, 'You can't do that,' and they said, 'We've tried that before,' and all of these reasons, and finally the good ones would say, 'Aw, get out of here—we'll see you after it's done.' "

Reginald H. Jones, retired chairman of GE, thinks that there likely is a generational difference in the willingness of managers to crawl farther out on the limb in demanding more responsibility and accepting more risk. "I suppose it's fair to say that in a sense you have a new breed developing now," he says. "You now have people, coming into middle management in particular, who were products of the college revolts of the '60s, and the whole Viet Nam era, an era in which there was a great deal of questioning of authority. That questioning of authority, that demand for a voice, if you will, the concern for a piece of the decision-making machinery that started at Berkeley and swept across the country, is now way back in the minds of those people who some 20 years later are now in middle and upper management. And while those people now wear three-piece suits and have shaved off their beards, they still are concerned with participation in the governing process."

Security and rewards are the twin foundations of a strong, healthy risk-taking business culture, says Frank Doyle, GE's senior vice president for corporate relations, who has responsibility for keeping tabs on that company's vast human resources. "Nobody is going to raise the risks unless you've raised rewards, and have also cushioned the risks," he says.

Doyle, for years one of the best labor relations executives in business, has thought a lot about the things that motivate employees and managers. "If you allow people to take chances, and if you punish failure, I mean really punish failure, people are really smart. . . . They make fewer and fewer mistakes," he says. "The only way you can do that is to take fewer and fewer chances. One of the communications devices that we use . . . is to try to avoid punishing people if their screw-up was one of going for something and not making it."

But the objective of rewarding risk-takers is complicated immensely by the problem of setting the targets against which success is measured. "We've been experimental," says Doyle, "but not very far-reaching." GE has tried gain-sharing, productivity bonuses, and other performance rewards for managers. But a risk-reward system should be based on factors that a manager has control over. "The problems we've run into, frankly, are that a lot of what happens to people at that level is driven by things completely outside their control," Doyle says.

"What we're trying to do here is being wrestled with by any company that has its eyes opened to the marketplace, and no company can raise their hand yet and say they've got it done," says AT&T's Kavner. "We're all wrestling with measurements that follow authority and accountability."

If risk-taking is now the managerial rage in corporations, that is not meant as a green light for mistakes, hip-shooting decisions, or managerial Russian roulette, however. And that needn't happen if those who take the risks also take responsibility for the results.

"People now do not expend a lot of wasted energy trying to make a bad idea work," says Doyle. "American industry is littered with examples of people who continued to pour money into something trying to make it work, even though with 30 seconds of thoughtful regard of the issue you'd say, 'Bad idea. Get off it.' If we make more mistakes, we certainly make them for a much shorter duration now. . . . I've watched this company and others spend lots of energy just trying to get it to stagger on long enough to claim it was a victory.

"You need a different kind of manager. It's a supportive manager who says, 'Go try it,' but close enough and supportive enough to say, 'Jack, look, we bet on you. You may be too close to see it—it's not working.' "

So an entrepreneurial culture requires a conveyor for ideas and an open gate at the far end. It needs managers who listen and respond and will accept challenges to the status quo; managers willing to risk failure in a good cause. And a system that rewards them, particularly when they fail.

And one thing more, Asch says. That kind of culture is going to run at a higher pressure and temperature because it is based on performance and swift decisions. It is a confrontational style of management at times, but when it is working, it is smoothed by a great deal of internal loyalty among team members. "It's just a question of personal style," Asch says. Self-confidence, humility, and a strong collaborative instinct are the ingredients. "I think there are people who have the potential to be like that," Asch says, "but have never been in a situation where that behavior has been rewarded."

"You'll die of your own weight if the only operating systems are the formal ones," Kavner says. "You have to have healthy, informal, trusting systems. People have to trust each other so that you can move the ball along. You have to have a general scheme of measurements and rewards that lay out a culture. And built into that is, 'OK, we trust you. You got that job because you're good at it. Go ahead and do it. And if you fail because you did the right thing, we're not going to punish you. Do it again.' "

# 14

## COCA-COLA

### Wagering the Crown Jewels

Sometimes a company can risk too much for the sake of change. When that happens, the best thing to do is to bite the bullet as quickly as possible and start over. Take Coca-Cola Co. Less than three months after the highly touted 1985 reformulation of the company's flagship brand—a change heralded by the firm as "the most significant soft-drink development in the company's 100-year history"—Coca-Cola responded to a considerable public backlash against the new product by reviving the old Coke. New Coke would remain on the market, but Coke officials conceded that they had gone too far when they tinkered with the 100-year-old company fountainhead.

The reformulation of Coke was the type of change few corporate executives would even contemplate: the revamping of one of the world's most famous and popular consumer products. Company testing had indicated that the new taste would be more popular than the old and, more significantly, than that of arch-rival Pepsi-Cola. But in the weeks that followed the change, a wave of consumer protest washed over the company, accusing it of tampering with a taste that was at the heart of

Americana. Though new Coke sold well in many parts of the country, clearly the nation wanted the old formula back.

So the company, in the words of one analyst, "having its cake and eating it too," announced that it would reintroduce the old formula as Coca-Cola Classic and offer both products to the public. The move stirred a huge amount of debate—had Coke, in a stunning Machiavellian stroke, planned this all along? But Coke officials would not admit to being so manipulative. They say they simply blundered, underestimating the public's emotional ties to the traditional taste of Coke—which, truth be told, really wasn't that different from the new taste. It's a case that will be taught in marketing and business courses for years.

But Coke officials believe that they may be able to turn the disaster around into a boon for the company. "What we have today is we have Coke and Coca-Cola Classic. Pepsi now finds itself sandwiched in the middle," says Coca-Cola Chairman Roberto Goizueta. "I like to quote an ancient Chinese proverb—which I made up—which is, 'He who gets sandwiched in gets eaten up.' . . . Assuming that our job and that of our bottlers is to sell more gallons of soft-drink syrup, and thus more gallons of soft drinks, we have never been in a better position to do that than we are today."

Time will only tell whether Goizueta's assessment of the world's taste for soda-pop is more correct on second thought than it was when the company decided to go with the new Coke. But the very risk-taking that prompted the reformulation of Coke reflected the recent era of change at Coca-Cola that is a far cry from the majority of the company's 100-year history. Since taking over as chairman of Coke in 1981, Goizueta has steered the once-sleepy company on an aggressive course, turning it into one of the most dynamic corporations in America. It is not only matching Pepsi-Cola move for move in the $50 billion worldwide soft-drink market through innovation and aggressive marketing, but it has moved boldly into other fields, most notably movie and television production, to capitalize on the booming growth of the leisure-time industries that Coca-Cola, in many ways, has always symbolized.

Shortly after taking over in 1981, Goizueta signaled the change that was to come with the issuance of a "Strategy for the 1980s," a slim 900-word pamphlet that, unlike many corporate manifestos, has proved remarkably prophetic. Not only did the strategic plan reaffirm the company's role as the world's dominant maker of soft drinks, but it also promised, "In the U.S., we will also become a stronger factor in the packaged consumer-goods business. I do not rule out providing appropriate services to this same consumer as well. It is most likely that we will be in industries in which we are not today."

Sure enough, in 1982 Coca-Cola took a giant step into a new field with the acquisition of Columbia Pictures Industries. The gamble paid off almost immediately when two of the studio's 1982 releases, *Gandhi* and *Tootsie*, became box-office and critical smashes. *The Karate Kid* and *Ghostbusters* later added to the string of hits. In partnership with Time Inc.'s Home Box Office unit and CBS, Columbia also set up Tri-Star, the first major new Hollywood studio in decades. In short order, Tri-Star added the hits *The Natural* and *Rambo*. Coke pushed Columbia aggressively into cable-television programming and production and has added additional entertainment-production companies with the simultaneous acquisitions in mid-1985 of television-production and syndication powerhouses Embassy Communications and Tandem Productions, and the 1986 purchase of Merv Griffin Productions, producer of the popular game show *Wheel of Fortune*. The company has pushed into other new fields as well, ranging from frozen foods to video games to music publishing.

Amid this flurry of activity, Coca-Cola has not forgotten the industry that gave it this platform for diversification. In addition to reformulating Coke, it has embarked on several other bold strokes in the soft-drink business. It broke with longstanding tradition to introduce Diet Coke— the first beverage other than the original to bear the Coke name—and turned it into the fastest-selling new soft-drink in history. Having proved that the Coke name could sell other products, the company in short order introduced Caffeine-Free Coke, Caffeine-Free Diet Coke, and Cherry Coke (not to mention a line of clothing with the Coke name printed on it). It began making a line of carbonated fruit drinks bearing the Minute Maid brand. And when rival Pepsico Inc. challenged the company's hold on the No. 1 spot in the gigantic and lucrative soft-drink industry with a surprise announcement of plans to acquire long-time No. 3 Seven-Up Co. in early 1986, Coke retaliated within weeks with an announcement that it planned to purchase the maker of Dr. Pepper.

Company executives say this frenzied activity was necessary to get the company moving at a faster, stronger pace than would have been possible without diversification. "There are times when you hit sort of a plateau, and your vision of the future is a little fuzzy," says company President

Donald R. Keough, who believes the company hit that point in the latter half of the 1970s. Though very successful, Coca-Cola was facing increasingly aggressive competition from Pepsi-Cola and Seven-Up that was limiting growth in what at the time was virtually the company's only business. And since Coca-Cola wasn't growing much, neither was the industry it dominated.

Its competitors were stronger than ever before—Pepsi's parent company was Pepsico Inc., one of the nation's strongest consumer-products companies; Seven-Up had been bought by tobacco and beer giant Philip Morris, Inc.; and Procter & Gamble was rumored to be considering bringing its huge marketing expertise into the soft-drink business. "When you're in the arena with Pepsico, Philip Morris, and, perhaps, Proctor & Gamble, you're in the major leagues," Keough says.

The solution decided upon by the new management team led by Goizueta and Keough was to apply Coca-Cola's own considerable worldwide consumer-products marketing skill to a new set of products. "We will not . . . stray from our major strengths: an impeccable and positive image with the consumer; a unique franchise system second to none; and the intimate knowledge of, and contacts with, local business conditions around the world," Goizueta said in his 1981 strategy statement. "In choosing new areas of business, each market we enter must have sufficient inherent real growth potential to make entry desirable. It is not our desire to battle continually for share in a stagnant market in these new areas of business. By and large, industrial markets are not our business. Finally, we shall tirelessly investigate services that complement our product lines and that are compatible with our consumer image."

The magic word, as Goizueta sees it, is leverage—using strength in one area to build business in another area. As long as the company had a frozen-orange-juice distribution system for the Minute Maid brand, for instance, why not feed other frozen products into the pipeline, as Coke plans to do? Similarly, the company's extraordinarily strong balance sheet—it had hardly ever borrowed for expansion—gave it a base for funding all sorts of new ventures. "If you look at almost everything we've done, perhaps the word leveraging is the most common denominator," Goizueta says. "We had a triple-A balance sheet. What the hell do you do with a triple-A balance sheet? If you don't use it, it's not much good. You don't pay dividends with the triple-A balance sheet. You have to use it." So Goizueta borrowed money against the strong base and made acquisitions to expand businesses and move into new fields, adding Coke's know-how and other resources to the financing. "We are leveraging the balance sheet, we've leveraged the trademark Coca-Cola, we're leveraging the Minute Maid trademark, we are leveraging the distribution system of Columbia," Goizueta says.

The company is hardly assuming that its new businesses will be as automatically successful as the soft-drink business it knew so well. Realizing that the movie industry is a hit-or-miss business, with more misses than hits, Coca-Cola has taken steps to spread the risk of operating Columbia Pictures. It has aggressively pursued joint-venture and partnership arrangements to finance new movie production and distribution, removing much of the risk of a box-office bomb, albeit at the same time diluting the profits from a smash. Additionally, the advent of cable television, home video, and other media have guaranteed markets and some income for even the biggest commercial failures—a safety net that didn't exist for the movie industry a few years ago. Perhaps Coke's biggest way of reducing the risk has been its participation in the Tri-Star partnership. The arrangement offers instant cable and network television outlets for the new company's movies, and doubles Columbia Pictures' annual slate of new releases—thus doubling the chances for a hit, while again spreading the risk for a flop. "I like to say you don't want to have a smashing hit," Goizueta says. "What you want is to avoid having a miss hit that can smash you." In addition, Columbia, as the distributor for Tri-Star movies, collects a 12.5 percent fee off the top, hit or miss—a very lucrative arrangement with the runaway hit *Rambo*, which by itself brought enough money to Columbia's distribution system in 1985 to cover the division's entire annual overhead costs.

The acquisition of Columbia Pictures gave Coke a springboard for other moves in the entertainment field. Through Columbia, the company gained an entrée into the video-game and television programming industries, and later acquisitions have added Big Three Music, a music-publishing firm whose titles include hits from movies such as *The Wizard of Oz* and *Rocky*; Embassy Productions, producer of such television hits as *Diff'rent Strokes* and *The Facts of Life* and syndicator of dozens of other shows; Tandem Productions, which produced such television classics as *All in the Family* and *Maude* and has more recently gone into motion-picture production; and Merv Griffin Productions, best-known for its game shows. In just a few years, Coke has become one of the five largest entertainment-media companies in the nation, and since the company has been rumored to be interested in virtually every major media company that has gone on the sales block in recent years, many analysts believe Coke will soon own the preeminent position in the entertainment industry.

Even as it garnered media attention for its moves in soft drinks and entertainment, Coke has been quietly looking to expand another area of its business. Hoping to capitalize on the success of its Minute Maid frozen orange-juice brand, the company has begun exploring opportunities in the frozen-food business, although its first venture, a modest foray into frozen pasta dishes, proved unsuccessful. Still on Goizueta's shopping list is a maker of frozen ethnic foods, with potential for national distribution, to piggyback on Minute Maid's marketing and distribution system. "We have in our frozen distribution system . . . an underutilized distribution system," Goizueta says. "And when you can distribute more product with basically your same expenses, you leverage and you make it very profitable."

Even as it has expanded, the company has trimmed away some previously unsuccessful attempts at diversification, most notably its Wine Spectrum division, which was sold to Seagram Co. in 1983 for $200 million. Coke found that for all its expertise in selling soft drinks, it just couldn't handle the hard stuff. "Even under the most optimistic long-range projections, the returns from our wine business were inadequate to justify our continued participation, given the many higher-yielding investment opportunities we see before us," Goizueta said at the time of the sale.

But while it has aggressively and enthusiastically pursued diversification, Coca-Cola has stirred things up most in its more traditional business. The company had hardly tinkered with its soft drink line since an Atlanta druggist mixed up the first batch of Coca-Cola in his backyard in 1886. Save for the introduction of such spinoffs as Tab and Sprite, the company had relied on natural growth and aggressive marketing to build its soft-drink business—a strategy that by no means had been unsuccessful. But with Pepsi, Seven-Up, and other competitors gaining ground, Goizueta stepped on the accelerator, introducing a raft of products in the first part of the 1980s, and culminating in the reformulated version of Coke itself.

The first of the new products was considered a highly revolutionary step. The company had always shied away from stamping the Coke name on anything but the original product, and in fact had named its diet cola Tab in the 1960s because it couldn't bear the thought of a product called

Diet Coke. Goizueta, however, broke the taboo. His reasoning was prag-matic—the sugar cola market was diminishing; the diet cola market was exploding. "Fewer and fewer people were liking Coke more and more," Goizueta says. Meanwhile, "the fastest-growing segment of the market did not have the Coca-Cola trademark." "The diet category was so ex-plosive and obviously something that was going to continue to grow over time," says Ira Herbert, Coca-Cola's executive vice president and head of corporate marketing efforts. "With a segment that big, and continuing to grow, it was really a very difficult thing for us to accept the fact that in that segment a brand named Coca-Cola would not be the leader. . . . We saw an opportunity to accelerate the growth and to end up in a very, very important segment of the market with our mother-brand name in the leadership role."

And so Diet Coke was born. The new soda was introduced with a massive advertising and promotional blitz in mid-1982, and the success was phenomenal. Within 18 months of its introduction, Diet Coke was the fourth best-selling soft drink in the United States, and it soon passed Seven-Up to become No. 3. It so shattered the old taboo against use of the Coke name that the cover of the company's annual report the year after it was introduced was illustrated by a picture of a giant Diet Coke label.

New products bearing the Coke name followed fast and furious: Caffeine-Free Coke, Caffeine-Free Diet Coke, and Cherry Coke were all successes, as Coke turned its flagship brand into what it called a "megabrand." Diet Coke got an additional boost a year or so after its introduction when the company reformulated it with aspartame, a new low-calorie sweetener that was better-tasting than the former sweetener saccharin and didn't have that ingredient's alleged onus as a carcinogenic substance. Aspartame-sweetened Diet Coke sold even better than before, as the diet soft-drink category of the soda market skyrocketed in the mid-1980s.

"Now, as we look at the marketplace and we see significant seg-ments—Cherry Coke, Caffeine-Free, and now Coke Classic, we think overall we will end up with a Coke posture in the market that will be significantly stronger than we can do with any single brand," Herbert says. In other words, the company was simply filling each niche in the soda business it could find with a different kind of Coke—and reaping all sorts of additional sales in the process.

Even before it released this flurry of new products, Coke was beefing up its system of independent bottlers, the backbone of the soft-drink business. After being bogged down with government challenges to the bottler system for several years, Coke went through a large-scale modernization and consolidation program. "We're going to live and die on the strength of the independent bottler system," Keough says. "We believe it's the best system, because the independent bottler is closest to the marketplace."

Finally, in 1985, Coca-Cola had the ultimate new product for its bottlers and other distributors. In tinkering with the taste of Diet Coke, Coca-Cola scientists had made another discovery—a new formula for Coca-Cola itself. The new mix was lighter and sweeter than the old—in short, an almost dead ringer for Pepsi-Cola, which was increasingly outscoring Coke in taste tests.

This was the supreme change for the company. It had made some slight changes in the top-secret "Merchandise 7X" formula for Coke over the years, generally to update sweetener and flavoring technology (and in 1903 to remove a trace amount of cocaine), but Coca-Cola still tasted substantially the same as it did when it was first concocted in 1886. The new change was so momentous that Coke's executives reportedly felt compelled to inform company patriarch Robert Woodruff on his deathbed of the impending move.

But to hear Coca-Cola officials tell it, changing the formula of the fizzy brown beverage was not a very difficult decision. "The decision, in fact, became one of the easiest we have ever made," Goizueta said when New Coke was introduced. Company-sponsored taste tests, somehow done in secret with 190,000 respondents, found that a majority of Coke drinkers preferred the new taste, as did a wider majority of Pepsi drinkers. That response all but ruled out the introduction of the new taste as a second brand, Goizueta says. "We would have had the best-tasting cola soft-drink in the market under a brand other than Coca-Cola itself," he says. "We would have had it under Coca-Cola II, or Coca-Cola Centennial, and . . . heaven knows how long it would have taken to build up market share. . . . What would have happened is, instead of being, now, Coke and Classic with Pepsi sandwiched in the middle, it would have been Coke and Pepsi, with Coke II sandwiched in the middle."

With that course of action ruled out, Coke decided to simply replace the new formula with the old. No one who experienced the hyperbole of the company's announcement—at a press conference held in the posh surroundings of the Vivian Beaumont Theater in New York's Lincoln

Center and televised throughout the world—would doubt that Coke never intended to bring back the old formula.

"Thousands of consumers across the width and breadth of this country have told us this is the taste they prefer," Goizueta told the press conference. "How could we leave such a winner, such a strongly preferred product, out of the market?" "Each of us has heard rumors about companies holding back product advances," Keough chimed in. "You know what I mean—cars that run on pencil shavings and batteries that never go dead. I have heard a lot of them, and they are all pretty silly. But it would be even sillier to deny consumers a better taste—a better soft drink. How could we deny Coke soft-drinkers a better Coke?"

Very altruistic. But industry analysts saw other factors involved. Pepsi was gaining ground on Coke, and such a bold stroke could halt the narrowing of the gap between the two—especially since the new taste was bound to attract many Pepsi drinkers. Too, the promotional blitz surrounding the introduction—to say nothing of the unbelievable amount of free publicity the change garnered in the news media—had to help sales. And some analysts suggested that the switch was not aimed so much at the American market but at the huge international market, where Coke could play on the new taste to accelerate the growth of its foreign sales. In any case, the reformulation reflected another plank in Goizueta's, "Strategy for the 1980s": "The unique position of excellence that the trademark Coca-Cola has attained in the world will be protected and enhanced as a primary objective."

It soon appeared that the company had done anything but "protect and enhance" its biggest source of revenue. The new formula did not produce the expected overall boom in sales, and indeed, in some areas, particularly the South, Coke's traditional stronghold, the consumer backlash was reported to have hurt sales. So Coke reversed position and brought back the old formula.

Some analysts saw the episode as a classic marketing blunder, right up there with the Ford Edsel. Others suggested it was a stroke of genius, allowing the company to position two subtly different drinks in the market and increase Coke's overall market share. The real story is somewhere in between, and offers a fascinating glimpse at the strengths and fallacies of marketing research, corporate psychology—and the fickleness of the American public.

For one thing, even though Coke had asked its 190,000 survey respondents whether they would forego the old Coke for the new taste, and got a positive response, the survey somehow failed to accurately measure the depth of their feeling. Goizueta likens it to trying to predict your reaction to the death of your father. "You know you're going to be sad," he says. "You're never going to know how sad you'll be, the depth of your sorrow, until he's dead."

Coke drinkers weren't just sad. They were furious. Letters and phone calls of protests poured into Coke's headquarters. Editorials lambasted the company. A Seattle man spent tens of thousands of dollars promoting a national effort to force the company to bring back the old taste. (Oddly, a taste test sponsored by a Seattle newspaper proved the protestor couldn't tell the taste of old and new Coke apart; meanwhile, new Coke enjoyed one of its biggest successes in the Seattle market.) The company discovered that the backlash had become so strong that people apparently had stopped drinking Coke strictly out of spite at the company's arrogance in telling them just what tasted best. "What we have here is a situation where we clearly ran into a psychological beehive that has reflected negatively on the new Coke to some extent," Herbert says. "There were certain areas where the hostility was so great that we were afraid it could . . . become lasting."

The hue and cry dominated the nation's conciousness for weeks— so much so that a woman wrote to the company that her 13-month-old daughter's first word was "Coke." Less than three months after the momentous announcement, the company finally caved in and announced old Coke's return. "It became a no-brainer," Goizueta says. Rather than attempt to dictate the public's taste, Coke would let consumers make a choice.

The capitulation appeared to be as much of a marketing stroke as the reformulation had been a negative. Public opinion seemed to shift markedly in favor of a company that would listen to consumer complaints. The letters now pouring into Coke headquarters praised the company— fully a third of the mail contained apologies from consumers who had complained in the first place. "One thing we have done in this Coke/ Coca-Cola Classic [situation]—we listened first to the consumers in blind taste tests, and then we listened to the consumers when they wrote letters," Goizueta says. "And I think in the packaged-goods business, listening to the consumer, if it's not the most important act of management, it's fairly close to being the most important one. We have not tried to impose something on them."

Perhaps the most amazing thing in the weeks following the return of old Coke was that sales of new Coke began escalating sharply. "Since we announced that Coca-Cola Classic is coming back, without even making it available, people started drinking Coke again," Goizueta said shortly after the announcement. "They were revolting against the idea that a choice was taken away." As long as consumers had a choice, then, they were happy, apparently. Goizueta likened the situation to Coke's switch decades ago from its traditional 6 1/2-ounce bottles to larger sizes—a move that was similarly criticized as being too great a break with the past. "Consumers just didn't like it. They wanted Coke in 6 1/2 ounces. But they could not react, because we had not removed the 6 1/2-ounce from the market. They removed it over time by not buying it," Goizueta says. "It was their option to abandon it. That's the difference. It will be their option to abandon Classic. But it will be their option. And they're right. That's one thing we've said—they're absolutely right and we were wrong.

"Today we have in Coke the best-tasting cola on the market," Goizueta says. "It beats Pepsi-Cola on the taste tests. It beats Coca-Cola Classic. We also have Coca-Cola Classic for those people who do not let their minds agree with their tastebuds. And there are a number of those." Indeed, since the reintroduction of old Coke, sales of the old formula are outstripping the sales of the new by a four-to-one margin.

So while American consumers make the choice between new Coke and old, the company will leave both on the market—and likely reap more sales than it would from either product alone. Coke officials call it the "megabrand" philosophy—that as long as products carry the Coke name, who cares which flavor consumers buy. Says Goizueta: "Two facts remain, when you remove all the dust, and that is that we are in the best position we have ever been to sell more gallons of soft drinks, and two, that we have without a doubt the strongest megabrand in the soft drink industry—any time, any place."

In the process, Coke has reversed the decline in the sugar-sweetened cola category—its original problem back when it began stamping the Coke name on new products. "The whole soft drink industry has been revitalized," Goizueta crows. "The sugar cola category, which was a dwindling segment of the industry, has acquired new life. . . . It's a very vibrant industry."

Still, Coke had cut it very close by tinkering with its flagship. Had its leaders not moved quickly to quell the consumer backlash created by the introduction of new Coke, the company might have been seriously, perhaps irreversibly damaged. But that, in a way, is the essence of change—to take risks, even when they are unpopular, and to adapt quickly to their consequences. For his part, Goizueta argues that Coke is a much better company as a result of all of the changes it has made in the past few years, despite the controversy surrounding many of them. "We realize that over the past few years we have unsettled some people," he says. "We unsettled them when we announced the Columbia acquisition. We were criticized then—now we are hailed as geniuses. Neither one is absolutely right. . . . We were criticized then and we unsettled people. We certainly unsettled them with Diet Coke, where we had desecrated the trademark. . . . Heaven knows with the new Coke, we unsettled people."

By making these disruptive changes, Goizueta contends, Coke is living up to one of the most important promises in its 1981 strategy manifesto: to increase the value of its shareholders' investment and to give them a solid return on investment—currently running at an impressive 20 percent a year.

Says Goizueta: "What is my job? Is my job to avoid flak in the press, be loved by the media? No. Is it my job to make shareholders very comfortable? No. My job is to make shareholders rich. That is the guiding light behind everything we have done."

# 15

# WALT DISNEY COMPANY

## Rekindling the Creative Spark

Few names in American business carry as much magic as the name Disney. It conjures up delightful images of Mickey Mouse, Dumbo, Pinocchio, and Disneyland—the kind of brand identification that any company would kill for. But for years, the Disney name evoked something else in the movie business: stodginess, failure, and a sense of being left behind the times.

Suddenly, as if transformed by a dash of the old Disney magic, all that has changed. Under the leadership of a bright young team of executives, Walt Disney Co. has come alive in the past couple of years to become one of the most vital, exciting, and successful entities in Hollywood. Moviemakers are clamoring to work for a company they once disdained, and the Disney name is once again becoming a dominant force in virtually all areas of entertainment.

It's as if one of Walt Disney's classic movies sprang to life: *Snow White*. After years of slumber, Disney is shaking itself awake and moving boldly into the modern world, its new management intent on making it the unchallenged leader in the entertainment field. It is a transformation that is shaking the company to its foundations—although the new leaders believe that preserving that foundation is critical to making the company successful. Disney's· transformation shows how a corporate culture can be both a source of great strength or a trap—if it's misunderstood.

Disney was the creation of its brilliant founder and namesake, a man who seemed to have an uncanny sense for understanding what Americans craved in entertainment. Mickey Mouse, Disneyland, classic movies such as *Fantasia* and *Snow White*—all sprang from Walt Disney's fertile genius. They were playful, wholesome, highly innovative examples of entertainment, achievements that set standards for every one else to try to emulate. The Disney name was synonymous with magical entertainment, but it was by no means a one-man operation—Disney's creative and production people were among the best in the business.

After Walt Disney's death in 1966, however, the company seemed to slump. Although Disney himself had said at the opening of Disneyland in 1955 that the park "will never be completed, as long as there is imagination left in the world," the sense of imagination seemed to have disappeared from Walt Disney Productions. The occasional hit like the Disney World or EPCOT theme parks were long-simmering projects of the founder brought to fruition years after his death, while most of the products of his successors were increasingly tedious G-rated movies that played to dwindling audiences. The Disney name, once boffo at the box office, had become poison. To get its first movie hit in two decades, with the mermaid fantasy *Splash* in 1984, the company had to release the movie under the Touchstone logo rather than its own.

The company's decline was traced to a group of managers that seemed bent on not offending the memory of Walt Disney. Under the leadership of long-time Disney employee Cardon Walker and then Ronald W. Miller—Walt Disney's son-in-law—the company meandered through the two decades after the founder's death with its output reflecting anything but the vastly changing culture of those years. Disney products seemed to be locked in a 1950s time warp, while other entertainment companies captured the "family" audiences that Disney was striving for— and had once all but owned. Movies such as *Star Wars* and *E.T.*, which seemed the embodiments of the qualities Disney once represented (indeed, their makers acknowledged that the films were tributes to the Disney magic) got made by other studios, while Disney's attempts to catch up were feeble imitations such as the disastrous *Tron*.

At Walt Disney Productions, it seemed, projects were being judged not so much on creative or artistic merits, but rather by one criterion:

"What would Walt have done?" The way the Disney organization answered that question seemed more often than not to be the antithesis of the daring, innovative creations of Walt Disney. The company also seemed as oblivious to changing entertainment-industry economics as it was to shifting creative tides—it all but ignored the goldmine of television, failed to follow other studios' moves to innovative financing techniques and the use of outside production talent, and was slow to capitalize on the vast opportunities new technologies like the videocassette player were opening in home entertainment markets. In spite of itself, the company remained successful—largely on the momentum of the theme parks Walt had built or planned and the occasional re-release of his greatest movie achievements—but it was a decidedly uninteresting firm. Miller made some tentative attempts to move the company along in the early part of the 1980s, with endeavors like Touchstone and *Splash*, but it was too little, too late.

Disney's wake-up call came from corporate raiders Saul Steinberg and Irwin Jacobs—although as might be expected of a company in such a deep sleep, it took a while for the message to get through. To the raiders, Walt Disney Productions was worth more dead than alive, a company that could be bought on the cheap—if you consider a couple of billion dollars cheap—and broken up and sold piecemeal for billions more, its extensive land holdings and treasure trove of movies sure to bring hefty prices. Steinberg purchased 12 percent of the company's stock in early 1984 and threatened a takeover, then backed off after Disney put up a fight—and agreed to pay him a $32 million profit in "greenmail" for his holdings. Part of Disney's anti-Steinberg defense, a planned acquisition of Gibson Greeting Cards Inc. for $315 million, attracted criticism from inside and outside the company—as well as the attention of another raider, Jacobs, who took a 6 percent stake in Disney with a takeover in mind.

With pressure mounting, Disney's management dropped the Gibson deal in August 1984. But Jacobs wouldn't go away. Speculation mounted on Wall Street that Disney, taking a scene out of one of its own cartoons, would summon a corporate "white knight" to chase the raiders away with a friendly takeover. Such a rescue, however, would have left Disney just another piece of a large conglomerate, perhaps gutting the company, in spirit if not in fact. But the drama had a surprise ending, orchestrated by major stockholder Roy Disney, nephew of the founder: Miller stepped aside and, with the approval of Jacobs and the Bass family, another large shareholder, was replaced by a new management team led by Michael D. Eisner and Frank Wells.

Eisner and Wells represent the new Hollywood as much as Disney's previous leaders stood for the old way of doing things. Eisner, who is in his early 40s, had run Paramount Pictures during that studio's boom years of the late 1970s and early 1980s, when it turned out motion-picture smashes like *Raiders of the Lost Ark,* and television hits like *Happy Days* and *Laverne and Shirley.* Eisner has a reputation as being a brilliant manager who could rein in Hollywood's often runaway production costs, but he also had a tremendous feel for the creative side of the business— for instance, an inspiration Eisner had after being pulled over by a California highway patrolman eventually became the gigantic box-office hit *Beverly Hills Cop.* Wells was a Rhodes scholar and longtime Hollywood veteran who had been one of the top executives of Warner Bros. for a decade before quitting the rat race for a year in his early 50s to attempt to fulfill a long-time dream of climbing the tallest mountain on each of the seven continents. Wells had made six of the seven and had his sights set on Mt. Everest when he was hired as Disney's president.

Eisner and Wells set out on nothing less than a complete makeover of Walt Disney Productions, doing everything from redecorating the company's delightfully Art Deco office complex in Burbank for the first time in decades to embarking on an ambitious television and film production schedule. "We've got a lot of things going on," Eisner says. "It's become a very active company."

The jury is still out, but the early results are impressive. After a year or so of clearing out the backlog of the old regime, the first products of Eisner and Wells' new vision for the company began coming to fruition in late 1985. The score so far: One hit movie (*Down and Out in Beverly Hills*), two hit television series (*The Golden Girls,* to which the company bought distribution rights, and *The Disney Sunday Movie,* with Eisner reprising Walt Disney's old role as host), a couple of hit Saturday-morning television series, and a series of successful new endeavors in theme parks, videocassette production, real estate, and other fields. It could well be argued that in less than two years, the Eisner-Wells administration produced more successes for the company than the two decades between the founder's death and their takeover.

The new executives came to the company with full knowledge of Disney's poor reputation in Hollywood. ("They were still making Don Knotts movies," Eisner grimaces.) But Eisner and Wells also brought fresh viewpoints and ideas, and they found things not quite as bad as they expected. "I think a lot of people here were waiting to do something, to get going" says Eisner, who first put forward the Sleeping Beauty metaphor for the company he took over. He says he found a corporate culture unlike most others and certainly those of oft-cynical Hollywood: one imbued with an upbeat family feeling left over from Walt Disney's time, a culture that has made Disney an almost legendarily happy company to work for, even in the worst of times. "The culture is catching," Eisner says. "Even if you've been innoculated against it, you can get it."

The trick, then, became to fuse that culture with a more modern outlook on the world. "The basic fabric of the company hopefully will remain, and on that fabric we will build a different company," Eisner says. "It's clearly a different company, but at the same time, the same company." To this end, Disney's new managers have become as aware as their predecessors of Walt Disney's legacy—but in a totally different way. Walt Disney stood for "enormous creativity," "uniqueness," and "enormous risk-taking," as Wells puts it. "He had the talent of stimulating and he had the talent of listening. And I'm sure he had a third, which was the talent of creating. That goes without saying."

So Disney's new leaders have tried to use the ghost of Walt Disney as a benevolent presence for change, rather than as a reason to not do things. "We've never sat around and looked at each other and said, what would Walt have done?," Wells says. "What we have rather done is say, What will work? What will be successful? What will please? What will draw people? What will attract people?"

Interestingly, Eisner and Wells defend their immediate predecessors in the Disney executive suite from the long-standing charges of complacency. On the contrary, the company's new leaders say, Walker and Miller took many risks, even though in many cases they involved little more than costly implementations of plans left behind by Walt, such as the $1 billion gambled to develop EPCOT. "There's much less risk-taking today than there was in the 15 years or so since Walt's death," Wells contends. "There isn't a modern practitioner of the somewhat arcane art of business-school management that would have ever built EPCOT. There probably aren't very many people who fall in that category who would have started the Disney [cable] Channel. . . . The people who went before us put in place assets that I don't think we would have ever had the guts to do, I really don't. And we're the inheritors of those. You would never build EPCOT if you sat there and brooded over a pro forma [financial statement]. You probably wouldn't have started the Disney Channel if you knew you were going to spend over $100 million to put it into place before you ever broke even, let alone earned back the investment, and if you were really wedded to the past you wouldn't have invented a new name and logo for a new movie division, so to speak, called Touchstone. They did all those things. We're just here to build on them."

But in laying down the architecture for that building, Disney's new leaders hope to revive Walt Disney's aura of creativity and innovation—adhering to the founder's passion for quality and taste but adapting that mandate to the new realities of the marketplace. "It's almost like the evolution of the English language," Eisner says. "You can go back to the derivations of Old English, of Middle English, of Shakespeare—you can see that it's there. It's not like a new language has been built. It's a new way to pronounce it."

Wells uses another metaphor. He sees Walt Disney's legacy as something akin to the United States Constitution—a set of values whose interpretation changes with the times, but still provides the basic precepts for that interpretation. "The whole point of the constitution is they wrote it broadly and vaguely and generally so that it could fit the times, it could fit whatever happened to the culture of the country, and the interests and the motivations," Wells says. "That's really all that Walt did. Walt set a tone that constantly changes in terms of real terms as to what people want to do and see and feel. . . . You've got to start every day of your life with the premise that the world, and its tastes and its entertainment values, change—and you must stay with them."

"We are here to match the legacy of Walt Disney, to match the culture of the Walt Disney company," Wells says. "They put us where we are today, and we're not going to turn our backs on them."

No longer is the main question about a new project "What would Walt do?" Instead, according to Wells, "We say, What will attract and interest and draw people to the parks? What will be entertaining to people? And [we] always ask the [next] question as well: Is it in good taste, because that's the one legacy we really do have—is it in good taste—and is it consistent with what Disney stood for? And if you can answer all those questions yes, you and I, I'm sure, will sit here today and say yes, Walt would have done that. There may be a lot of other people that wouldn't [agree], because they're going to judge it by what Walt would have done in the mid-60s and the mid-50s. But I'm telling you, there's no question, if you read about his life and read about what he did and said, he was always in front of everybody else, and I hope we will be too."

Even as they are trying to keep Walt Disney a vibrant part of the company that bears his name, in some cases Eisner and Wells have found that remnants of the patriarch's style of doing things have held the company back—albeit in the most innocent of ways. Eisner says that upon joining the company, he began hearing stories from old-timers about what a wonderful storyteller Disney had been—a quality that drove many of the company's most classic works, but also created some modern problems. When Eisner began looking into how the company was creating cartoon features, he discovered that standard operating procedure was to eschew a formal script and begin production by drawing up storyboards—rough drafts of how the action will progress. To Eisner, that seemed to be a strange way to make a movie. "I don't understand it," he says. "The storyboards are not particularly interesting, and don't hold together . . . all the things I learned in English 101 about beginning, middle, denouement, and structure are not there. And then the more I've been here, the more I hear these great stories about what a fantastic storyteller Walt Disney was . . . I've heard it everywhere: He can mesmerize a room with his storytelling, he can mesmerize a group of children—he just had a great way of telling stories, obviously. And I finally realized—that there *was* a script, but it was an oral script. . . . Walt Disney, who made one film every four years himself, sat in a room with a bunch of his guys and he'd tell a story. He'd tell his version of Snow White. Now he's dead and gone, and they've never realized. They say, 'There was no story, there's no script, we just—we—just sat around the room and talked about it.' Well, that's not true. Walt Disney read the script to them, and they wrote it down."

"The process was great. I accept the process, but there was nobody who could replace Walt Disney," Eisner says. "There was nobody who was as good as Walt Disney. . . . You hit one maybe every generation. And most of those guys, of the one every generation, don't have all the other things that Walt Disney had."

So now, two decades after Walt's death, Disney's animation department is finally learning how to function in a more conventional manner. "We don't have anybody here now who can tell a story the way Walt Disney can tell a story," Eisner says. "So what are we doing? We are changing the way animation is done. We are going to go outside and hire a writer to come in and write a story." Eisner doesn't worry that the scriptwriters will lack Walt Disney's vision—they'll just make up for it. After all, Eisner says, "If we had Walt Disney, we wouldn't need anybody else. If I could do what Walt Disney could do, we could save a fortune in scripts."

Unquestionably, Eisner and Wells have brought their own styles of management to Disney. Within days after Eisner's appointment as chairman in September 1984, Eisner gathered six of the company's most creative talents for a Sunday morning meeting at his house that within a few hours produced three ideas for Saturday morning cartoon series— a potentially lucrative field in which the company, for all its reputation as a cartoon maker, had never participated. "You've got to gather the people and then you've got to get them all excited and come up with the ideas," Eisner says.

That Sunday morning meeting is an example of one of Eisner's favorite ways to get things done—a sort of "encounter group," as he calls it, with creative people and ideas bouncing off one another to come up with winning concepts. Often, he says, the best ideas don't come until the very end, but he is confident they will emerge. "I've gotten more done in the last five minutes of a five-hour meeting than in the first four hours and fifty-five minutes," Eisner says. Wells calls Eisner's creative meetings "gong shows," because every so often someone will playfully stand up and "gong" a bad idea. "I have never seen such an interchange and interplay of ideas," Wells says. "Good ideas rise to the surface, and you must not ever feel inhibited to do that. I don't know that they were inhibited before we got here, but I do know that one of the things we've stood for is a good idea no matter who it comes from. If it's there you know it, you feel it, you do it, no matter where it comes from."

Still, you sometimes have to prod people a little. Shortly after becoming Disney's president, Wells held a meeting with members of the company's marketing staff to seek new ways of marketing Disneyland, Disney World, and EPCOT—which, incredibly, had never been the subjects of formal advertising and marketing campaigns by the company. The meeting was not a success, Wells remembers. "I went around the table, and frankly it was kind of stony silence. I said, 'This is not a satisfactory meeting. We're going to come back tomorrow, you 15 people, and I want each of you to have at least one idea.' And I left." His point was made. The next day, the marketers presented him with 43 ideas on how to sell the theme parks to the public. "Every one of them was new and fresh and different," Wells says. Most were implemented immediately. Among the ways the company began communicating with its customers better were road shows featuring Disney characters that traveled across the country promoting the parks, and the publicizing of a new "800" number for park information that generated requests for half a million brochures in just a few months of operation in selected markets. With many of those 43 marketing ideas now implemented, attendance at the Disney parks is running substantially ahead of previous figures.

The changes in the company's processes are as subtle to an outsider as the seemingly cosmetic change Eisner and Wells made in the company's name in early 1986, from Walt Disney Productions to The Walt Disney Co.—reflecting the company's increased scope. What the changes in the company mean to the end product, however, is easily measured. And while it is too early to tell whether the new Disney can begin generating *Star Wars* and *E.T.*s on a regular basis, Eisner and Wells have clearly improved the company's output.

One of the first things they did after taking over was to take a hard look at the Disney projects that were already underway when they took control of the company—with a particular eye toward "black holes" that were draining money and creative talent without much prospect for a successful finished product. "We went through it with a strong rake," Wells says. The result was a $166 million write-off of investments in projects "which we believe do not have continuing value in relation to newly defined corporate strategies and emerging business opportunities," Eisner and Wells wrote in a letter to shareholders in the company's 1984 annual report. "There isn't a black hole left after the write-offs we went through," Wells says.

What's left over, Eisner and Wells believe, are Disney's healthiest projects, to which they are adding more opportunities. Eisner is quadrupling the ouput of Disney's film-production division to 12 to 15 movies a year, moving the company away from the cartoons and Don Knotts features that have been its staples for years and into more movies like *Splash*—hopefully with the same measure of success. Among the projects under way are projects starring comedienne-singer Bette Midler and Shelley Long, the star of TV's *Cheers*, and new movies by the writer of *Beverly Hills Cop* and the team that made the comedy smash *Airplane*—the kind of sophisticated movie-making talent Disney had seemed to shy away from in the past. Although Touchstone will likely be the label for most films made by the company—the Disney name will be reserved for family-

'oriented fare—Eisner says he sees virtually no limit to the kind of movies
the company can make.

Those working on the Disney lot in Burbank report a new atmosphere
of interaction and pooling of ideas rare in Hollywood these days—but
not unheard of in the old days in the friendly Disney culture. Screen-
writers can share scripts, directors can exchange ideas, and new concepts
are encouraged—a big change from today's Hollywood, where some of
the most original ideas often seem to be remakes or sequels. The studio
also is attempting to develop its own corps of young writing, directing,
and acting talent—another throwback to the golden days of Disney and
Hollywood.

But other things brought by Eisner and Wells to Disney are decidedly
modern. Take the way the company finances its movies. No longer will
Disney finance all of its projects in-house—a practice no other major
studio has done for years. Spreading the risk as other studios have done,
Eisner is using co-financing deals and other devices to pay for the company's moviemaking. One of the first strides in this direction was the
successful offering in mid-1985 of Silver Screen Partners II, a set of
limited partnerships offered to small investors by E. F. Hutton & Co.
that raised $150 million to help finance future Disney productions. Such
outside financing arrangements reduce the studio's risks in the case of a
flop, although they also spread the profits from a hit.

Eisner also is going outside the company for creative and production
talent. One of his first hires was Jeffrey Katzenberg, another former
Paramount executive, to run Disney's motion-picture and television division. Katzenberg, one of the movie industry's most highly regarded
young executives, is known in Hollywood as "The Golden Retriever" for
his uncanny ability to sniff out a good deal. Katzenberg, in turn, brought
in still more outsiders to give Disney's film and television operation its
first infusion of new talent in years. "There's a willingness to go outside
that may not have been there before," says Eisner—himself the only
outsider to head the company in its history.

At the same time he is building up the movie business, Eisner is
directing the formation of an aggressive new television production unit
that he hopes will make Disney a major television presence much as was
his previous employer, Paramount. "Disney must have the Disney name
and the Disney kind of family entertainment back on network television,"
he says. To Eisner's mind, that primarily means comedy—and notably,

the only successful new comedy of the 1985-86 television series was Disney's *Golden Girls*. "I think this company is suited to do comedy television," Eisner says. "We have to get into the *Cheers*, and *Family Ties*, and *Webster*, and *Happy Days*, and *Laverne and Shirley*, and *Mork and Mindy*, and *All in the Family*—whatever it is." Disney's expansion into television will also include the syndication of the many *Wonderful World of Disney* and other television shows that sit in the company's archives. To date, this treasure store has never been exploited, for reasons that aren't really clear. Eisner has changed that.

In addition, Eisner has begun cracking the company vault for more aggressive re-release of Disney's other treasures—movies like *Pinocchio*, *Fantasia*, and *Snow White*. Violating the long-standing company commandment, Thou Shalt Not Overexpose, Eisner has begun pushing some of these classics into the marketplace, either through re-release or into the lucrative videocassette and cable markets. "It's almost like having a plethora of riches," Wells says of the company film library. "You tell me when the next generation of children, measured in six- or seven-year increments, is not going to want to see *Snow White* and *Bambi* and *Dumbo* and *Jungle Book* and *101 Dalmatians* and *Pinocchio* and *Alice in Wonderland*, and on and on and on, and that's the time I'll check out." One outlet for the classics is the Disney Channel, the company's cable-television venture, which is already turning a profit and is becoming a principal vehicle for the display of the company's creative output, new and old.

Eisner and Wells are also turning their attention to Disney's theme parks, perhaps the most consistently successful of the Disney empire's enterprises over the years. Rock star Michael Jackson did a short 3-D movie-musical for showing at the parks, *Star Wars* creator George Lucas is working on a ride based on that series of movies, and several other new attractions—the first in years—are in the works. "There is no question in our minds that Walt would have done that," Wells says. Also on the drawing board is at least one more Disney park—European Disneyland, near Paris—to go with the three in the United States and Tokyo Disneyland. The company has also announced plans for a new attraction near EPCOT and Disney World in Florida that will kill two birds with one stone: A large studio complex that would provide tourists with a way to see how movies are made—as well as giving the company some sorely needed facilities to handle its huge increase in movie-making. And Disney's new leaders are also applying to the theme park business some of the innovative financing ideas they've brought to bear on the movie side of the company—they will likely sell one or more of the theme parks to an investor group and then lease it back under a long-term management contract, with valuable cash-flow and tax benefits.

Eisner and Wells also are studying ways to exploit the holdings of Arvida, a real estate subsidiary purchased as part of the defense against Steinberg, although the company has said it will probably divest many of its land holdings. Eisner says he wants to be in the entertainment business, not the real estate and housing business. "Land as a recreational commodity, great; land as a housing commodity . . . we're not going to be there," Eisner says. Still, one area of housing has appeal—hotels. Eying the huge amount of lodging that has sprung up on the fringes of Disney World and EPCOT, the company will attempt to get in on that action by expanding its hotel holdings in the area. In an effort to generate new ideas for use of the company's vast land holdings, Wells put together another meeting of the minds a few months after joining the company. This one brought together architects, sociologists, land planners, environmentalists, and academics to give fresh perspectives on land use.

When you look at it closely, Eisner's and Wells' manifesto for change at Disney is not really very radical. Rather, it attempts to capitalize on the company's existing strengths as a purveyor of general entertainment—and to exploit those strengths to the maximum possible. In many cases, the plans interact, a realization of one of Disney's classic, but lately underutilized strengths—the ability of a successful movie character, say, to be the basis for a Disney World attraction and for merchandising efforts. Think of Mickey Mouse, and the number of ways the company has generated business from his image—everything from movies to the Mickey Mouse Club to lunchboxes. Disney hasn't had a similar creative and marketing coup in years, while E.T. and Cabbage Patch Dolls have turned into gold mines for other companies.

Disney now hopes to recapture that by creating new characters that hopefully will spawn television series, movies, merchandising, and theme-park attractions. Wells says he hopes in a few years "that in addition to Mickey, Minnie, Donald, Goofy, Pluto, and the other Disney characters, we have a dozen that were equally a part of the national cultural psyche." Already, one product of the Sunday-morning meeting at Eisner's home— a Saturday-morning cartoon show based on characters called Wuzzles— has generated a successful line of toys. Such merchandising opportunities, and link-ups of the company's characters with other companies' merchandising or advertising needs and abilities, appear limitless. "Every single day there is a new matching up of the assets, the characters, the history of this company that Walt Disney and our predecessors built with the modern-day business world," Wells says. "No one should be this lucky. It's absolutely incredible."

Everywhere they look, Eisner and Wells see opportunities that the company has not previously tapped. They're like kids in a candy store. "You could spend a lifetime just in the core businesses that you've got," Wells says. "You could build a movie and television company, you could build the Disney Channel, you can put new characters into consumer products, you can find new assets for Arvida to run, and most of all you can develop Walt Disney World and build another park in Europe. You're talking five lifetimes of just what I've said, of work to do." Add in spin-offs, new businesses, acquisitions, and other opportunities, and Wells says, "I guess my only wish is that I was 30 to do this now instead of 53, not for any other reason than that it would just be fun to keep doing this for the rest of my life."

"Our eternal frustration is and always will be that we can't move fast enough," Wells says. "There are still so many things to do that are so obvious, that demand a lot of management time, but the basic restrictive fact of life of this company is that we just don't have enough time to do all the things that clearly or obviously should be done. That is not cockiness. . . . You know what has to be done, in some respects you know your priorities, so the limitation is time and management and putting people in place to get those things done."

The changes brought by Michael Eisner and Frank Wells to Walt Disney Co. bode well for the future growth of a company that is already quite large—approaching $2 billion in revenues. Eisner and Wells see that size as advantageous to the company, giving it the muscle to do what it needs. But they also are trying to maintain the corporate culture they found when they took over. "We have to act like a giant company. You can't act like a small company," Eisner says. "The question is whether or not we can evolve into a giant company without losing that family feeling."

Clearly, the combination of new blood and the Disney culture is a potent, infectious one. Longtime Disney employees show a new enthusiasm about the company that is matched by their chief executives. "There's no more fun in this world than this company," Wells says with a boyish grin. "Michael and I are still like two little kids. We call each other up and say, 'Listen to this!' . . . The great joy of this company is the new businesses and the new challenges and these incredible things that only a man like Walt Disney would put into place, almost without regard for how profitable they would be. The question he essentially asked is, what can I do for this world, and Michael and I were lucky enough to inherit that. And what you have to do is match that challenge and legacy up against the realities of a public company and the shareholders and all the rest." In fact, Wells says, it's as much fun as climbing mountains— although he still has his heart set on conquering Everest.

Sleeping Beauty, then, is coming awake. As Eisner and Wells direct Disney's changes, they say they are more cognizant than ever of the legacy left them by Walt Disney. But they believe it is a legacy that can be used positively to promote the company's growth, rather than to inhibit it. And for all their enthusiasm, Disney's new leaders are proceeding with a caution one might have expected from the previous regime. "I want to keep my foot on the throttle, but I'm real quick to move from the throttle to the brake," Eisner says. "Where there's not going to be a change is going to be in striving for a certain kind of quality expectation." Similarly, Wells says, "There are any number of times we have come down on the side of remembering we're the Disney company, and making a decision you might not make were you in any other company. . . . You really do have a larger responsibility when you carry that name around."

Despite that once-constrictive restriction, change is apparent all around at Walt Disney Productions, change the company never asked for, but from which it is hoping to benefit. Eisner argues that Disney might have changed regardless, particularly given the directions in which his predecessor, Ron Miller, had slowly begun to lead the company. "The change was coming. I don't think I brought the change," he says. "It was inevitable."

But Eisner acknowledges that that change was hastened by events. "They had a forest fire here," Eisner says. "Sometimes it takes that kind of firestorm to let everybody know that change is not only in the wind but has to be done."

# 16

# GENERAL MOTORS

## Reinventing the Wheel

By tradition, nearly a thousand of the most important executives of General Motors Corp. gathered every two or three years at the luxurious Greenbrier Hotel in White Sulphur Springs, W.Va., for a briefing on the state of the company. The sessions typically were treated like councils of war and clothed in secrecy: The drapes were pulled, name tags checked, and participants warned not to repeat what they saw and heard. Not that that would have been a problem. The customary fare was a tedious procession of boilerplate speeches and amateur humor. Golf, cards, and socializing were the real business of the Greenbrier conferences.

That at least was the tradition until Roger B. Smith became chairman of GM in January 1981. At the first Greenbrier meeting he presided over, in April 1983, Smith had a grim message for the troops. "We got down there, got everybody in the same room, 850 people, and laid out our missions, our objectives, and our strategy," Smith says. There was nothing secret about it. "We told them, 'For Chrissakes, when you leave here you'd better go home and tell the people we're up to our ass in trouble and we've got to start doing things differently.'"

Smith, as good as his word, is steering General Motors into the most dramatic change in direction in the company's long history.

The shocks began early in 1982, forming a timeline of change: In March of that year, Smith sits down for dinner at the Links Club in Manhattan with Eiji Toyoda, chairman of Toyota Motor Co., the leader of the Japanese auto industry that has poured more than 20 million cars onto American shores since its recovery from World War II.

The GM chairman has an audacious idea. Knowing that GM cannot compete with the Japanese in the subcompact car market because its production costs are too high, Smith proposes a historic joint venture: GM will sell subcompacts built by Toyota in a surplus GM plant in Fremont, Cal. The venture would give Toyota a way to boost its U.S. sales, outflanking the restrictions on Japanese imports. For its part, GM would gain a valuable close-up look at Japanese management methods. And if Toyota succeeds in negotiating a less costly labor agreement with the United Auto Workers, it could give GM leverage in its own negotiations. Toyoda accepts, and over the cries of outrage from GM's American competitors, the deal goes through. The company is named New United Motor Manufacturing Inc., or NUMMI, and the cars—Novas— start coming off the line in December 1984.

The scene shifts. It is 1984 and John Gutfreund, the managing director of the New York investment banking firm Salomon Brothers, has arrived in Dallas to call on H. Ross Perot, the bantam Texan who founded Electronic Data Systems Corp. and built it into a billion-dollar computer-systems firm. The reason Gutfreund has come to Texas—the thing he won't mention over the telephone—is to bring Roger Smith's proposal to buy EDS. Despite Perot's initial misgivings, he is won over by Smith's vision of how the computer company could knit General Motors' far-flung operations and outposts together electronically, achieving tremendous gains in efficiency and control. For $2.55 billion, EDS becomes part of General Motors.

A year later, General Motors is making another acquistion. After a secret auction that attracted some of the biggest names in American industry, it has come up the winner in the bidding for Hughes Aircraft Co., the legacy of eccentric billionaire Howard Hughes—a company with leading positions in electronics, defense contracting, and systems management—all central to GM's future.

The scene shifts again to Spring Hill, Tenn., a little town 30 miles from Nashville. On July 29, 1985, the town and the rest of the world learn that it has won a nationwide contest to become the site of GM's $3.5 billion Saturn car project, the crowning attempt by GM to overtake the Japanese in auto-manufacturing prowess. The Saturn is Smith's "clean-sheet" experiment to set aside the way GM does business now and to replace it with the most advanced production processes, computer systems, and work force relationships the company can come up with. Then Saturn will become the model for the rest of the company.

NUMMI, EDS, Hughes, Saturn—four dramatic symbols of the revolution Smith and his top associates are attempting at the world's largest industrial company. Convinced that GM's old ways are fatal in the supercharged competition that lies ahead, Smith is dead set on changing the way the company works, from its goals and master strategies to the minute policies, rules of thumb, and informal understandings that govern daily life inside the company. Competitors Ford Motor Co. and Chrysler Corp. are essaying the same kinds of changes. But at GM the changes are broader and bolder, because of its sheer size and economic power.

General Motors was the model for industrial organizations of the 20th century: powerful, stubborn, monolithic, and authoritarian, its prosperity based on the relentless march of its assembly lines, symbols of the great economies of scale created by mass production.

If Smith's campaign succeeds, GM will become the model of the 21st-century manufacturer. Its competitive strength would be built on an entirely different foundation—the world's best manufacturing technology; computer networks to link design, production, inventory control, and every other major function and operation; and a radically different approach to human relations within the plant, one designed to make every employee a contributor to the company's success.

Five years into his term, Smith can see only the first signs of victory, not the final outcome. "We won't get the real test for a while. We're kind of in between," Smith says. "We know we're getting things done we need to get done, but it will be a little while." The real test will be GM's ability to cut the five-year development time for new cars almost in half, giving it the fastest response time to market conditions of any auto maker in the world. Clearly there have been stumbles and setbacks along the way, and Wall Street analysts fault GM for lagging behind even its U.S. rivals in productivity and profit per car—not to mention the Japanese. Smith argues that this reflects the greater size and costs of the transition GM has undertaken. The revolution won't be completed before

Smith's scheduled retirement in 1990, but the revolution is under way, and there is probably not a nerve anywhere in GM's sprawling corporate body that hasn't been pinched, jangled, or severed in the process.

"We've done it a thousand times in the corporation [in the past five years] whether it was the way they managed people on the assembly line, or how they did their daily jobs," Smith says. "And we tell them we've got farther to go than we've come." It's not easy getting the message across. "Moan. Groan. Insanity!" comes back the response from many parts of the organization, he says. But Smith is adamant about forcing change on General Motors and its people. "You have to go around and pound their fingers off the rock and tell them, 'Let go and swim across the stream. You're not going to drown.' "

It was GM that appeared in danger of drowning when Smith and President F. James McDonald took over in 1981. Although the world's leading auto maker had rebounded from a harrowing $760 million loss in 1980, it owed a significant part of that recovery to the voluntary limits on Japanese imports arranged by the Reagan administration in 1981. But unlike most of his peers in GM, Smith was convinced that the huge losses GM had suffered were not the result of outside forces alone.

The fact was that GM was being beaten at its own game by the Japanese, whose devotion to quality and productivity in manufacturing had produced an enviable reputation with car buyers and a cost advantage of $1,500 to $2,200 per car compared to GM and the other American auto makers. Smith believed that gap could not be closed unless drastic changes were made in its operations. In a company whose executives instinctively put on their self-confidence before they step into their shorts in the morning, that message was a hard sell.

If GM's size and power were a symbol of 20th-century American manufacturing, so was its self-confidence, and that, perhaps more than anything else, had gotten GM into such deep trouble, according to Alex Mair, the recently retired GM vice president who headed the company's technical staff. For most of the postwar era until the 1980s, GM had sold virtually every car it could make, except during recessionary periods, thanks to a organizational system that for its time was unmatched. GM believed it was an American institution—"Baseball, hot dogs, apple pie, and Chevrolet," were the words to a long-running advertising jingle. But the more successful GM got, the less attention it paid to why it had succeeded.

Ross Perot says the reason was simple. "General Motors and the entire

American automobile industry had a big respite from competition. Detroit was the automobile capital of the world," he says: Talk about hot dogs and baseball, Perot says. "They owned bat, ball, gloves, both teams, the stadium, and the lights. It's hard to lose, right? It got so bad that they tried to get divisions to compete with one another"—Chevrolet vying with Pontiac, Oldsmobile with Buick, and so on. "Now we've got a whole generation of people who think that's what competition is," Perot says.

"A company in that position might not notice major changes taking place," Mair says, because success breeds a nearsighted contentment with the status quo. And that attitude, in turn, stifles the thing that GM needed most—an inventive, entrepreneurial culture, where people with ideas weren't afraid to offer them and demand attention. To succeed, Smith's revolution had to win on two fronts. Both the manufacturing processes and the attitudes of people throughout the corporation would have to be turned in a completely new direction.

"This requires the development of all-new technology, and I really underline the word *all*," Mair says. GM's future depends in large part upon the gains in productivity that must come from changes in the technology of manufacturing—the ability to form and machine things faster, to design and build machines that stay running longer and perform more reliably, and the introduction of "smart" robots equipped with sensors and vision systems to build cars. "That's where the gains are going to be made," Mair says.

The second task of the new technology is to control the torrent of information of all kinds that flows through the company. This is the task that has been given to Perot and EDS, and Smith has shifted GM's 8,000 data-processing scientists and programmers over to the Dallas-based company, along with the responsibility for GM's vast computer systems, which include more than 100 IBM mainframes and thousands of other programmable terminals. In ten years, Smith's goal is to bring every piece of machinery and every operation in GM's plants—materials handling, metal machining, assembly, inspection, maintenance, and all the rest—under the control of computers. For American companies, handicapped by high labor costs and an economic system that is poorly attuned to the global economic challenge, the management of information has jumped out as a potentially vital advantage in the struggle to improve productivity and lower costs.

GM is also counting on technology to add value to the cars it sells—something its management thought it knew how to do. One of the industry's fundamental business calculations was deciding what features could be added to entice customers to spend more money. But while Detroit was still fixated on power windows, fancy moldings, and plush interiors, foreign competitors were taking affluent customers away with efficient high-performance cars. GM now knows it will have to compete on performance, and technology is the key to that.

In an effort to advance technology even further, Smith has set up the Trilby project at GM, an exercise involving 100 scientists and technicians who have been charged with rethinking the entire technology of the automobile, even down to reconsidering the number of wheels it rides upon. Among other things, the Trilby project is expected to produce designs for onboard computer systems for cars that could deliver the best possible performance during normal driving and help the driver keep control in emergencies by providing split-second coordination of steering, braking, and engine systems with the driver's own reactions. "Should the steering and brake systems know how fast the car is going and should they somehow respond to that?" asks Robert A. Frosch, the former head of the National Aeronautics and Space Administration who was hired by GM to head its laboratories. "If the answer is 'yes,' how do you make sure [those systems] fit with the responses and desires of the driver?" Such is the challenge of the Trilby project, Frosch says.

"There is a collection of revolutions that are coming together," he adds. "There is the computer hardware and software revolution, there are the software insights into human thinking, there's the sensor business, which incorporates sight and touch, there's the telecommunications revolution." To regain its competitive position, GM must be in the forefront of each of these revolutions, extract what it needs, and piece the parts together.

The much-ballyhooed Saturn project is an important product of that synthesis. Imagine an auto worker, an automotive engineer, a plant manager, and a union shop steward sitting down together to decide the best way to manufacture a car, with no old procedures that must be followed and no outmoded work rules in the labor agreements. Suppose they were free to search for the best way to get the job done, using the most advanced technologies in sight. Those are the rules for the Saturn team, established as a separate subsidiary within GM to give it the independence it must have to succeed.

"It's not a car, it's a process," GM Vice Chairman Howard Kehrl says. "And the process in this case is a reevaluation of all we thought was correct." The Saturn company, which hopes to be producing 500,000 subcompact cars a year by 1990, will be an experimental station for dramatically new approaches to car-making. "Without the Saturn project we don't stand a chance against the Japanese," Smith insists.

One of the likely casualties of the revolution at Saturn will be the traditional assembly line, a fixture of the automaking culture since the time of Henry Ford and the Model T. The assembly line was a source and symbol of Detroit's former affluence, the heart of mass-production economics, with 10,000 parts attached one at a time by thousands of workers stationed along a three-mile-long conveyor that could move only as fast as the slowest operation. To keep the line going there could be no shortage of parts, so huge inventories were kept on hand—and in its years of plenty, GM didn't worry much about the cost. At its peak, GM sold more than 1.5 million Chevrolet Impalas a year, an incredible turnout that dictated a style of production emphasizing uniformity and repetition.

Saturn, designed for different times, will not be built that way. Final assembly of the Saturn will involve no more than 15 major parts or segments, such as an entire front end with grill, headlights, fan, and radiator assemblies attached. Each of these components will be assembled separately, by GM or its suppliers, and transported on a tightly controlled schedule to the final assembly site. A new generation of assembly line robots equipped with machine "intelligence" and vision systems will determine what kind of car is approaching, what kind of weld is required, for instance, and where the weld must go, and then it will test itself to make sure the job was done right. GM is counting on all of these changes to radically alter a basic measure of productivity—the number of employee hours required to build one car. The labor content per car now ranges from 175 to 200 hours, compared to 100 hours at most Japanese auto plants. Saturn's mission is to lower it to 30. The modular assembly will permit smaller production volumes, allow faster changeover to new models, and promote a far greater responsibility on the auto worker's part for the quality of the product.

There is a basic motive running through Smith's costly search for technology through the acquisition of EDS, the $5 billion purchase of Hughes Aircraft, the joint venture with the Japanese robotics company, Fanuc Ltd., and the other smaller high-tech companies GM has snapped up. Given the size of GM's bankroll, there wasn't too much in corporate America it couldn't afford, but Smith wanted no part of the conglomerate game (indeed, he has turned down overtures from oil companies that wanted to come under GM's wing). Instead, he wanted technology that tied in directly to the company's mission of car and truck manufacturing. As Perot observes, there is nothing GM can do that will be more profitable than making cars, if it can do the job right.

GM is paying for the change. Its earnings for 1985 suffered because of the heavy spending to modernize today's plants and perfect the technology for tomorrow's even more automated plants. "I've known for a long time we were going to earn less," Smith says. Of course, he adds, "I could produce phenomenal earnings for GM" by cutting back on research, thinning the ranks of technicians and management who are the revolution's cadre. But it would be a farce, he says. It would destroy GM's future.

As the company tries to corral new manufacturing technology, Smith also is pushing GM's scientists and engineers to be alert for spin-off products and services that arise out of its automotive work. "My other plan is to take some of those talents, add to that what we can pick up from the outside, and grow a whole new era of diversification for the corporation," he says. Eventually, those new businesses should account for nearly 10 percent of GM's revenues, Smith says, and 10 percent of GM would be, by itself, one the 50 largest companies in the United States.

The diversification that the entire electronics industry is waiting for is the expected offspring from EDS and GM. Perot's company is building an electronic network to link the engineers at their design terminals with cutting machines on the factory floor—a product that can be sold to factories around the world. The same goal has been set for the information management network the company is building. "We're not only talking about $3 billion in GM data-processing businesses today," Perot says. "We're talking about eventually building the world's largest data- and voice-communications and artificial intelligence system. We're not just talking about processing payrolls and records and doing inventories; we're talking about providing the technology and software for robotized assembly lines and other uses that would astonish you."

The gains that Smith wants from technology can't be achieved just by buying robots, writing software code, and adding more computerized design terminals. They require a change in basic attitudes throughout the corporation about the role of technology, Mair says. That was driven home to him a few years ago during a tour of a GM plant just after it had been reequipped with state-of-the-art machining equipment, the powerful, complex tools that drill and shape metal castings to produce auto components like engine blocks. The efficiency and productivity of these tools is measured in terms of their machining rate: how fast the tools can remove metal from the piece they are working on.

Looking at this "brand-new, fantastic machinery," Mair had a jarring flashback. He had worked at the same plant, the Chevrolet factory in Flint, Mich., in 1939 as a brand-new GM engineer. For some reason, the machining rates from that time had stuck in his memory. Incredibly, he realized, the rates for the new machinery, decades later, were essentially the same. "Brand-new machinery!" he exclaims. Mair told the technicians at GM's advanced manufacturing operation to find a way to increase the machining rates. They faced a familiar hurdle that had blocked progress for those 40 years and more, not only at GM, but at its competitors' plants as well: Machining generates heat. If the drills or lathes used to shape the metal piece run too fast, they would produce so much heat that the piece could be distorted. It was a simple physical fact that engineers assumed would always limit machine-tool speeds.

A fresh look and a lot of costly research demonstrated a simple but ingenious way around the old conventional wisdom: If the machining was done at much faster speeds than previously, the metallic chips would disappear so rapidly that the heat would not be transferred to the piece of metal. The chips would be hot; the piece would not. Others have reached that conclusion, but none have carried it as far as GM, Mair says. Now, after five years of research and development, GM is achieving machining speeds that exceed previous technology by several orders of magnitude, giving GM what it believes is an important competitive advantage in this part of automobile production.

"We got full support," Mair says, crediting Smith for recognizing the importance of the research. "I think we would have been unable to do that 10 years ago in General Motors, because it would have taken too much effort."

Such gains in manufacturing productivity are representative of another revolution underway at GM, as at other companies. Until the 1980s, the management formula followed at GM and elsewhere was based on stretching out the life of equipment as long as possible, to limit manufacturing costs. The competitive edge was gained in marketing and product design—not in manufacturing productivity, GM thought. It was an approach that worked just fine until Detroit encountered the Japanese, whose forte was manufacturing technology. "Somebody had gotten better in the two areas that really count, quality and cost," Mair says. Before the 1980s, it would have been too difficult to persuade GM's management that a breakthrough in manufacturing technology could be worth the cost. "We would have had very little opportunity to say, 'We'll dramatically exceed the world,' " Mair says. That barrier no longer stands.

But brute technology is not enough. The challenges of the 1980s require sweeping changes in the culture, management style, and labor relations within the company. And the changes Smith has instituted have been germinating in his head for years.

In the mid-1970s, Smith was picked to run a new planning effort called the corporate directions group. The other executives involved weren't keen about it, he recalls, "so I had a real chance to go in and fuss around with the thing." Smith and a trusted lieutenant, GM strategic planner Michael E. Naylor, pursued the questions of GM's competitive position. "It took us years and a bunch of false starts to really understand the system and what it could do and what it couldn't do," the GM chairman says. "It was there we realized there were some things we were doing that were going to lead us into big trouble."

By the 1980s, GM's management structure had become fossilized under the weight of its bureaucracy. One chronicler called it "a vast white-collar assembly line"; GM was making decisions like it made autos, with even the smallest queries having to travel from office to office, through layers of bureaucracy, before a decision was made—and then passed back down the line. It was a system that buried innovation and penalized those who bucked the status quo. "We thought somewhat restrictively, because we were getting all the business anyway," Mair says. As a result, it became uncomfortable to try to push a new idea all the way into the wall, if necessary. "Even if people had some ideas, they weren't going to go rushing forward with them if it had a risk of them not doing well," he says.

When Smith took charge of GM in 1981, the plan he and Naylor had worked on since the mid-1970s was ready. It had three simple but essential goals: to reward innovative thinking, to develop new methods for making and selling cars, and to decentralize decision-making. But Smith understood that a change this basic could not be achieved by issuing orders from the chairman's office. It had to be built into the system somehow. The answer presented itself in a major project GM's president McDonald had begun shortly after taking office—a thorough study of the company's organizational structure. "Jim McDonald is the guy who should get the credit," Smith says. "One of his basic concepts on that was, while we could mandate the change from the top, what the change would be would have to come from the bottom up." That led to a survey of GM management, conducted by consultants McKinsey & Co., to overcome any shyness executives might have felt about speaking their minds. And some of the responses surprised Smith and McDonald. "There were more people out there that thought we needed to change— and were willing to change," Smith says.

With their responses in hand, Smith and McDonald announced in 1983 the biggest structural reorganization of GM since the consolidation of the company in the 1920s under Alfred P. Sloan Jr. The two man-ufacturing fiefdoms, Fisher Body and the General Motors Assembly Di-vision, were abolished. Control of production was placed in the two new divisions created by the reorganization, Buick, Oldsmobile, and Cadillac in one group (BOC), and Chevrolet, Pontiac, and GM of Canada (CPC) in the other. With this step, the people responsible for designing, man-ufacturing, and selling the cars were all within reach of one another. Each division head was allowed to organize the group to his liking. "We'll see which one works," Smith says.

The goal of the reorganization is to push decision-making out of GM headquarters and down into the plants. "Before," the GM chairman says, "most of our people were running a real authoritarian system, where the guy says, 'This is what we're going to do.' " Often, that decision was simply the way things had always been done. "They just muscled it into being the right decision," Smith says. "But technology wasn't moving as fast then." The ever-increasing speed of technology today has put a pre-mium on speed of decision-making, demanding flexibility and an ability to come up with and apply fresh ideas.

Nothing like this revolution has been attempted before by a company the size of GM, and though it has at times caused a great deal of confusion and wasted energy, it has been accepted for the most part, according to Smith and other GM leaders. "It's a combination of things—things we were dreaming we could do," Smith says, and things that had to be done. "The harsh reality was the damn place was on fire and it didn't take a genius to say, 'For Chrissakes, somebody get a fire extinguisher.' "

The change in technology at GM may well be matched by a shift in management's relationship with the United Auto Workers. In preparing the plan for Saturn, a GM-UAW-Saturn study group covered 2 million miles around the globe to look at different strategies of labor-management relations, compensation, and employee relations—ideas it could weave into the Saturn project. "This is an attempt to gather up all of the good from everywhere else and to put it into one place," says Stephen P. Yokich, who heads the UAW's national organizing unit.

The result is a pay system at Saturn that scraps the time clock, the hourly wage, and, if it works to the maximum, much of the contentious distinction that has existed between the salaried and hourly workers in the plants. Saturn's workers will be paid on a salaried basis according to the complexity of their assignments and the skills and training they have mastered to carry them out. In addition, GM and the UAW have agreed that the initial responsibility for doing the job right lies with the assembly team on the spot—not a handful of supervisors eyeballing the production line. With that responsibility will come a more flexible set of work rules. "It's a change in the way management sees the union," Yokich says. "They finally realize that we have brains and not just backs." There is some dissent within the UAW about the union-management partnership at Saturn from union members who feel it will destroy labor's separate identity and thus its organizing ability. But if Saturn succeeds and becomes the pattern, the labor-management relationship in manufacturing will have entered a new era.

An equally long leap is planned for GM's managers at Saturn, who will have to function in what Smith calls a "paperless plant." It's an exaggeration, but it captures his absolute determination to cut the enormous paper trail inside GM and replace it with a computerized network created by EDS. In that future plant, Smith says, "We don't use any paper with our suppliers. We're on line by computer with them. There are no invoices. There's no receiving documents. No matching of slips. No purchase orders, requisitions, releases against that. It's computer-driven."

When a customer orders a Saturn, then, the order will be electronically communicated by the dealer to all levels of the Saturn production and marketing process. "If we do it right, one of the tire companies will get an order for a Saturn," Smith says. "The computer will start making tires at the supplier's plant, deliver them to the Saturn plant at just exactly the right time to go on that car, and as it goes out the door, money is going to go on deposit for the tire company at a New York bank. All without a piece of paper."

"It's impossible to do right now," Smith admits. "EDS knows that's going to be a tremendous undertaking." There may be 30 or 40 basic management systems within GM, each generating its own crush of paper, punch cards, and printouts—systems that control the design and construction of parts as small as the brackets that hold a fender on, for example. "We use $8 billion worth of what we call expense material," Smith says, "material that's used in a car but is not something that goes on a car. I'm talking about cutting oil, drills, motors that drive assembly lines and drill presses, welding tips, ad infinitum. There's over 1 million items. We're the biggest Ace Hardware store in the world. Now, we think, if we could get one corporate-wide system for that . . . we could see tremendous gains."

The greatest obstacles may be human, not technological. At this point, Mair says, GM is having trouble with older managers who are comfortable with paperwork and are having an awful time operating without it. "There are people that write a letter to come to a meeting and they go into a lot of detail, all the agendas," he says. "Everybody is afraid they'll miss this array of information.

"That also has generated a comfort in a big company where people say, 'I can't get all this done, I got all this paper I've got to read.' It makes a nice facade for not having all your things done," Mair says. "We're going to have to figure out how to disseminate the information far more effectively. Many hours of work at GM is spent muddling through what you think you're supposed to know."

"The whole system is going to have a flow of information that literally drives our whole company," Smith says. "But instead of having that flow through 2,964 reports that are issued hourly, daily, weekly, monthly, yearly, the whole system runs through [a computer] and you intercept it. If you want to know how many blue cars we built yesterday, you can get that out of the system. But you aren't going to get a report on your desk every day. It isn't going to be new skills, it's going to have to be attitudes and approach. Running your mind with what you need to run it on.

"If you get the guy educated in such a way that he doesn't have to rely on paper, get his crutch away from him, as it were, and let him see what he can do . . . it's fantastic," Smith says. "He's got time to think about other things instead of running through a great big pile of papers to get his work done."

But like every other part of the revolution Smith has instigated at GM, the change must be cushioned and regulated to keep the sheer disruption and anxiety from stopping the whole process. "What would happen in the Post Office if all the postal workers got their work done in 45 minutes every morning?" Smith asks. "They'd be terrified, wouldn't they? They'd all look around and say, 'Who's going?' So you need some other kind of incentive. The way we see to do it is to start with a thing like Saturn, where you don't have some of those built-in traps and things that hold you back." And, he hopes, Saturn will become the model for the company.

How do you get along without paper? How can the dependency be broken? Mair says he doesn't know yet. One thing is clear to him, though: There has to be greater personal trust among managers, so that they don't need a supporting piece of paper as evidence on an issue. The paper trail really says a manager doesn't trust a colleague. "You have to delegate authority," Mair says, "and go with Roger Smith on the risk."

# 17

## BORG-WARNER

### Blending Manufacturing with Services
### to Take Advantage
### of the Changing Environment

Most people would be hard-pressed to say exactly what it is Borg-Warner Corp. does. Although its name offers no clues, some might guess that it's one of those old-line industrial outfits that crank out automobile parts and other bits and pieces used in manufacturing various industrial products.

Well, that's half right. Borg-Warner does do those things. But it also has become a major player in such nonindustrial fields as consumer and industrial financing, industrial-plant security, and courier and armored-car services, all in the name of protecting itself from the financial downturns that regularly beset the rest of its businesses.

By reducing its dependence on the nation's declining manufacturing sector and hitching itself to faster-growing service industries, Borg-Warner has anticipated the changes that are reshaping the entire American economy. In many ways an embodiment of the current metamorphosis of the American industrial landscape, Borg-Warner now finds itself straddling both the old manufacturing businesses that were its base for years and the up-and-coming service economy. In doing so, Borg-Warner has found success—but it also has gotten a firsthand glimpse of many of the problems the economy as a whole is finding in making the transition between manufacturing and services.

Borg-Warner's shift has been presided over by James F. Beré, a cheerful, leprechaun-like executive in his early 60s whose decidedly humanistic views about management and about a corporation's place in society are as different from most other chief executives' as is the path on which he's steered his company. And for a man running one of the nation's largest companies, Beré also has a less than rosy outlook for the role of big corporations in American business life. "The growth in this country is not going to be the big company," he says. "The best we are going to do is rearrange our companies, so we can stay viable."

Beré has surely done that with Borg-Warner over the past few years. Before he began tinkering with the company, it was not unlike any of a host of other Midwest industrial titans—a fairly faceless supplier to the automobile factories of Detroit, and one of the bigger ones at that. When it was formed in 1928 by the merger of four auto-parts companies, it made transmissions, clutches, carburetors, and any number of other bits and pieces of automobiles. Over the years it diversified into other areas as well—most notably heavy-duty plastics (its Cycolac plastic is used to make the shell of most telephones), chemicals, and industrial pumps. Anonymously supplying its products almost exclusively to other manufacturers, Borg-Warner's only exposure to the general consumer market has been York air conditioners and, for a time, Norge appliances.

Beré took over as chief executive in 1972. Within the next two years, the company was hamstrung by a major recession, caused by the Arab oil embargo, that rocked the industries the company served and sent sales and earnings into a tailspin. As went Detroit, so went Borg-Warner, and after years of steady growth, the domestic auto industry was entering a period of rough times. Earnings, which had been marching steadily higher for years, slumped from $71.3 million to $50.8 million in 1974, and then to $44.5 million the next year. The company was forced to lay off thousands of employees. Borg-Warner seemed to be taking its place among the dozens of other big industrial companies in smokestack America that were about to fall on a long period of hard times.

To avoid such a fate, Beré and Borg-Warner's other executives began thinking in the mid-1970s about moving the company away from its older businesses into something a little more stable. "In our manufacturing, in our self-analysis, it became very apparent that unlike many companies, most of our product lines were on the mature side of their life cycle or curve," Beré says. "Where our products were mature, we were affiliated with the automobile industry, which we were anticipating to change, but not as severe a change as it was. . . . That was the genesis of our thought: that we'd better change."

It wasn't a terribly original idea. Many other companies, severely battered in the same period of time, had the same thought. Many of them diversified into high-technology fields such as computer equipment and electronics, with varying degrees of success. But Borg-Warner held back. After looking at several high-tech industries that were then becoming very hot—notably electronics—it finally decided to stay away from those fields. These businesses had become so popular, Beré says, that prices of young high-tech companies were quickly being bid up by other old-line manufacturing companies looking for diversification opportunities. (Borg-Warner has in the years since, however, made a number of small equity investments in high-tech electronics companies to gain exposure in those fields.)

At first, Borg-Warner didn't seem completely committed to the idea of diversification. In 1978, Beré made an attempt to increase his company's stake in the auto-parts industry through an attempt to merge with Firestone Tire and Rubber. Firestone's customers were similar to Borg-Warner's—and so was its susceptibility to economic cycles and the vicissitudes of the auto industry. Although Firestone was a fairly cheap buy—at that time it was staggered by a controversy over tire safety—a combination of Firestone and Borg-Warner didn't seem to make a whole lot of long-term sense, especially in light of Beré's desire for diversification. Fortunately for the company, the deal ultimately fell through. "I'm glad we did not make it," Beré now says of that foray, "because we would have been in something we didn't want to be in."

What Borg-Warner wanted to be in, it finally decided, was something to give it protection from the ebb and flow of its traditional businesses. "In studying our company, we found out we were highly cyclical," Beré says. "We also noticed something that disturbed us immensely: When we had a boom—if that's a proper word—we never went quite as high as other companies. But when we had a recession, we went deeper." So steady, stable service industries seemed just the thing.

The company didn't look very far for inspiration. As early as 1953, Borg-Warner had diversified into the service arena—although nobody called it that back then—when it formed the Borg-Warner Acceptance Corp. (BWAC). The division was initially set up to provide financing to purchasers of Borg-Warner's York air conditioners and Norge appliances, but it soon expanded to provide credit services to other companies. Over the years, it carved out a niche for itself among the nation's large financing companies by choosing to concentrate the bulk of its business in towns and cities with populations under 200,000, giving it greater control over its operations. The division thrived—even through the severe 1974-75 recession that deeply hurt so much of the rest of the economy, as well as its corporate parent.

During that recession, BWAC continued to grow at a rate of 15 percent a year—while the rest of the company was stagnant, at best. So Borg-Warner began exploring other service fields that would provide similar growth and countercyclical stability. "Since we had one service company, we felt quite comfortable that we should proceed on that basis," Beré says. "There was a recognition that a higher incident of the Gross National Product would be in the service side of industry. . . . Staying in manufacturing possibly would have been more difficult or a higher risk for the company than going to services."

Best of all, service businesses were not subject to the kinds of ups and downs Borg-Warner was used to. In bad times as in good—sometimes more so, depending on the field—service businesses tend to be extremely steady performers, if managed effectively.

Borg-Warner decided against trying to increase its presence in the service field by trying to vastly expand BWAC; Beré felt the credit subsidiary could not handle the kind of rapid expansion that he was looking for (although BWAC is today one of the nation's dozen or so largest financing companies, providing credit for individuals and corporations to buy everything from appliances to industrial equipment). Rather, Beré had another idea. "The strategy . . . was to buy a good small company in the service industry that could grow nationally," he says.

Beré didn't have any specific kind of service industry in mind—like high-technology, the "service" tag is hung on all manner of companies. "We have some board members who would like to say, tell us specifically what you're going to look for," Beré says. "We much preferred to put a concept out there and, from a pragmatic point of view, have found out what's available within our range." And so Beré let it be known on Wall Street that Borg-Warner was interested in moving into something in the service field. What the investment bankers brought back, at first, was not very attractive. "At that juncture, it was in vogue to look at insurance companies and other things," Beré says. "We lost our courage on insurance companies, again because everybody was working from the same planning book, I guess, and there was too much demand for those companies, and we didn't want to pay those prices."

But there was another company available—Baker Industries, a New Jersey-based company with a variety of interests in the field loosely defined as "protective services," encompassing such areas as security guard services, alarm systems, and the Wells Fargo armored-car business. The timing was perfect: As the economy fell apart in the next few years, crime went up, and the demand for security services mushroomed. "If you look back at protective services," Beré says now, "it couldn't have come at a better time for us in the whole context of security in our society—there was almost this total disruption in law and order, which most of us don't like to talk about, but the fact is that's what it was. Everybody was doing their own thing, and as a consequence, people were concerned, and there was a great demand to have these guard services. I'm just impressed at Christmas: You go down to any urban area in the United States, big cities, and what do you see in front of a store and walking the store? Security. Not the Chicago police or the Philadelphia police or the Washington police."

As a result, Baker's business has skyrocketed. With the acquisition of the Burns security-guard operation and the Pony Express courier service, Borg-Warner's overall protective-services revenues are now about $1 billion annually—quintuple Baker's revenues when Borg-Warner acquired it. Through its various divisions, Baker provides security systems for nuclear power plants, industrial fire-protection equipment, couriers and armored cars for the transport of important documents and money, and guards for everything from department stores to the 1984 Olympics and the Michael Jackson Victory tour.

The shift to services came just in the nick of time. Borg-Warner all but breezed through the two recessions of the early 1980s. To be sure, its more traditional businesses stumbled a bit, but just as intended, the strength in its new-found services businesses carried the company. "They still perceive us as an automotive supplier and wonder why we're not having trouble like the other companies," Beré was able to say midway through the devastating 1981-82 recession. "But we're not really an automotive supplier."

Borg-Warner's revenues and income streams are now just about evenly divided between manufacturing and services businesses, leaving it a much more balanced company. And Borg-Warner has not abandoned its older businesses as it has expanded the service side of the corporate portfolio. Unlike other companies that sold off old-line businesses to make room for new endeavors better fitted to the changing economy, Borg-Warner not only retained virtually all of its more traditional businesses, but committed itself to investments in plant modernization and kept a tight rein on costs in the runaway years of the late 1970s. Those two strategies gave it a strong foundation for growth when the economy bounced back. It didn't hurt that the company lucked into a few goldmines—such as Detroit's switch to front-wheel-drive cars, which tapped Borg-Warner's considerable transmission-making expertise, and the hot-selling Pontiac Firebird and Chevrolet Camaro, which were equipped with Borg-Warner automatic transmissions that provided handsome revenues.

"We decided to stay in manufacturing, to try to upgrade our manufacturing as well," Beré says. "We thought that the greatest revolution from our point of view would be taking the new high-tech . . . and applying that to our present production. . . . I'd be very disappointed if we weren't extremely aggressive in being part of the revolution in manufacturing to become competitive on a worldwide basis."

By modernizing and automating its production facilities, Borg-Warner managed to make productivity gains that in many cases kept the company viable in increasingly competitive manufacturing fields. The validity of that philosophy can be seen in the results of Borg-Warner's automotive-parts division: after losing money in 1980 as the auto industry slumped, the division rebounded to record years in 1983 and 1984 with the auto industry's recovery. In fact, when the services side of the company stumbled a bit in 1984 as the result of competitive pressure on some of Baker's operations, the company's resurgent older businesses carried Borg-Warner upward.

The company also has continued a series of tough cost-containment programs begun during the 1974-75 recession. One way Borg-Warner kept strict controls on its older businesses as it diversified was by deciding early on to use very little debt in funding the new acquisitions. "I did that for the simple reason that it was an internal discipline for us," Beré says. Not only did it force the company's managers to operate their businesses in as lean a manner as possible, it also served as a check against a huge, unwieldy acquisition that would force the company to incur a great deal of debt with questionable reward. "We didn't do some of the foolish things, and we kept our powder dry," Beré says.

The company also hesitated in cutting away some of its older, struggling businesses—sometimes to its benefit. In the late 1970s, when Wall Street and some executives within the company were clamoring for Beré to cut loose the firm's troubled chemicals division, he resisted. "We decided to stay in it—and three of our competitors went out of business," Beré says triumphantly. In other cases, Beré allowed temporarily moribund operations to continue to draw on the corporate coffers for growth, in order to allay employee fears that the axe was about to fall. "As soon as people see you not putting more capital in, they become very paranoid, and they say, 'Oh, you're selling me,' " Beré says. "It's very difficult, and you have to be very lucky."

Still, Borg-Warner's shift in emphasis has not been without difficulties—many of them problems symptomatic of the entire economy's accelerating shift towards a service orientation. Perhaps most significantly, the change demanded a whole new management style from a company whose managers for years had been running factories—and generally proved unable to make the switch, according to Beré. "I came to a conclusion that you're not going to get a manufacturing person to be strongly service-oriented," he says. "That infuriated me in a way, and also frustrated me, in that we were engineers and manufacturing types, but basically, every business is to serve—there is no business without serving some service or product. And our people, rather than go to the service side, namely the aftermarket in automotive, they were much more interested in selling to Detroit, the big order. Our pump people were much more intrigued in being in a big new power plant than they were in [seeking smaller, more customized orders].

"I was convinced that if you wanted to be in the what I call the service side of the economy, which is labor-intensive rather than capital-intensive, it had different nuances of management style," he says. One of the biggest problems was fundamental to the difference between manufacturing and service businesses: In manufacturing, one of a manager's key goals is to reduce labor costs, while by contrast, service businesses are based on labor.

"All of our people were trained to really eliminate labor in capital-intensive businesses," Beré says. "As soon as you have seven persons working a machine, you want to find a way to have six working. . . . Labor in capital-intensive (businesses) is a variable cost."

"When you're people-intensive, now you come to a different style of leadership, of motivating those people, and having checks and balances that are being observed. That's the big difference. I think the other difference of management style is what I would term attitude. There's a perception in our ethic that says you're really not working unless you're producing something tangible. And that takes on a whole new air of motivational devices to do that. . . . In fact, there's interesting psychology—I think we have people who almost put people as second-class citizens if they were in the professions, or teaching, or even in the church side or writing side. So that's a big difference in how you motivate."

Borg-Warner's service acquisitions were made not only to put the company into the services sector, but to acquire managers who could function best in the new fields. "Most of our manufacturing people would be very comfortable in service until they had their first crisis," Beré says. At that point, he says, the managers would find out that what worked in dealing with a manufacturing crisis was all wrong for a crisis in a service business. For instance, while a variety of manufacturing ills can be cured by getting people out of the process and automating, the same prescription in a service business can be a disaster, since service businesses usually revolve around people.

Still, Beré believes that there are keys to running a manufacturing business well that are just as important to a successful service business, even though the management styles differ. One example of this is business controls. Keeping tabs on productivity levels in service-oriented businesses is difficult—many managers whose sole experience is in manufacturing would argue that it is impossible—but experts believe innovative forms of measurement can allow companies to chart service-industry productivity. Beré agrees. "You have to control the business," he says. "I don't want to sound inhuman in this, but basically what you're doing is controlling human beings, and you have to have immediate feedback in a service business, because if that productivity goes down by those persons, you [have to] see it immediately."

And while it finds its way through the brave new world of managing service industries, Borg-Warner is reminded constantly how tough things can be in its older businesses. While the operations of most service industries are pretty much contained within the boundaries of the United States, Borg-Warner's industrial businesses compete in an international arena. "Some service businesses—ours are typical—are essentially combinations of localized operations, and can still build substantial positions within a single country," Beré says. "But I cannot think of a manufactured product that is not already or potentially subject to massive global competition. . . . Many markets are becoming more global than national, and the trend to multinational operations is growing. . . . National boundaries are becoming largely academic when it comes to business." Borg-Warner has attempted to cope with the globalization of its markets in several ways. It has sought out alliances for foreign business, so far without major success. It has aggressively expanded its operations abroad, to give itself manufacturing and marketing presence in the nations in which it does business (the cover of the company's 1984 annual report was a map of the world, with flags marking the nations in which it has operations). And Beré has become a tireless crusader, as a member of the Business Roundtable and other organizations, for the notion of free international trade, or fair trade, as the term has been modified in the 1980s.

In addition to diversifying Borg-Warner into new fields, Beré has hedged the company's bets in another rather unusual manner. Over the years, Borg-Warner has bought significant interests in Hughes Tool Co., a maker of oilfield equipment, and Echlin Inc., a manufacturer of replacement auto parts—in a sense, playing the stock market, on a long-term basis, with funds unneeded for its own corporate development. These passive investments, each greater than 20 percent of the companies' total stock outstanding, gave Borg-Warner an opportunity to count a share of the companies' profits in its earnings statements, giving it the financial benefits of being in two additional industries without having to worry about running the businesses. However, any losses suffered by the companies also count against Borg-Warner's bottom line, and when Hughes' and Echlin's businesses turned down in the mid-1980s, Borg-Warner began reevaluating the relationships. In 1985, it sold its interest in Echlin, saying it wanted to invest the money elsewhere, but hung onto its Hughes stock for the time being.

Beré has achieved his goal of revamping Borg-Warner so that half of its business is in services. But he's not done yet. If you want to bet on what kind of service company will be the next added to Borg-Warner's collection, put your money on a temporary-help agency. "I'm convinced that the next great market growth is temporary help," Beré says. But his concept of temporary employment goes beyond the normal clerical fields associated with such agencies. He believes changing demographics and social mores, the high costs of providing employee benefits and other factors could open markets for temporary or part-time positions for professionals such as lawyers, writers, or engineers. In times of economic trouble, such a business could be a windfall, as companies drop full-time professionals but need such specialized help on a part-time basis.

Such an acquisition would further change Borg-Warner. But it will help fulfill the prophecy of the company's official history, published in 1978, just as Borg-Warner was beginning its diversification into services. Borg-Warner, according to the history, is "a company that has been different in every decade of its existence, and will be different again in the next one." Beré, with one revolution under his belt at Borg-Warner, sounds like he'd rather the next one be a little less acute. Says he: "I, for one, would like to see a change in a company without it being noticeable that it is a change."

# 18

## BALANCE LONG-TERM AND
## SHORT-TERM PRESSURES

Jim Beré talks about what it was like to go to a meeting of Wall Street securities analysts during the years when he was shifting Borg-Warner's emphasis from manufacturing to services: "The first criticism was, 'You as management do not have the long view. Tell us about your long-view strategy,' " Beré remembers. "[That was] Question No. 1. Question No. 2: 'What are you going to do next quarter?' "

That dichotomy is one of the most frustrating to American management today. On the one hand, executives of leading-edge companies are trying to chart a long-term course, trying to make the changes and investments needed to adapt their companies to a changing world. On the other hand, the investment community is clamoring for instantaneous results—in the form of improved earnings—not three years down the road, but in the current quarter, if you please.

More often than not, the stock market—the principal source of funding for all public companies—is swayed by company performance, generally as measured by quarterly earnings. If a company has a poor quarter, for whatever reason, its stock tends to react negatively. To avoid that, executives are chary of making the investments or write-offs required to change a company.

It is the curse of the public company. "One problem with U.S. industry is this constant concern with the next quarter, which is brought by the fact of the investment public," Coca-Cola Chairman Roberto Goizueta says. "I cannot think of a more stupid mechanism than the stock market on the short-term. I cannot think of a wiser mechanism than the stock market on the long-term."

Some companies have circumvented this problem by going private, taking their stock off the market and placing it in the hands of a small number of private investors who might be more patient about a company's growth and willing to listen to and understand management's explanations that a short-term dip in earnings is necessary for the long-term good of the company.

But not very many large companies are able to exercise that luxury. It takes a courageous manager to mollify short-term pressures while working for long-term improvement of the company. "We manage somebody else's store, and therefore we have to fulfill a certain kind of street mentality, we have to be acceptable to the financial world," says Walt Disney Chairman Mike Eisner. "At the same time, we can't manage the company quarter by quarter. The ability not to look at the [stock-market] tape—that's a great discipline. Where's the stock? Don't look at it— I'm not going to look at it today. The fact of the matter is you can't manage a company day by day. You have to manage it over the long-term."

"In the United States, I think, managements are too concerned about short-term profits, quarter to quarter—they don't look at the long-term needs of the business," says Gould Chairman Bill Ylvisaker. IBM Chairman John Akers says, "I have a 10-year horizon, personally. So I'm not particularly concerned about first-quarter 1985 earnings. I mean, I'd work hard on them, but I'm much more interested in 1986 and 1987 and 1988. We've always run this business in the long run with a long view, and we continue to."

Irving Shapiro, the former Du Pont chairman, says, "The well-managed company recognizes that the real function of management is long-term, not short-term, and each CEO is preparing the way for his successor. He's benefitting from what his predecessor did. I don't want to overstate it—obviously, there is a little bobbing and weaving through all of this. But basically, the thinking is long-term. There's no other way to run a large business."

The long-term/short-term dilemma may never have been sharper than it is now, with so many companies having to make hard choices affecting their survival at a time when economic and competitive challenges have never been greater. The task is made even harder by the short-term unpredictability of such vital factors as tax policy, energy prices, and foreign-exchange rates.

How to resolve the long-term/short-term issue has long been debated in the nation's executive suites. Some managers bow to the pressures, forego needed investments, and play straight to the stock market, pumping out high quarterly earnings and inflating the price of their stock—until they bleed the company dry and force new management to take painstaking steps to restore long-term opportunities, if there are any left at that point.

Rather than follow that destructive course, executives of most leading-edge companies say they try to cope with long-term/short-term pressure by taking pains to explain long-term strategies and intentions to stockholders and the investment community, in the hope that sophisticated owners and analysts will understand and deal with investments in the company accordingly.

But some executives argue that dwelling on the long-term can be just as damaging as a preoccupation with short-term performance. The danger then, they say, is that a company becomes so obsessed with hitting some long-range goal that it neglects to take care of its current businesses. Or, a company can find its long-term targets so hard to hit that it keeps shifting its aim—and bumbles along confused for years, embracing and abandoning one strategy after another. "You can't run an enterprise that is free of short-term pressures," GE's Jack Welch says. "If you do, you'll end up over-investing and doing a lot of other things. You've got to balance both of those. . . . That's why you get paid as a manager—to make that trade-off appropriately, and live with the decisions that trade-off brings about."

That is what Welch and others preach—balancing the long-term and short-term pressures. "Every manager, in every company, at lower levels, will tell you, 'You know, if we didn't have to make this year, 1989 will be terrific,' " Welch says. "Well, there might not be an '89."

Placating the long-term/short-term demons is a major concern of any company that is trying to fundamentally change itself to compete more effectively in today's world. Managers must be able to satisfy Wall Street, employees, customers, and other constituencies that the short-term effects of change will be more than made up for by the long-term benefits. Borg-Warner went through several lean years while it spent money to acquire the service companies that now are among its most successful divisions, and all the while, Beré had to keep convincing securities analysts that he was doing the right thing. Ylvisaker has made the same plea to the investment community as he has revamped Gould in recent years and earnings have been battered in the process. Most securities analysts have wound up believing him, and have recommended the stock as a long-term play. "I think it's a question of explaining to the investors," Goizueta says. "If you tell them, 'This is what I'm doing,' and you develop credibility with them, I think the smart investors will stay with you even though you have a bad quarter." It's the old dictum of No Surprises. "Surprises they cannot take," Goizueta says. "They'll take discomfort, but surprises they cannot."

The pressures are not so great when changes are only being made to part of a large company, but they exist nonetheless. General Electric has made a series of investments in recent years that had no immediate positive impact on short-term profits—indeed, they cut into profits—but may have great potential for long-term gains. GE didn't have to spend $38 million modernizing its dishwasher production facility in Louisville, Ky.—but the investment paid off in the long run in a sizeable increase in market share and more efficient production. To Welch, such investments are like rocks—they don't appear to change much over a short period of time. "I don't think you look back at rocks over 24- or 36-month timeframes," he says. "They need a longer time horizon."

The importance of these long-term investments cannot be trivialized. "Let's take almost every one of our core businesses," Welch says. "One can argue, without the right investment, without the right moves, we could be less strong in those businesses five years from now than we are today." GE's $6.4 billion purchase of RCA is another example—pricey in the short term, but of value in the long run as it adds technology and other new strengths to GE.

General Motors has also bet on the long-term with its recent acquisitions of Electronics Data Systems and Hughes Aircraft. The nearly $8 billion spent by the company on those deals will reduce GM's earnings for years to come—but Chairman Roger Smith and other GM executives believe the company will reap far greater benefits from EDS and Hughes for years beyond the financial dip incurred to purchase them.

Long-term investments can be critical to the development of new technologies and products that simply cannot be brought to market, or made profitable, in a short period of time. G. D. Searle had to wait for over a decade to develop and gain federal approval for its revolutionary low-calorie sweetener, aspartame—and is now cleaning up the market with the product. Similarly, Sony took losses for years on its Beta videotape technology while it waited patiently for a market to develop that gave the company a big payoff on the technology.

Sony's patience, though, is representative of a legendary quality of Japanese companies—that they are willing to take losses for years on a product in the name of establishing a market. In steel, in automobiles, in pharmaceuticals, in countless other products, Japanese companies have gained a notoriety for taking an extremely long view of the world, biding their time and losing billions of yen—albeit often with government support—while they wait for markets to come around to their products. Because of differences in the Japanese system—principally that its companies are financed by bank loans rather than by stock—it would be difficult for United States companies to emulate the Japanese example of ultra-long-term strategy. "As long as we stay with our kind of an enterprise system, we can probably never go as far as some other countries can in sacrificing the short run for the long run," RCA Chairman Thornton Bradshaw says. He uses the Japanese steel industry to illustrate the point: "After the war, the Japanese had a target for steel. It took them about 10 years to get there. During that 10-year period of time, their so-called shareholders, which were mostly the banks, sat still. They didn't have any eruptions at their shareholder meetings, they weren't paying dividends, etc. We can never do that. American business is the art of treading that fine line between short-term results and longer plans."

Still, in some instances, an American company with enough resources can handle the long-term, money-losing development of a product it is sure will be a big winner somewhere down the road. One of Du Pont's most important technological breakthroughs over the past 20 years or so has been its super-strength Kevlar polymer, which is used to make everything from military armor-plating to bullet-proof vests to high-strength tires. Yet after more than 20 years of development, Du Pont has just begun to turn a profit on Kevlar. The company has waited patiently for markets for the material to develop—and the payoff is finally at hand. "It's taken all that time to build up the end uses and get the quality up, to the point where you can start realizing benefits," says Shapiro. "Any management that was thinking short-term would have said, long ago, 'To hell with this—we'll all be dead before we see profits.' And yet I don't have any doubt in this world this is a major technological breakthrough that will both have great end uses and will also make money in the late 1980s and 1990s and thereafter. That's the game you're in. You're long past the period when you come up with quick new discoveries that pay off in a year."

Imbuing managers with the motivation to make correct long-term/ short-term decisions is a task that faces most companies. Many firms have taken steps in recent years to adjust compensation systems to give managers an incentive to stay on a long-term course. AT&T and GE have begun experimenting with compensation plans that peg pay to long-term performance of the manager's unit. "Money, title, standing in the organization [are] based on how well they've grown their businesses, rather than creat[ing] an artificial pressure for them to move on and run some other business," says Frank Doyle, GE's senior vice president for corporate relations, the executive responsible for human resources at the company. "It takes that whole long-term/short-term trade-off fallacy and dumps it, because if you leave a manager in place long enough so that he is going to be measured on both the short- and the long-term, then he makes that trade-off, and he makes it probably in an optimum way."

Another thing companies are doing to reduce short-term temptations is throttling back on stock-option plans that gave top managers incentives to go for short-term hits. Too often, it seemed, executives would manage a company for short-term gains that would boost the price of their stock, and then take the money and run, leaving the residual problems to the managers that followed. "I always used to make the case when I was running Du Pont that the easiest way for me to look like a great manager in a hurry was simply to cut back on R&D," Shapiro says. "You could get several hundred million dollars in a hurry. Nobody would notice the difference until 10 years later. Yet if I had done that, I would have regarded myself as a fraud as a CEO."

Kathleen Asch, who is managing the AT&T Epicenter entrepreneurial venture, believes that a long-term outlook can give a manager time to more thoroughly read a market and adjust accordingly. "I think the longer payback horizon allows people to make less risky decisions, because they can fire, and then wait for the volley and then adjust, so they have enough time to react in a slower fashion," she says. "If you don't do it, you'll be dead sooner or later, because the corporation will close you down. If you do hit it, you're a hero. Yet the corporation is traditionally populated with people who haven't had to make those decisions and aren't aware of those trade-offs."

Some experts believe that the relatively short average tenure of American chief executives is partially to blame for long-term/short-term imbalances, by limiting these executives' accountability for long-term decisions and encouraging them to manage for results over a relatively short timeframe. "I would venture to say that if you looked at all those older-line companies, the CEOs of most of them have stepped into these positions at the age of 55 or 60," Ylvisaker says. "Now, if you're realistic about it, what impact can a guy have in five years on top? Very little. So his measure of performance, unfortunately, is the stock price, which is governed by his quarterly results." This leaves very little reason, Ylvisaker believes, for an executive to attempt to make changes in a company that might have a long-term payoff. "He keeps doing what they've been doing," Ylvisaker says. "Deep down, he knows long-term it's not the right thing to do, but changes aren't made."

Ylvisaker, like others, is an advocate of longer terms for chief executives, where possible. Like most of the top executives in the companies examined in this book, Ylvisaker came to the top post at Gould relatively young. That's one of the reasons he chose 44-year-old James F. McDonald as his designated successor in 1984. "I could have picked somebody who may be more experienced," Ylvisaker says. "That wasn't the right thing to do. You need somebody who can be making decisions for the long-term that are going to impact the company, and not the short-term, and not to have to worry about what happens quarter to quarter or the price of the stock quarter to quarter." For similar reasons, many companies are leaving managers in place for longer periods at lower levels, not just to give them more experience in running a particular business—which has its own rewards—but to force upon them accountability for that business' performance over a longer period of time.

An even greater threat to the long-term/short-term balance has appeared recently in the form of corporate raiders like T. Boone Pickens Jr. and Carl Icahn. Arguing that some companies are waiting too patiently for long-term payoffs that will never come, these raiders have launched attacks on managements designed to create immediate profits for stock-holders—not the least of whom include the raiders themselves.

The raiders argue that they are only trying to force a company to raise the value of its shareholders' holdings to something approximating the company's theoretical, or book value, or to force complacent managers to better rationalize their philosophies for the companies' futures. Indeed, in some cases, such as Walt Disney Productions and Martin Marietta, a takeover raid can be a good thing for waking up a somnolent management or forcing needed changes in a company's organization. "In a sense, the raiders are playing a good role, as much as I dislike some of them personally," Bradshaw says. "They are shoving managements that ought to make changes and won't make the changes without being shoved."

But many experts believe that the damage inflicted by the raiders in the interest of short-term gain usually is highly detrimental to long-term prospects, as companies have wriggled out from the raiders' grasps by taking on monumental amounts of new debt to finance repurchases of stock or to take other measures to repel the raiders. In order to get rid of Pickens, and then Icahn, Phillips Petroleum Co. in early 1985 skewed its debt-equity ratio to a whopping 75 percent from a previously conservative 20 percent in order to raise money to buy back about half of its stock. Phillips' chairman admitted to being a "born-again debtor"; other observers feared that the company had put itself into a financial hole from which it would be lucky to recover—especially as oil prices slipped in the months that followed and crimped cash flow.

"When they merely result in borrowing from the future to pay the present, then we are really, I think, losing our balance on that tightrope between present benefits and long-range benefits," Bradshaw says of the raiders. "You're overleveraging the United States. It is parallel to the federal deficit. And then all we need is some kind of downturn in the economy, an increase in the interest rates, and we could have a string of extraordinary failures that could really shake the United States economy and the world economy."

Some of the perceived culprits in the rise of the raiders are not far removed from the Wall Street research analysts who press companies about the next quarter's profits. They are the institutional money managers, controlling billions of dollars worth of pension funds, insurance-company investments, and the like, playing to a scorecard that measures their success by their ability to post big gains in their portfolios over a short period of time. The raiders have been a godsend for these stock-market players, offering the potential for a short-term run-up in stock price that can gild a money-manager's career. The institutional investors' strength on Wall Street—they now own well over half of the stock on the market—has become more and more powerful over the years, and no one seems to know how to make them less of a factor. "It's almost as though you're having a chemical reaction and there's nothing you can do but measure it and see what's happening," Shapiro says. "The institutions look at a situation and say, 'Well, we don't care who owns this, who runs it—if it's taken over next week, we'll get X dollars and we'll vote for it.' That's probably a bit of an overstatement, but that's the trend that's going on. And so the institutions in a very large sense are really the sponsors of much of the change that's going on, and if you think about it, they're going to play a larger and larger role in corporate America, simply because the pension funds and all of that are growing, and the prevailing wisdom is you're better off investing in equities than debt long-term. So that money pours in."

In a sense, it's ironic—whereas in Japan, institutional ownership of companies allows them to concentrate on long-term growth without hec-toring by stockholders, a different kind of institutional ownership of American companies is, in many cases, working to the detriment of long-term management strategies.

But executives say that the institutional investors can be placated if a company can do a convincing enough job of selling Wall Street on its long-term prospects. If the money managers understand a company's long-term plan for the future, executives say, they will buy the company for that reason, and resist short-term temptations. "My experience is, when you talk to the institutions, if you've got a sensible case to make about what you're doing long-term, they're enthusiastic," Shapiro says. "On the other hand, if you're doing a cop-out and trying to explain short-term failures with a lot of razzle-dazzle about the long-term, then they're very cynical. So if you play it straight and you've got a decent story, they'll be responsive."

Not only does the stock market demand short-term results, but Congressional tax policy-makers have picked up the theme. The landmark 1981 tax law, for which business had lobbied so hard, created unprec-edented tax rewards for corporate investment in new plant, equipment, and research activities. Many companies took advantage of these tax breaks, only to face a political backlash directed at a handful of prominent companies like GE, which had succeeded in eliminating their federal tax bills entirely.

The experts are still arguing whether the benefits of tax breaks for corporate investment exceed the costs in reduced tax payments. But a reduction now would clearly increase pressures for short-term profits, weakening prospects for the long-term.

General Electric drew particular criticism from politicians and commentators, who labeled the company a tax scofflaw when it was revealed that GE had paid scant tax for several years while it took advantage of such tax breaks and poured money into new plant and equipment investments. Welch gets very defensive about the subject, arguing that the long-term results of the investments far outweigh any reduction in the amount paid by the company to the United States Treasury. "No one has yet said that General Electric did anything other than invest $18 billion," Welch says. "They use words like 'loopholes' and 'tax-dodging,' but no one has ever said we didn't get the productivity, nobody said our margins didn't grow 30 percent, none of those things. Nobody said we didn't create or save 200,000 jobs. People said we didn't pay taxes. That's the wrong argument." The tax credits, Welch contends, "certainly made it more attractive for us to invest. Our investments certainly created a more competitive General Electric. A more competitive General Electric certainly sustained more jobs than it would have without doing that."

The long-term/short-term debate, then, involves management philosophies, the way corporations raise capital by issuing stock, and other complex, yet fundamental, issues inextricably intertwined with doing business in the 1980s. How well a company can balance these various forces will play a crucial role in getting them onto the leading edge of American business and keeping them there.

# 19

# LEADERSHIP

## The Essential Ingredient

Just as the 1980s has produced a new kind of business environment, it is also producing a new kind of business leader. This new generation of chief executives comes from a variety of backgrounds, but most of them have common traits: They tend to be hands-on managers who have risen from the ranks—more knowledgeable about their companies' operations than many CEOs of the past. They tend to put a premium on being flexible and moving quickly, to fit the fast-changing environment in which they are guiding their companies. And they tend to be aggressive and unafraid to make the changes they believe are needed to put their companies on the leading edge.

But most of all, these executives are driven by a far-reaching vision for their companies. The concept of the organization man, the professional manager, has given way to a more intuitive, involved manager who truly is a leader, who is able to assess the changing environment, can see where a company has to go to take advantage of that environment, and can chart a course that can get the company to that goal, pulling legions of employees along the way.

According to former Du Pont Chairman Irving Shapiro, today's leaders require a combination of skills, many of them intangible. "You start out with certain givens in any business—intellectual ability, experience, leadership qualities, acceptance by the organization," he says. "Then you get to the intangibles and you get to wondering about what kind of gut judgment does this fellow have? How will he behave under adverse circumstances? That's the real test. Any damn fool can do it when things are going well. But how do you stay with it and keep things right when you're really in trouble?. . . . I've seen fellows who look like the greatest guys in the world and yet when the crunch comes, they fold."

The ideal top executive, Shapiro says, is not necessarily the smartest executive or the most polished, but rather the rare person with an indefinable blend of leadership qualities. A successful organization, it has been said, requires three kinds of individuals: a dreamer, a businessman, and a son-of-a-bitch. In today's best leaders, these disparate qualities are merged.

Two leading chief executives, GM's Roger Smith and GE's Jack Welch, epitomize the new breed of corporate leader—even though it's unlikely that a Hollywood casting director looking for someone to play a titan of Big Business would waste a second glance on either man.

Smith, the revolutionary who is standing General Motors on its head, is a man of average height, a folksy manner, and a redhead's impatience. He could easily have stepped out of a Norman Rockwell cover for the *Saturday Evening Post.* On any scale of charisma, Smith doesn't come close to Chrysler Chairman Lee A. Iacocca; in contrast to Iacocca's polished shtick, Smith's rhetoric is spiced with homely expressions like "By golly" and "Holy Toledo" that sound more like a car dealer's lingo than a CEO's. And Smith is just what the business school savants have been urging American corporations to stay away from in recent years, a financial executive—a bean-counter—the kind who allegedly has too little feel for the factory floor or the marketplace to supply the leadership needed in the 1980s, according to the experts.

Welch also seems a somewhat improbable leader at first glance. His selection as the top man at GE in 1981 surprised outsiders, primarily because the contrast with his predecessor, Reg Jones, was so great. Throughout the 1970s, Jones was one of the nation's best-known, widely quoted, and most influential business leaders, a tall, patrician figure whose nickname "Reg" was pronounced, it was said, with a hard "G"— as in God. Welch, on the other hand, is a chronic nail-biter with a slight stammer to his working-class New England accent. The only child of a railroad conductor, he grew up in Salem, Mass., got a Ph.D. from the University of Illinois and landed at GE in 1960 as a chemical engineer with its plastics division, then a backwater of the corporation.

Both Smith and Welch began at the very bottom of their companies' management ladders armed only with their individual armor—their intelligence, ambition, values, and personal strengths and weaknesses. By separate paths, both Smith and Welch made it to the top of their companies, and have become role models for business leadership in the 1980s just as Jones was in the 1970s.

Even more than their immediate predecessors, Smith and Welch vividly demonstrate the power held by Fortune 500 chief executives. Barring the unexpected, each of them will preside for a decade or more over a huge, multinational corporation with more economic power than many of the world's nations. They control billions of dollars in assets; their policies affect hundreds of thousands of employees; and they collect million-dollar salaries, to match their power. But there are limits to that power, faced by every chief executive who tries to cause a huge organization to alter its course. "Every company has its own culture, and there are no two that are just alike," Jones says. "I think that there's no question but that a CEO very definitely has an impact on that culture, just as an Iacocca has reestablished the morale at Chrysler, just as a Roger Smith is sparking a new dynamism and entrepreneurialism at General Motors. But at General Motors, Roger is finding that it's hard to change that behemoth around. It's kind of like taking a supertanker and doing a 360-degree turn with it. You do it one degree at a time. It's not like turning a Honda."

A wise CEO will recognize the limits on his or her power, Jones says. "The CEO finds it much easier to work, as a carpenter would say, with the grain rather than across the grain. You can change a corporate culture, but you do it largely by working with that culture and not counter to it, and you have to face up to the realization that any change will come slowly."

Kenichi Ohmae, manager of the Tokyo office of McKinsey & Co., the consulting firm, describes the challenge this way: "A river is flowing in one direction, and as the land grows, it shapes a valley. Now if you find out for some reason that's the wrong valley, it's very difficult for this same water to go to other valleys. . . . A corporation has a certain way of doing things. Inertia is building up. And therefore simply telling them that this is the wrong valley . . . doesn't work. We have to find ways to move the whole inertia and mass into other valleys." And that's a big, tough job.

Both Smith and Welch are somewhere in the middle of that huge task, and the returns are still being counted. But unquestionably, they have seized the opportunities presented them by fate, luck, and their own abilities, and have become catalysts of change.

In Smith's case, there weren't many hints in his career that he would try to carve out a new valley for the world's largest automaker when he got the chance. The Roger Smith who took control of GM in 1981 struck some who dealt with him outside of GM as the quintessential company man, diffident and very respectful of the actions of his predecessors—and not particularly sure of the future. "It's pretty hard to make the case that anybody could anticipate this bookkeeper type coming in to the top job and saying, 'To hell with the past, this is a whole new world out here and I'm going to take this company in that direction,' " Shapiro says. "You'd expect him to be a conservative financial man, particularly a little guy who is not a very articulate spokesman, and who isn't going to bedazzle any group of people by his personality. And yet, somewhere in his makeup is the ability to sort things out and say, 'I'm not going to be a caretaker, I'm going to do something.' "

It isn't likely that GM knew what it got that day in 1949 when it hired Smith as an accounting clerk, with his MBA degree from the University of Michigan. The child of a middle-class family in East Detroit whose father was a small-town banker and business executive, Smith got his first taste of the automobile industry working one summer on a Chrysler assembly line while he was in high school. After serving in the Navy in World War II, he joined GM. A workhorse and unabashed company man, Smith's perseverance and absorption of detail carried him up through the organization until the opportunity came to join GM's financial staff in New York City under then-GM Chairman Frederic G. Donner—like Smith, a bean-counter. The custom then was to select a financial man to serve as chairman, based in New York, with the presidency reserved for an operating executive in Detroit.

In New York, Smith built a reputation within GM as a sponge for facts, who would do the jobs nobody else wanted, and in time, a dependable troubleshooter and adept planner. And from the vantage point of Donner's staff, overlooking all of GM's operations, Smith developed an eye like a medical internist for the company's strengths and weaknesses, its muscle and fat and hardening arteries. The experience was invaluable, and Smith was on an upward path at GM in the early 1970s when he got two assignments that helped propel him into the chairman's job.

One of the tasks was running GM's decidedly unglamorous nonautomotive products and defense businesses. Smith soon shocked the higher-ups by urging that GM get out of one of the businesses he supervised: the Frigidaire appliance division. As he and others tell it, it became clear to him that the company's appliance business was doomed. That was close to heresy in a "can-do" executive culture like GM's, which didn't know the word quit—or wouldn't admit it if it did. "We had sent manager after manager down there with the challenge to straighten Frigidaire out," Smith says. "When I got there, I came back and said, 'There's nobody can turn that around; what we ought to do is get out of it.' I remember I talked to Eddie Cole [GM's president then] and he said, 'That's the wrong attitude. We'll fix it. I'll come help you.' I said, 'Eddie, don't waste your time. It's unfixable. There's no technology, there's not anything that's going to get us away from the competitive position we're in.' He said, 'But we made it work in the past.' I said, 'Yeah, and we had a two-to-three-year technological lead on the rest the industry. Now we put a new dishwasher in Houston and seven weeks later the competition's got it in Dallas. There's no such thing as a technological lead that would support the labor-cost differential [favoring GM's opposition].' Smith eventually prevailed and Frigidaire was sold, a decision Smith and GM never regretted.

Smith loves to tell that story. It reveals in him the capacity for taking a tough, unsentimental look at the company's strengths and weaknesses, a special quality that was a key factor in his selection as chairman. "Up until then, I think General Motors had never thought there was something they couldn't just do," Smith says. Today, that discipline runs through Smith's strategy for GM—it explains why he turned to a joint venture with Toyota to produce competitive subcompacts for the American market, and why he is so intent on curing GM's competitive weakness through costly investments in technology.

Smith's other crucial early-1970s assignment came from then-chairman Richard Gerstenberg, and it enabled Smith to probe deeply into the company. "In 1972, Dick Gerstenberg put me in charge of a thing we called the corporate directions group," Smith says. The other top executives assigned to the project were "not really keen about it," Smith says, "so I had a real chance to go in and fuss around with the thing." The experience gave Smith a valuable feel for what made GM tick when he emerged as the front runner for the chairmanship a few years later.

When Smith took over, GM was suffering the pain and embarrassment of its first loss since 1921. Smith's response came straight from his accountant's instincts. GM laid off 172,000 auto workers. Another 27,000 white-collar workers also lost their jobs. A pall fell over the company each week, when the pink slips were delivered. Subordinates who tried to slip sloppy staff work past Smith encountered his rough side and some paid for it by demotions or sackings.

Many of his early moves as CEO were marked not by brilliant new thrusts, but by embarrassing gaffes, particularly his handling of the United Auto Workers contract negotiations in 1981. First, he mistakenly announced that cost savings won at the bargaining table would be passed on to customers—sending a signal to would-be car buyers to sit back and wait for lower prices. And on the day the UAW contract was signed, with its hard-to-swallow wage concessions, Smith announced a new bonus plan for 6,000 executives. "The timing made you wonder whether he was part of this world," auto analyst Maryann Keller said at the time.

What onlookers didn't yet see in Smith was his vision of the threat to GM and his determination to do something about it. As Smith saw it, a business-as-usual response wouldn't make it, not with the internal problems and competitive pressures bearing down on GM. Its costs weren't competitive, its product-response time was too slow, its quality wasn't good enough, and budget-cutting alone wouldn't do the job. "I don't think that, 'Ding-a-ling-a-ling', the bell rung," Smith says. Rather, his plan for the company was a culmination of the things Smith had dreamed of doing and things he knew had to be done.

From this plain-spun man came a series of dramatic moves—"lulus," he calls them—that were designed not only to answer specific competitive problems but also to shout the news of change down GM's corridors. The company's controversial car-building partnership with Toyota was the first "lulu." Then, when the technical operations staff came up with the Saturn car project, Smith recognized its power as a catalyst to focus the company's attention on the need for change. He insisted on making it a separate corporation, able to seek new relationships with GM's two powerful, crucial constituencies, the United Auto Workers union and the GM dealer network. And he is using Saturn to attack the rigidity of the GM bureaucracy by insisting on a "paperless" corporation. The acquisition of EDS (with the embrace of Perot as a new member of GM's hierarchy) and the purchase of Hughes Aircraft were risky but powerful symbols of change. "Everybody laughed at the EDS acquisition, that he paid too much for it, that it was the wrong thing to do. I bet my money on Roger being right on that one," says Shapiro. "He's done the same thing with Hughes Aircraft," adds Shapiro, who served as chairman of the finance committee of the Howard Hughes Medical Institute, which sold Hughes Aircraft to GM. "Short-term, he's bought a defense business. Long-term, he's buying a huge technical organization. The game turns on people, and he's got some of the great resources in the country now."

There have been smaller "lulus," as well. As Alex Mair, GM's former vice president and research director, tells it, it was Smith's foot on the throttle that brought one unusual discovery at GM's labs into the marketplace. The product is Magnaquench, a remarkably powerful industrial magnet, ten times stronger than conventional iron magnets. As soon as he learned of it, Smith recognized its potential as a success story. Mair recalls Smith's immediate attachment to the magnet. "Roger Smith came out to the research lab and got it going so fast we had to put something together," he says. The lab was making only about five grams a day of the product for its experiments, but to sell it commercially, the researchers would need to scale production up to several tons a day—and they hadn't figured out how. But Smith insisted they'd find a way. "He said, 'You'll work that out, especially if I get you some help,' " Mair recalls. "We had to stand on our heads." But they succeeded. "We've had some chairmen that if we'd showed them that, it would have had no meaning," Mair says. "But Smith said, 'That stuff hangs on everything.' "

"There's something about Roger on this," Mair continues. "He right away could see all sorts of things we could use this thing for. And he's the chairman. . . . I'm not sitting here complimenting Roger, but that was one that probably would have taken a couple more years, as good as it was, to get going." Magnaquench became a success story—one GM's scientists had been looking for for a long time.

Where did Smith's surprising talent for leadership come from? That's a question Ross Perot asked himself shortly after agreeing to sell his company to GM. It wasn't an idle question. Among other things, the financial considerations were immense: Perot still owned 45 percent of EDS, and the GM offer promised him 11 million shares of GM stock, ultimately. But Perot, who regards the computer services company he founded as a kind of extended family, says the threshold issue

for him was what kind of company was GM—what kind of man was Roger
Smith.

"I, of course, know nearly everybody that runs the big companies in
this country," Perot says. "A lot of them do fit into a pretty standard
mold to be personally unattractive to me. Certainly the people that I call
the corporate gypsies I have no use for at all, because they float from
company to company, taking and not giving much. . . . Now suddenly
here we are with this nice, warm, friendly, informal guy who started at
the bottom, like everybody else in General Motors, worked his way to
the top, knows where all the valves and switches are and knows where
all the bodies are buried. And he's like us. He knows his business. He
has spent his career building one company—he is dedicated 'to that
company."

"I watched Roger for a few months and I said, 'Now this is an interesting guy,' " Perot says. "And I said, 'What makes Roger Roger?' "
The first thing Perot found was that Smith's father, E. Quimby Smith,
was a resourceful businessman who opened a bank in Ohio, and when
the Depression did it in, bounced back to start a copper-tubing company
that prospered. "So there the seeds are," Perot says.

But there were other factors. "All over the automobile industry,"
Perot says, "there are people who are frightened of electronics." But not
Smith—he's fascinated with the potential of that science to revolutionize
the automobile industry. Where did that come from? "As a young enlisted
man in World War II in the Navy, he was an electronics technician.
Very important," Perot says. "See, before he learned to be afraid of it,
he learned to understand it. . . . Then you say, O.K., here's a guy that
came up crunching numbers. Where did this leadership come from?"

Perot also found that answer in Smith's wartime experience. Smith
served aboard the flagship of Adm. Arleigh Burke—"Thirty-knot Burke,"
the sailors called him, one of the legends of the Pacific naval war, so
nicknamed because he always kept his task force moving at flank speed.
"This is a guy that sailors would walk off the edge of a cliff for," Perot
says. "He was not a remote, distant figure. He was a guy down there."
And that's the way Smith comes across to the GM people he deals with,
Perot figures. "Arleigh would stand around and talk with the sailors on
a very direct and personal basis. You watch Roger, he does the same
thing. I think Arleigh Burke had an enormous impact on Roger's leadership style."

John T. Connor, former chairman of Allied Corp. and a GM director who served on the committee that picked Smith, told author Cary Reich in the *New York Times Magazine* in 1985, "It was clear to us that Roger Smith was aggressive, impatient, very bright, very thorough—and someone who would step on toes from time to time. I thought he would be someone who was willing to make changes, even in a bureaucracy as entrenched as GM's."

But Shapiro doubts that many people anticipated how many toes Smith would trample nor how far he would go to overhaul GM's bureaucracy. "No one could have forecast that," Shapiro maintains.

By contrast, Jack Welch was not as much of a surprise to GE. He had long had a reputation as someone who did things a little differently and more aggressively than other managers. When Welch arrived at GE's plastics department in Pittsfield, it was anything but a plum assignment. "An optimist was a guy who brought his lunch to the plastics division," recalls Tom Morton, managing editor of the *Berkshire Eagle* in Pittsfield. "It was not a place where people wanted to work." But that never slowed Welch. "He was this little wise-ass Irish kid who had the magic touch," Morton says. "He was the brash young man in town. He knew where he was going, and you'd better get out of the way."

Welch rapidly established a reputation as a hard-driving overachiever with a knack for creating little empires for himself as he barreled through GE's stodgy bureaucracy. From the very beginning, GE veterans say, Welch had an unusually keen appreciation of where the company's strongest competitive edge would come from—its scientists. In his early years, his beat-up Volkswagen was almost a fixture in the parking lot of GE's technology center at Schenectady, N.Y., a short ride from Pittsfield. "I never saw anybody who would utilize the research and development center in his product work as effectively as Jack Welch," Reg Jones says.

Scrimping for every dollar, new employee, and edge he could get, Welch became famous for "bootlegging"—sneaking money for a new project from another part of the operation. Often he was prodded and protected by a strong mentor, Charles Reed, a legendary GE manager who encouraged Welch's risk-taking. Welch racked up a string of successes, among them the development of Noryl, a tough industrial plastic that moved from the laboratory into the market under Welch, becoming a foundation for a thriving plastics business at GE that has grown to more than $1 billion in annual sales. By the time he was in his mid-30s, Welch was running a billion-dollar chunk of GE, including the plastics business and other operations. Within a few years, he was put in charge of the company's lighting group, its consumer-products business, and its huge credit and financial services operation. In 1979, he was made vice chairman of the company, and two years later, in April 1981, he won a tough competition with two other top GE executives for the opportunity to succeed Jones. He was 45.

"If you looked at his track record in each business he had approached, he had taken it on as if he was the entrepreneur/owner of the business. And it had totally consumed him, in terms of his interests, his capabilities, his time, and so on," Jones says. "I also saw in Jack a tremendous amount of drive, and against this era of slower growth . . . we were looking for speed. And that drive was going to help us achieve that speed."

At first glance, it might seem that Welch has repudiated Reg Jones, by dismantling Jones' beloved planning system, by unloading Jones' key acquisition for GE, the Utah International mining company, and by shaking up many other things that his predecessor had left for him. But don't suggest that to Jones—he says that's exactly what he wanted Welch to do, that conditions were changing so radically that GE's top executive in the '80s had to be completely different from Jones in the '70s.

"I think Jack was no mystery," Shapiro says. "He won out in a very severe race because he's exactly what Reg Jones wanted. And even though Jack has undone what Reg put together, Reg was wise enough to recognize that what was needed was a guy who was as bright, tough, and aggressive as Jack."

Like Smith, Welch has tried to send a seismic jolt through a huge enterprise—forcing the elephant to dance, as GM people refer to it. Yet Welch, like Smith, stresses that the leader can only begin a process of change, push it, and feed it. For change to really occur, they say, it has to take root within the organization. "I think today this is not a company of Jack Welch," the GE chairman says. "I've been here a long time. I'm becoming relatively an old hack at this job. I think the changes one instills to begin with create a vision, a belief. But then it becomes . . . a bunch of people doing it"—disciples, if you will, who spread the word. Not surprisingly, Welch cherishes, and champions, lower-level managers at GE who share his penchant for innovation and entrepreneurship, and indeed, in many ways, he seems to want to create a company full of Jack Welches, aggressively running their businesses like he's aggressively running the corporation.

Jack Welch and Roger Smith are two men from ordinary stock who have reached the apex of two of the world's most powerful organizations and who have come to epitomize the new style of management for the 1980s at large corporations. Today's leading-edge chief executives are visionary, daring, aggressive managers who do not flinch from the hardest decisions affecting the very foundations and identities of their organizations.

# ACKNOWLEDGMENTS

Our contention throughout this book that American business is changing at a rapid pace has been amply illustrated by the changes that have affected the companies in the book since this project was begun. In just the few months since the first draft of the manuscript was completed, two companies mentioned in the book have changed their names; others have slightly changed their course; a few have made important acquisitions or divestitures; and two—General Electric and RCA—have joined forces in a $6.3 billion merger. In the months between completion of the manuscript and publication, odds are there that still more change will occur. Still, the book is as up to date as we can make it.

This book is the culmination of several years of reporting on American corporations, in the course of which we have conducted hundreds of interviews that formed the raw material of the book. More specifically, a number of executives gave freely of their time to talk with us over the past 18 months in greater depth about their companies and management styles and their perceptions of how American business is changing. Those conversations are at the core of this book. These executives included Jack Welch, Mike Carpenter, and Frank Doyle of General Electric; former

GE chairman Reg Jones; Roger Smith, Alex Mair, and Ross Perot at General Motors; Tom Pownall, Larry Adams, and Norm Augustine at Martin Marietta; Robert Kavner, Ian Ross, Morris Tanenbaum, John Segal, William Stritzler, and the Epicenter venture group at AT&T; Mike Eisner and Frank Wells at Walt Disney Productions; Bill Ylvisaker at Gould; Thornton Bradshaw and Bob Fredericks at RCA; Howard Love and Fred Tucker at National Intergroup; Jim Beré at Borg-Warner; Roberto Goizueta and Ike Herbert of Coca-Cola; Lew Lehr at 3M; John Young at Hewlett-Packard, and current and former du Pont chairmen Ed Jefferson and Irving Shapiro.

In arranging these executives and obtaining other information, we were aided by a number of corporate public relations executives, including Jack Batty and Larry Vaber at GE, Don Postma and the late R. T. Kingman at General Motors, Bill Harwood at Martin Marietta, Pic Wagner, Dick Gray, and colleagues at AT&T, Erwin Okun at Disney, Gerry Corbett at Gould, Tom Ross of RCA, Bill Thompson and associates at National Intergroup's Washington office, Patricia Yoxall of Borg-Warner, and Tom Gray and Randy Donaldson of Coca-Cola.

This book could not have been written without the support of our editors at the *Washington Post*, including Ben Bradlee and Len Downie. In particular, Frank Swoboda, the *Post's* assistant managing editor for financial news, was an enthusiastic supporter of this project from its inception, generously allowing us time off to work on it, pushing us to do stories that added to it, and generally egging us on; he is the ideal boss. A number of our colleagues on the *Post* financial staff also helped out by working with us to gather information that eventually found its way into the book. We're sure that these excellent reporters—in particular Caroline Mayer, David Vise, Warren Brown, Michael Schrage, Neil Henderson, and Merrill Brown—will recognize a quote or two in these pages. Other colleagues at the *Post* and the *San Francisco Examiner* held down the fort while we took time off to complete our work.

This book would not have been written had not Jay Acton spotted a story on General Electric in a Sunday edition of the *Washington Post* and wondered whether it could be the basis for an entire book on changing companies. Jay, then, was as much inspiration as agent, and he was terrific in both roles. His staff at Edward J. Acton Inc. also deserve thanks for always being there when we had questions about this new field of book-writing. Leslie Meredith, our editor at McGraw-Hill, and Lisa Frost,

Assistant Editor, were most helpful in suggesting changes to improve the manuscript.

Finally, Jane Styles Potts and Marty, Alex, Chris, and Martha Behr provided constant love, encouragement, opinions, refreshment, and tolerance to the two authors in their midsts. We couldn't have done it without them.

Mark Potts
Peter Behr

San Francisco
Falls Church, Va.

# INDEX